openly gay personnel, increasing the diversity of the forces to serve the goals of both military effectiveness and social equality. He also critically examines the increasing presence of private security contractors in the battle space as replacements for uniformed members of the armed forces, which is a threat to the historic linkage between service in the interest of security and citizenship rights and responsibilities. This volume is particularly timely given the recent lifting of the ban on service by openly gay personnel and the opening of ground combat occupations and units to women. Readers interested in these issues will have difficulty, as I did, putting this book down."

David R. Segal, professor emeritus of sociology, founding director, Center for Research on Military Organization, University of Maryland

"This important work is a major contribution to American military history. It candidly explores the major questions and controversies concerning the relationship among citizenship, social identity, and military policy from World War II to the present with a candidness and clarity based on comprehensive research and thorough understanding of all aspects of the subject. All those concerned with issues related to the human dimensions of national security will profit from reading it."

Ronald H. Spector, professor of history and international affairs, George Washington University

"In his latest book, William A. Taylor provides an excellent, well-documented, and readable analysis of military service in this country from World War II to the withdrawal of American military forces from Iraq. This book should be required reading for those citizens, scholars, and public officials concerned about balancing national security and individual liberty."

Lawrence Korb, former assistant secretary of defense for manpower, reserve affairs, installations, and logistics

"Who serves in the United States military? Why do they serve? How do they serve? A serious and honest examination of these immensely important questions is critical to current and future discussion of transforming, overhauling, or drawing-down the American military. William A. Taylor's *Military Service and American Democracy* is essential to this discussion. Perceptive and persuasive, Taylor insightfully places the evolution of American military personnel policies amid the distinctive clash between American security needs and individual freedom in a free society."

William Thomas Allison, professor of history, Georgia Southern University

Military Service and American Democracy

MODERN WAR STUDIES

Theodore A. Wilson
General Editor

Raymond Callahan

Jacob W. Kipp

Allan R. Millett

Carol Reardon

Dennis Showalter

David R. Stone

James H. Willbanks

Series Editors

Military Service and American Democracy

From World War II to the Iraq and Afghanistan Wars

WILLIAM A. TAYLOR

UNIVERSITY PRESS OF KANSAS

Published by the University Press of Kansas (Lawrence, Kansas 66045), which was organized by the Kansas Board of Regents and is operated and funded by Emporia State University, Fort Hays State University, Kansas State University, Pittsburg State University, the University of Kansas, and Wichita State University

Library of Congress Cataloging-in-Publication Data

Names: Taylor, William A., 1975– author.
Title: Military service and American democracy : from World War II to the Iraq and Afghanistan Wars / William A. Taylor.
Description: Lawrence, Kansas : University Press of Kansas, [2016] | Series: Modern war studies | Includes bibliographical references and index.
Identifiers: LCCN 2016028674
ISBN 9780700623204 (cloth : alk. paper)
ISBN 9780700623211 (ebook)
Subjects: LCSH: United States—Armed Forces—Recruiting, enlistment, etc. | Draft—United States—History. | Military service, Voluntary—United States—History. | Democracy—United States—Citizen participation.
Classification: LCC UB323 .T39 2016
DDC 355.2/230973—dc23
LC record available at https://lccn.loc.gov/2016028674.

British Library Cataloguing-in-Publication Data is available.

Printed in the United States of America

10 9 8 7 6 5 4 3 2 1

For the millions of Americans who have served in defense of democracy abroad, whether as conscripts or volunteers, and for the ideal of American military service that has also served in defense of democracy at home, at times unevenly and unwittingly.

To my wife and children

Renee M. Taylor

Madison G. Taylor

Benjamin A. Taylor

The only defense of democracy is to make it work so successfully for the benefit of the mass of men that they will be willing to die rather than to give it up.[1]—Paul H. Johnstone, March 1947

Is there any type of important policy that is essentially military, and not civilian, in nature? Can a line be drawn between military and civilian policy, with the purpose of keeping each out of the sphere of the other? If so, should the dividing line be defined by Executive delegation, by statute, by Congressional or public pressure, or by military *esprit de corps*? On the other hand, are military and civilian policies so mixed that the problem is rather to organize the relations between civilian and military authorities; if this is so, on what principle of delegation can the dividing line be drawn— and who should do the delegating?[2]—Harold Stein, 27 November 1951

Too frequently the debate on this issue is posed in terms of "Is the AVF working?" That sets it off on the wrong track. The debate should always begin with "What is the best way for the U.S.A. to procure people for the Armed Forces?" That avoids implying the AVF is the only way. A draft assures that the right number of people in the right mix of quality serve in the right place when they are needed. Military service is important for the sociopolitical fiber of our country. All should share in service as well as benefits. Really, the military is the only place in our society where people of all backgrounds (race, socioeconomic, political, education) are thrown together and forced to get along and work together. It is an experience that benefits individual, group and country.[3]—Robert F. Froehke, 23 June 1983

Also by William A. Taylor

Every Citizen a Soldier: The Campaign for Universal Military Training after World War II

CONTENTS

ILLUSTRATIONS

ACKNOWLEDGMENTS

The English poet John Donne wrote, "No man is an island, entire of itself; every man is a piece of the continent, a part of the main."[4] It is in this spirit that I acknowledge the many debts that I owe to colleagues, friends, and family resulting from this book.

Robert S. Ehlers Jr., a colleague at Angelo State University, encouraged me to write this book and first introduced me to Michael J. Briggs, editor-in-chief at the University Press of Kansas. Mike believed in the project from the start and provided guidance, counsel, and encouragement throughout the entire process. He and the whole team at the University Press of Kansas were a joy to work with. Andrew J. Bacevich and David R. Segal, peer reviewers at the book proposal stage, imparted sage direction. William T. Allison, Robert L. Goldich, Beth Bailey, and Major General (retired) Dennis Laich reviewed the entire work and offered numerous helpful comments and steady inspiration. I am humbled and honored to have received all their cogent insights and invaluable recommendations for improvement. Ronald H. Spector and Lawrence J. Korb remain gracious mentors and steadfast supporters. I am thankful for their constant backing and very positive endorsements.

At Angelo State University, president Brian J. May joined Donald R. Topliff, provost and vice president for academic affairs; Susan E. Keith, dean of the College of Graduate Studies; Paul K. Swets, dean of the College of Arts and Sciences; and L. Casey Jones, chair of the Security Studies and Criminal Justice Department, in championing my work and demonstrating great university leadership. Angelo State University awarded me a Faculty Research Enhancement Program grant that contributed to this project and funded research at the National Archives and Records Administration, U.S. Air Force Historical Research Agency, Richard M. Nixon Library, and Gerald R. Ford Library. Katie Plum, director of the Office of Sponsored Projects, guided me through the maze of research grant funding with lucid advice and steady assistance. At Porter Henderson Library, Maurice G. Fortin, executive director; and Mark A. Allan, assistant director for research and instruction services; offered extensive library resources and commandeered rare books through interlibrary loan. Colleagues Bruce E. Bechtol Jr. and Anthony N. Celso afforded sound counsel and good company. Thomas G. Nurre Jr. widely marketed my work,

Daniel J. Meyer Jr. contributed my university photograph, and Purnell J. Curtis provided exceptional technology support. My student research assistants, Ashley N. Tanner, Hunter B. Granzin, and Joseph B. Plachno, inspired me through their continual pursuit of knowledge. They, along with my many other undergraduate and graduate students, always reminded me of the vital connection between teaching, research, and service.

A grant from the Harry S. Truman Library Institute funded extensive research at the Harry S. Truman Library in Independence, Missouri. Michael Devine, Lisa A. Sullivan, and Samuel Rushay were tireless helpers. Randy Sowell and David Clark delivered invaluable aid by locating pertinent records there, while Janice Davis contributed high-quality photographs of key personalities involved in this story. A grant from the Dwight D. Eisenhower Foundation sponsored productive research at the Dwight D. Eisenhower Library in Abilene, Kansas. Meredith Sleichter administered the grant and supplied cheer during my visit. Kevin M. Bailey offered useful suggestions about relevant records at the library. A grant from the Gerald R. Ford Presidential Foundation underwrote wide-ranging research at the Gerald R. Ford Library in Ann Arbor, Michigan. Jeremy Schmidt coordinated the grant, greeted me at the library, and proved most attentive to my project. Stacy Davis delivered outstanding archival support and steered me through a plethora of primary source documents. The library's ability to run subject searches that produce accurate folder-level detail on particular topics was especially helpful. A General and Mrs. Matthew B. Ridgway Research Grant from the U.S. Army Military History Institute allowed far-reaching research at the U.S. Army Heritage and Education Center in Carlisle, Pennsylvania. Thomas L. Hendrix directed the grant, and Greta Andrusyszyn fielded numerous research inquiries. Richard L. Baker was remarkably accommodating at the center, even allowing me access to research before the archives opened to the public, while Michael E. Lynch shared helpful suggestions and encouragement. A University of North Texas Libraries Special Collections Fellowship sponsored research in the special collections archives in Denton, Texas. Morgan Gieringer coordinated the logistics, publicized the fellowship, and arranged for my public lecture there, and Courtney Jacobs procured the relevant primary sources. A Moody Research Grant from the Lyndon B. Johnson Foundation backed extensive research at the Lyndon B. Johnson Library in Austin, Texas. Amy Barbee and Samantha Stone administered the grant, while Claudia Anderson and John Wilson provided exceptional archival support.

At the National Archives and Records Administration, Paul Brown presented expert guidance through Record Group 220 and Record Group 330. He also deciphered the War Department decimal system as it related to U.S. military service. At the U.S. Air Force Historical Research Agency, Maranda Gilmore and Tammy Horton were most helpful, while Stephen A. Bourque provided excellent company. At the Richard M. Nixon Library, Dorissa Martinez afforded adept archival aid, specifically steering me through the massive subject files within the White House Central Files. She also explained the intricacies of the Nixon Administration White House Special Files and White House Central Files and the differences between executive and general classifications. Finally, she called attention to useful material on Martin Anderson's pivotal role for the Nixon administration in the transition to the all-volunteer force (AVF). Jon Fletcher supplied high-resolution photos of significant personalities in the Nixon administration and furnished relevant captions for them. Jeffrey Kozak and Cara Sonnier at the George C. Marshall Library did likewise for public figures in the Roosevelt, Truman, and Eisenhower administrations.

My parents, Richard A. Taylor and L. Diane Taylor, instilled in me a love of learning that persists. My sister, Alison M. Eck; brother-in-law, Bryan A. Eck; and niece, Sophia G. Eaton; offered constant backing and inspiration. My wife, Renee M. Taylor, and my two wonderful children, Madison and Benjamin, deserve the most thanks. It is to them that I dedicate this book. Their love and support has always sustained me.

Any errors that remain are mine alone.

ABBREVIATIONS AND ACRONYMS

AFQT	Armed Forces Qualification Test
AVF	all-volunteer force
CWO	Chief Warrant Officer
DACOWITS	Defense Advisory Committee on Women in the Services
DADT	"Don't Ask, Don't Tell"
DOD or DoD	Department of Defense
EUCOM	European Command
FECOM	Far East Command
FY	fiscal year
KP	kitchen police
M&RA	Manpower and Reserve Affairs
NAACP	National Association for the Advancement of Colored People
NPS	non-prior service
PSC	private security contractor
ROTC	Reserve Officers' Training Corps
SPARs	U.S. Coast Guard Women's Reserve (*Semper Paratus,* Always Ready)
UMT	universal military training
VOLAR	volunteer army
WAAC	Women's Army Auxiliary Corps
WAC	Women's Army Corps
WAVES	Women Accepted for Voluntary Emergency Service

Military Service
and American
Democracy

CHAPTER ONE

CAMP RED CLOUD

Normal was the day at Camp Red Cloud, South Korea. The weather was cold, as was usually the case, and members of the 2nd Infantry Division conducted military training. For one soldier, 28 October 2014 marked the culmination of more than four decades of military service. Chief Warrant Officer 5 Ralph Rigby celebrated a major milestone for himself, his family, and coincidentally America. On that crisp fall day, Rigby retired after 42 years of military service. Because he was the last continuously serving draftee in the U.S. military, his retirement also marked the end of an era. Born in Auburn, New York, Rigby was drafted in 1972 when he was only nineteen years of age. Encouraged by his mother Dorothy to accept his fate, apply his efforts, and achieve his goals, Rigby did that and more. When President Richard M. Nixon ordered all draftees released from the army, Rigby elected to continue his military service. Over the years, the army repeatedly promoted him, first to sergeant first class and then to warrant officer, eventually vaulting him to the pinnacle of chief warrant officer 5. In a crowded room at Rigby's retirement ceremony, Major General Thomas S. Vandal, commanding general of the 2nd Infantry Division, remarked, "Chief, you have truly been a bargain for the American people and our Army; a giver who has sacrificed much for the sake of our nation." Indeed. Expressing his thanks to his many friends and colleagues present, Rigby quipped, "After all, being drafted was the closest I have come to winning the lottery. . . . If I had the chance to do it all over again, I would."[1] While the event marked an immense individual accomplishment, Rigby's retirement also denoted a significant landmark in the history of American military service. It served as an indelible reminder that U.S. military service since World War II has witnessed many manifestations. For many Americans, especially those born after the advent of the all-volunteer force (AVF) in 1973, the draft was and is a distant concept. As Chief Warrant Officer 5 Ralph E. Rigby's retirement demonstrated, however, its legacy remains today.

This book analyzes U.S. military service from World War II to the conclusion of Operation Enduring Freedom. It is a broad history that details the many personnel policies that have shaped, controlled, and defined military service during that time period. My purpose in writing this book

Major General Thomas S. Vandal, commanding general of the 2nd Infantry Division, presents Chief Warrant Officer 5 Ralph E. Rigby an encased flag as a token of appreciation for his 42 years of dedicated service in the U.S. Army during his retirement ceremony at Camp Red Cloud, South Korea. 28 October 2014. (U.S. Army, courtesy 2nd Infantry Division Public Affairs Office)

is to explore two pivotal questions regarding U.S. military service: who serves in the military, and how. The first question delves into individual and group identity. At various times, official personnel policy has excluded certain groups from military service. As a result, military service has been an arena of contested citizenship, one in which American values have been tested, questioned, and ultimately redefined. Over time, this process resulted in greater inclusiveness and expanded opportunities in military service.

The second question involves the oft-forgotten dichotomy between national security and individual liberty in American democracy. These two competing ideals have existed in constant tension throughout recent American history, especially since the emergence of the United States as a world superpower after World War II. U.S. policy makers faced difficulty in justifying any form of compulsory military service, primarily because of the value of individual liberty in American democracy. They often succeeded, however, at implementing compulsory military service. Even though the nation's first peacetime draft commenced in 1940 and continued in varying forms and to differing degrees until 1973 (except for a brief interval in 1947–1948), a generation of Americans has grown up in the absence of compulsory military service. To many Americans, therefore, debates regarding various forms of military service are a foreign concept. My hope is that this book serves as an indicator of the duality of U.S. military service since World War II; it has been roughly equal parts conscript and volunteer.

My central argument in this book is that modern American history witnessed constant debates regarding military service: whether it was to be compulsory or voluntary, who served, and what was the best method of providing personnel for the nation's defense. This process of defining military service through personnel policy, reconstructing it based on practical, political, and social pressures, and expanding it to eliminate inequities illuminates the role of military service as a litmus test for American values. As a result, military service promoted citizenship, opportunity, and equality. In this sense, military personnel policy served as the nation's conscience, bringing difficult and uncomfortable questions about American values into sharp relief. While I explore social and political factors throughout, my focus is military personnel policies. My hope is that the book will prove useful for scholars, students, and general readers interested in military service in modern American history.

The book benefits from extensive primary source research, including visits to the National Archives and Records Administration, Library of Congress, George C. Marshall Library, Harry S. Truman Library, Dwight D. Eisenhower Library, Lyndon B. Johnson Library, Gerald R. Ford Library, Richard M. Nixon Library, U.S. Army Heritage and Education Center, U.S. Air Force Historical Research Agency, and University of North Texas Libraries Special Collections. During my research I have assembled, presented, and analyzed a vast array of primary sources including letters, personal papers, memoranda, government reports, congressional hearings, and oral history interviews, as well as historical books, magazines, and newspapers. Throughout this book, I endeavor to present these archival materials directly to the reader, allowing the words and deeds of participants to be front and center. The book also synthesizes existing literature on military service, much of it narrow in either chronological or topical scope. As a historian and security studies scholar, I am indebted to colleagues in a variety of fields. American civil-military relations generally and military personnel policy specifically are truly multidisciplinary fields. They encompass the work of historians, sociologists, political scientists, and psychologists, among others. Eminent scholars such as Samuel P. Huntington, Morris Janowitz, Charles C. Moskos, Andrew J. Bacevich, Beth Bailey, David R. Segal, Eliot A. Cohen, Lawrence J. Korb, and Robert L. Goldich, among many others, have shaped the contours of the field for decades and continue to do so. In this volume, I emulated this multidisciplinary approach. For example, I examined treatments such as Samuel A. Stouffer's massive G.I. survey during World War II, Leo Bogart's analysis of Project Clear surveys during the Korean War, and Department of Defense surveys associated with a repeal of the "Don't Ask, Don't Tell" (DADT) policy during Operation Enduring Freedom to illuminate insights into U.S. military service that augment political, social, and policy understandings derived from archival research. Such an interdisciplinary approach makes this study useful for historians as well as colleagues in other disciplines interested in the dynamic and contested nature of military service.

I organized the book into ten topical chapters that follow a chronological order, each analyzing a particular debate about military service in recent American history. This first chapter introduces the topic and sets the overall context for the book. Chapter 2, "The Selective Service Idea," provides an overview of the nation's first peacetime draft, instituted in 1940; the subsequent unprecedented expansion of the Selective Service System during World War II; and implications of both for military service in the United States. Chapter 3, "A Sound and Democratic Principle," examines the impact of World War II on military service in the postwar environment. It analyzes the campaign for universal military training (UMT), the ascendance of selective service over UMT as the basis for postwar national security, and initial attempts of military personnel policy to grapple with race after World War II. Chapter 4, "Freedom to Serve," considers changes in military personnel policy between World War II and the Korean War that dealt primarily with the desegregation of the military. Policy changes during the Truman administration initiated this watershed, and developments on the battlefield several years later during the Korean War cemented it. The chapter explores the Gillem Board, the Fahy Committee, and rapidly burgeoning military personnel requirements of the Korean War. Chapter 5, "Who Serves When Not All Serve?," analyzes U.S. military service from the Korean War to the early Vietnam War. It studies such important milestones as the Gesell Committee and the Marshall Commission that respectively considered issues of equal opportunity and equity within military service. Chapter 6, "Conscription Is a Tax," scrutinizes the transition from the draft to the all-volunteer force. This momentous change occurred among heightened mobilization, impassioned debates, and tremendous uncertainty. Its importance cannot be overstated. Chapter 7, "More Than Ever Before," examines the results of the transition to the AVF, including the consequential increase of women in military service partly spurred by the loss of draftees and a shortage of male volunteers. As the U.S. military discarded the draft, it lost a valuable source of personnel: draftees and draft-motivated volunteers. Reserve components suffered the most. One offset to this conundrum was an expanded role for women in military service. Chapter 8, "To Serve in Silence," studies early debates surrounding the "Don't Ask, Don't Tell" policy in the 1990s and its subsequent repeal in 2010. It considers the relationship between sexual orientation and military service, the debates about it, and changes in military personnel policy that ensued. Chapter 9, "An Uneasy Relationship," investigates the ascendance of private security contractors and considers political, ethical, and strategic implications of the privatization of force. As military personnel shortages surfaced during Operations Iraqi Freedom and Enduring Freedom in Afghanistan, the utilization of private security contractors dramatically increased, with negative consequences. Chapter 10, "The Nation's Conscience," concludes the work with some reflections and questions regarding the AVF today, especially its political, economic, and social repercussions. In it, I argue that military service has played a valuable role in American society since World War II as a litmus test for American values. Discriminatory military personnel policies accentuated problems in a unique way due to the symbolic power of military service. As a result, military service often sparked debates about problems elsewhere in American society and often spurred further change. In this way, military service has often proved the nation's conscience, for better or worse.

This work is important for four reasons. First, this contribution places current debates regarding the AVF in historical context. Many recent observers have questioned it from a variety of perspectives: political accountability, economic feasibility, social representativeness, and civil-military relations, among others. It is instructive to remember that current conversations regarding military service are only one episode in a much larger historical discussion regarding who serves in the U.S. military and how. Situating the current dialogue in its broader historical context benefits both contemporary and historical examinations of the vital and fluid relationship between military service and democracy in America. Second, it is a useful reminder that U.S. military service since World War II existed under fairly equal periods of compulsory and voluntary constructs. The duality of military service exhibited a unique and intimate tension; national security and individual liberty have crested or receded in relative importance, depending on the historical context. Therefore, it is crucial to remember that the AVF is not the only military service that the United States has utilized in the recent past. Third, this volume outlines the crucial impact of military service on American society, especially in terms of framing debates regarding who serves, why, or why not. The book illuminates how military issues, in this case personnel policy, impacted society. While many of these effects were unintended consequences, they nonetheless had far-reaching results within American democracy. Even though the smoke of battle exhibits more dramatic consequences, military service as an ideal in American society also had effects all its own. Practical, political, and social pressures, as well as the constant need for personnel to fill the ranks of the military, led to perennial debates, contested conceptualizations, and redefinitions of who served. Ultimately, military service functioned as a litmus test of American values and expanded opportunities within military service as a result. Finally, this book demonstrates an irony about American civil-military relations. When the military has been considered in isolation, observers have often correctly characterized it as a traditional and conservative organization that was resistant to change. The unique nature of American civil-military relations, however, has ensured another characteristic. Civilian leaders have often been able to reshape and reform restrictive military personnel policies precisely because of the organizational characteristics of the military: strict civilian control, deference to authority, adherence to orders, and rigid vertical hierarchy. In context, these factors resulted in malleability. When military service reflected values inconsistent with American society, civilian leaders were able to hammer, forge, hone, and polish military personnel policies so that they more accurately reflected the nation's conscience.

I hope that this book will stimulate broad questions and motivate additional research into U.S. military service and its important relationship to American society. Overall, *Military Service and American Democracy* contributes extensive historical context to current debates that are central to illuminating the complex relationship between military policy, politics, and American society.

CHAPTER TWO

THE SELECTIVE SERVICE IDEA

The Selective Service System has as its foundation little groups of neighbors in every one of the 3,070 counties or parishes in the United States. These neighbors in every county make up the 6,443 local boards. On them is placed with an utter and complete confidence the primary responsibility to determine who is to serve the Nation by training for the armed forces, and who is to serve in industry, agriculture and government. All must serve. This decision of where the registrant shall serve is, in wartime, often a question of life or death.[1]—Lewis B. Hershey, 1942

The United States of America has just successfully concluded a global war which strained her manpower, industry and material resources to the utmost. Every citizen of the democracy was called upon to exert the utmost effort as part of the National team. That every citizen did so, to the limit of his and her ability, is history. The natural and artificial resources of any nation are dependent upon and re-reflect the vigor of her manpower. An intelligent patriotism is imperative, if the nation is to vindicate the past, maintain the present, and rise to its future destiny.[2]—Gillem Board, 4 March 1946

During the emergency of World War II, the Selective Service idea of decentralized or local operation was in operation six and one-half years from September 16, 1940 to March 31, 1947. It began with about 15 months of peace, came to maturity during three and three-fourths years of war and terminated 19 months after victory. On the mobilization side, the 6,443 local boards of the System accomplished the stupendous task of registering 50,680,137 men, classifying and reclassifying

36,677,024 who were liable for military service, gave physical examinations to or forwarded for physical examination around 20,000,000 and secured the induction of 10,022,367.[3]—Lewis B. Hershey, 1948

The year 1939 witnessed the founding of future technology juggernaut Hewlett-Packard, the publication of John Steinbeck's now classic *The Grapes of Wrath*, and the first NCAA basketball tournament, where in the finals the University of Oregon Ducks handily defeated the Ohio State Buckeyes by a score of 46 to 33. It also marked the beginning of World War II, a conflict that defined modern American history and propelled the United States toward becoming a world superpower. World War II also fundamentally shaped U.S. military service in the modern era. Beforehand, the nation's military was quite small; relatively few individuals experienced peacetime military service, and the ideal of military service lingered in the shadows of American society. All that changed with the outbreak of global war.

The U.S. military in 1939 was woefully understrength. A few examples prove the point. While the army's planned strength at that time was 375,000 soldiers, it could only muster 242,648. Other military services experienced similar shortfalls. The navy had 156,500 sailors, well short of its goal of 182,000. The reserves planned to maintain 192,000 members but could only assemble 157,000 reservists. While the army was the most understrength, the air components proportionally lacked more personnel. Military leaders sought 7,000 personnel dedicated to army air but could only enlist 2,800 aviators. Navy air fared worse; a paltry 2,602 naval aviators answered calls for 16,000 personnel. The National Guard stood closest to its authorized strength, with 245,000 guardsmen on the rolls compared to a goal of 251,000. This situation put total Americans serving in the military in 1939, including the reserves and National Guard, at 806,550, well short of the nation's peacetime goal of 1,023,000. Such low figures were overwhelmingly due to funding constraints rather than inability to recruit. By the time Japan attacked Pearl Harbor on 7 December 1941, the U.S. military had tripled in size, and by 1945 it topped 12 million soldiers, sailors, airmen, and marines.[4]

As war clouds loomed on the horizon, the U.S. military began to swell in size. The establishment of the first peacetime military draft in American history commenced a march toward unprecedented mobilization.[5] On 20 June 1940, Edward R. Burke (D-NE) introduced the peacetime draft bill on the floor of the Senate, and James W. Wadsworth Jr. (R-NY) presented a companion measure on the floor of the House of Representatives the following day. Contentious debate in Congress and throughout American society ensued; the United States was not yet at war, and many Americans argued that conscription was a last resort only to be implemented during conflict.[6] As Lewis B. Hershey, the eventual director of the Selective Service System, later recalled, "The debate on the bill in the forums of public discussion and on the floor of the Congress, indicated the uncertainty of our national public opinion and the confused crosscurrents of neutrality, non-belligerency, defense, and war." In the midst of these "confused cross-currents," President Franklin D. Roosevelt signed the peacetime draft law on 16 September 1940. Known colloquially as the Burke-Wadsworth bill after its two congressional sponsors, the Selective Training and Service Act of 1940 operated in peacetime from 16 September 1940 until 8 December 1941; when the United States declared war on Japan, it operated in wartime thereafter. This act inaugurated the first time in U.S. history that peacetime conscription was law.[7] The milestone also elevated military service to a universal obligation among American males in both theory and reality. Section 3(a) declared, "Every male citizen of the United States and every other male person residing in the United States, who is between the ages of 18 and 45 at the time vested for his registration, shall be liable for training and service in the land or naval forces of the United States."[8] Such a provision redefined military service in America; it also reestablished the Selective Service System that over the course of the next several years inducted millions of Americans into military service.[9]

Even though the United States was formally at peace when Congress passed and President Roosevelt signed the selective service law, World War II had already erupted and fierce fighting was occurring around the globe.[10] On 1 September 1939 war erupted in Europe when Germany invaded Poland. Although the United States was not yet formally at war, Hershey characterized the act as "passed in the shadow of war" and acknowledged, "It was passed as a precautionary measure to prepare ourselves for what seemed to our national leadership a situation of grave national danger." After President Roosevelt signed the act into law, mobilization proceeded quickly. On that same day, he ordered all males in the continental United States between the ages of 21 and 35 to register

Director of the Selective Service System Major General Lewis B. Hershey (middle), Georgia Neese Clark, and Secretary of the Interior Oscar Chapman at the Washington Hotel for a meeting. 6 September 1950. (Courtesy Harry S. Truman Library)

with the Selective Service System. Roosevelt then appointed a national advisory committee composed predominately of civilians to plan "the procurement of manpower for our National Defense under the Compulsory Military Training bill."[11] Roosevelt named Frederick J. Osborn as chair and appointed members Wayne Coy, W. H. Draper Jr., Joseph P. Harris, Floyd W. Reeves, and Channing H. Tobias.[12]

On 23 September 1940, Roosevelt issued an executive order that implemented the Selective Service System. The sixty-one-page document covered in minute detail the system that conscripted American men into military service during peacetime. Mentioning the specificity in Roosevelt's order, the *Los Angeles Times* reported, "It even contained a diagram, definitions of singular and plural, told the type of furniture to be used in registration offices and the type of telephone calls that would be allowed." More important, Roosevelt tasked state governors to create the infrastructure of the peacetime draft, including a state executive for selective service and organization of local draft boards, one for approximately every 30,000 residents. Roosevelt left no doubt with governors as to the significance he placed on the request and the peacetime draft: "The Congress has made its historic decision after careful consideration and full debate. The procurement and training of our man power under proper administration, fairly and without fear or favor, is undoubtedly the most important single factor in our entire program of national defense. I ask your every help."[13]

A flurry of executive orders swiftly established rules and regulations that guided the implementation of the Selective Service System.[14] On 4 October 1940, Roosevelt clarified classification, selection, and financing of the draft, and ten days later he appointed University of Wisconsin chancellor Clarence B. Dykstra the national director of selective service. On 18 October Roosevelt detailed physical standards; four days later he outlined the process for delivery and induction of draftees. Two successive registrations occurred. The first occurred on 16 October, and contemporaries characterized it as "the first peacetime registration for military service in American history." It resulted in 16,565,037 total registrants by 30 June 1941.[15] The second registration occurred on 1 July 1941 and registered anyone who failed to register the first time and any males who had since turned twenty-one years of age. On 31 July 1941, Roosevelt appointed Lewis B. Hershey director of the Selective Service System.[16] By 30 September 1941, the two registrations resulted in 17,370,355 Americans registered with the Selective Service System.[17]

Once the Selective Service System classified them, local boards selected approximately 1 million Americans for military service and inducted them into the armed forces. Even though the Selective Service System had national and state headquarters, the organization was local in character, with 6,443 local boards that classified, selected, and delivered registrants for induction into military service. There were also 279 appeal boards and 650 medical advisory boards. Local characteristics ensured that the Selective Service System reflected American society. Ironically, the Selective Service System voluntarily administered compulsion: "All the members of these various types of boards and the Government appeal agents and examining physicians served on a voluntary basis without pay or reimbursement of any kind." By 8 December 1941 the Selective Service System had registered 17,388,000 Americans, classified 15,418,710, and inducted 921,722 of them into military service. It also placed roughly 2 million additional Americans in Class I, defined as "persons [who] were (1) in military service, (2) immediately available for military service, or (3) awaiting local board examination."[18] Therefore, in slightly longer than one year, the peacetime draft registered more than 17 million Americans, placed close to 1 million of them directly into military service, and made 2 million more of them available for it.

The Selective Service System also motivated many Americans to enlist for military service. Hershey, the foremost authority on the draft at that time, explained: "Recruiting under these conditions has its roots in the liability to service placed on registrants by the Selective Service law. The extent of recruiting would not be possible except under these conditions. Registrants took time by the forelock and used the period prior to being drafted to make their own choice of the arms and services. In short, it was not a free recruiting or enlistment situation. The gentle pressure of the Selective Service was ever present." Even though such "gentle pressure" was a powerful and omnipresent force during the peacetime draft, it still left the vast majority of Americans deferred from military service. Of the more than 17 million registrants, the Selective Service System deferred 12,138,710 Americans from the peacetime draft for a variety of reasons, most because they had dependents.[19] The draft, however, was still the critical mechanism that allowed mobilization for World War II. "As in World War I, the draft was the principal source of military manpower, inducing many men to enlist and providing directly more than 10 million, or 61 percent, of the 16.5 million men who donned uniforms," concluded one extensive military personnel study that covered the entire period of the World War II draft, from its peacetime inception on 16 September 1940 until its expiration on 31 March 1947.[20]

From the outset, the army needed personnel far more than any other military service; therefore, the draft was more crucial to the army. To demonstrate this, all of the nearly 1 million Americans inducted into military service during the peacetime draft served in the army. Hershey admitted, "No requisitions for men had been received from the Navy or Marine Corps, but their recruiting programs have benefited immensely from the existence of the Selective Service Law." Such a close relationship between the army and the draft was due to its relative size, as the army at that time was roughly 2 million men. By comparison, the navy and marine corps combined numbered only approximately 500,000 men; the air force was not yet an independent military service.[21]

The peacetime draft received favorable ratings in public opinion polls; more than 90 percent of respondents agreed that "the draft has been handled fairly." George Gallup, widely considered an expert in the field, commented, "After watching the operation of the Selective Service draft for nearly 7 months, the American public, in a Nation-wide survey of opinion, has passed an overwhelmingly favorable verdict upon it." Gallop further explained, "The sentiment of the people is almost unanimous that the first peacetime draft in the history of the country has been handled fairly in their communities. . . . Fewer than 1 in every 10 persons interviewed in the survey said they thought the draft had not been fair, and their objections were largely based on personal grounds rather than on over-all policies or basic principles."[22] Such positive public sentiment boded well for the herculean task of full mobilization that remained ahead.

Even so, the draft faced significant challenges. From the start of the peacetime draft, the tension between compulsory and voluntary military service was both palpable and problematic. The two constructs coexisted for less than one year after U.S. entry into World War II. On 5 December 1942, President Roosevelt issued Executive Order 9279, which ended the recruitment of men ages eighteen to thirty-seven and instead required the draft to provide all enlisted personnel within this age group.[23] This decision to forbid voluntary military service did not end competition among the military services for men. The navy and marine corps continued to recruit seventeen-year-olds, whereas the draft could only induct eighteen-year-olds. In addition, the marine corps often stationed officers at places of induction, who touted the corps to draftees. Roosevelt's executive order illustrated another historical lesson, though: since World War II, voluntary methods largely proved insufficient to provide sufficient personnel for America's major wars.[24] U.S. policy makers and military leaders often exhibited optimism that voluntary methods eliminated the need for compulsion, but confidence gave way to compulsion when confronted with significant personnel requirements of large wars. Therefore, U.S. military service from World War II to the present exhibited a split personality. During that time frame, military service existed roughly evenly between compulsory and voluntary constructs. From 1940 to 1947 and again from 1948 to 1973 the Selective Service System loomed large and cast the shadow of compulsion across the land.[25] From 1973 until the present, the voluntary construct reigned supreme, although important questions about its sustainability remain.

The shift to compulsion began in peacetime and quickly thereafter eliminated voluntary enlistment. It also cast a spotlight on other areas of American military service that demanded attention. As the Selective Service System inducted increased numbers of African Americans into the military as a result of the peacetime draft, many African Americans rightfully made a direct connection between military service and expanded opportunities.[26] Partly in response to these social pressures, the Selective Training and Service Act of 1940 specifically forbade racial discrimination in the mobilization of personnel for military service. The official Selective Service System history noted that the act "contained the basic legal prohibitions against racial discrimination." It further explained that "any person, regardless of race or color, between the ages of 18 and 36, shall be afforded an opportunity to volunteer for induction into the armed forces of the United States for the training and service prescribed." A second provision proclaimed that "in the selection and training of men under this act, and in the interpretation and execution of the provisions of this act, there shall be no discrimination against any person on account of race or color."[27]

These two provisions in the law were ideals, not reality; racial discrimination was endemic to the military services at that time. The resort to compulsion, however, illuminated disparities in military service far more intensely than voluntary service. In order to achieve widespread public acceptance and to avoid criticism, the Selective Service System sought no official racial discrimination. The military services continued to discriminate, but increased inductions of African Americans challenged the military services to grapple with the issue of race in a way that the comfort of peace failed to cause. As a result of increased numbers of African Americans, intensified pressure from civil rights leaders, and heightened civilian oversight from the president and Congress, the military services relented into expanding opportunities in the form of more military occupational specialties (MOS), additional training prospects, increased military schools, and, ultimately, military desegregation. From the reestablishment of the Selective Service System, there was a racial relations division within the office of the director led by an African American army lieutenant colonel that sought "to eliminate any conditions causing racial discrimination, to improve relations between the races in their contacts with the Selective Service System, and otherwise to promote satisfactory racial conditions." The compulsion inherent in the Selective Service System necessitated good public relations for the system, for Congress, and for the president; in turn, that compelled extra attention to racial matters in U.S. military service, especially racial discrimination by the military services. Such a situation presented an opening wedge promoting a fairer environment within the Selective Service System and forced a crack within the historical discrimination that the military services had

Stressing the need for interracial solidarity in the postwar world, African American and white soldiers got together as part of the army's general educational program at a heavy bomber base in Italy. 1 March 1945. (U.S. Army, courtesy Harry S. Truman Library)

been more than content to perpetuate. African Americans were by far the largest minority group in military service during World War II: "Negroes constitute the largest proportion of the racial groups under discussion and 84 percent of the inductions of this group." From November 1940 to October 1942 the Selective Service System inducted 336,253 African Americans, compared to 11,652 Puerto Rican Americans, 8,018 American Indians, 7,429 Filipino Americans, 5,369 Japanese Americans, 4,578 Chinese Americans, 413 Hawaiians, and 17,156 Americans classified at that time as "others." Therefore, the predominant racial issue for civilian and military leaders who worked on mobilization and military personnel policy at that time was how to mobilize African Americans. By one estimate, African Americans "in 1940 constituted 9.7 percent of the population and 10.4 percent of the total registration"[28] and thereby represented a significant source of military personnel.

Partly due to the early connection between the draft and hopes for racial equality in military service, the draft increased the proportion of African Americans in the military.[29] Some African American newspapers heralded this dynamic as an opportunity to expand further African American participation in military service. Prior to Japan's attack on Pearl Harbor, the *Kansas American* declared, "There are now some 65,000 of the finest young Colored men in our armed forces; as our country's military needs expand thousands more will answer the call to colors. These young men, like their young fellow white Americans, stand ready, if need be, to give their life's blood for the cause of democracy." The newspaper proclaimed, "They have a right to expect nothing less than full democratic treatment. We must look forward and work for the day when there will be no barriers in the way of Colored youths to full training and advancement opportunities in the navy, the Air Corps, and the Army. We must look forward and work for the day when no man who offers his life for the defense of democracy will suffer segregation on account of color."[30] Over the course of the war, the number of African Americans in military service increased dramatically. Official records of the Selective Service System indicate that African Americans "were an important source of manpower for the armed forces in World War II as is shown by the fact that a total of 1,056,841 Negro registrants were inducted into the armed forces through Selective Service as of 31 December 1945. Of these, 885,945 went into the Army, 153,224 into the Navy, 16,005 into the Marine Corps, and 1,667 into the Coast Guard." Official records further specify, "These Negro inductees made up 10.9 percent of all registrants inducted into the Army (8,108,531), 10.0 percent of all inductions into the Navy (1,526,250), 8.5 percent of all Marine Corps inductions (188,709) and 10.9 percent of all Coast Guard inductions (15,235). Thus Negroes, who constituted approximately 11.0 percent of all registrants liable for service, furnished approximately this proportion of the inductees in all branches of the service except the Marine Corps."[31] African Americans played a significant role in military service during World War II, with over 1 million inducted. This total was representative of the liable age group (10.9 percent versus 11.0 percent) and once again demonstrated the army's unique connection to compulsion because it was the most personnel intensive of the services and therefore the most impacted by personnel policy.

Partly as a result of the increased numbers of African Americans in military service, especially within the army, civilian leaders urged consideration of the implications of race for military personnel policy. On 27 August 1942 the War Department established an "Advisory Committee on Negro Troop Policies," known colloquially as the McCloy Committee after its chair, Assistant Secretary of War John J. McCloy. Members included

Inspector General's Office representative Brigadier General Benjamin O. Davis; Assistant Chief of Staff, G-3 (Operations) Brigadier General Idwal H. Edwards; Assistant Chief of Staff, G-1 (Personnel) Brigadier General Donald Wilson; Services of Supply representative Brigadier General Joseph N. Dalton; Army Ground Forces representative Colonel Edward Barber; and Army Air Forces representative Colonel John H. McCormick. The McCloy Committee's purpose was to serve "in an advisory capacity to the Secretary of War on Negro troop policies."[32]

The McCloy Committee collected information on military personnel policies regarding race and combed through masses of personnel policy documents outlining race. It concluded that a "separate but equal" policy governed military service and recorded, "It is the policy of the War Department that the services of Negroes will be utilized on a fair and equitable basis." The committee also determined, however, that the War Department found no fault with a segregated military: "The policy of the War Department is not to intermingle colored and white enlisted personnel in the same regimental organizations. This policy has proven satisfactory over a long period of years and to make changes would produce situations destructive to morale and detrimental to the preparation for national defense."[33] The specific duties of the McCloy Committee were to "inform itself on all phases of the subject," form recommendations "to assist in developing a cogent and consistent War Department policy," and "aid Commanding Officers of Negro troops" through the dissemination of their findings.[34] McCloy resolved that high-level attention to race as it related to military service and a basic change in military personnel policy were needed. As a result, he recommended "the designation of a first-class officer or group of officers of high rank with the special assignment of planning for the use of Negro troops. In the past, the subject has been rather unpopular and change has taken place as a result of yielding to pressures rather than on the basis of forward planning." McCloy argued that the formation of this new advisory group should also include a change in policy. As Davidson Sommers, assistant executive for the group, declared, "However, I do not think that a mere study, even by a highly qualified officer, would be sufficient. Some indication of direction from high Army levels is needed as a basis for the study and I think this requires a basic change in policy. I recommend that the basic Army policy be changed to call for eventual non-segregation and assignment of Negro troops solely on the basis of ability and that the designated officer be directed to plan on this basis."[35] Although it would not take effect until later that fall, the result was the creation of the Gillem Board that the latter part of this chapter discusses in depth.

As World War II raged, military personnel requirements increased, and compulsory military service became the only sanctioned method to fill the ranks, civilian leaders became increasingly involved with military personnel policy. One example was the War Manpower Commission, which attempted to pressure the military branches to remove race as a consideration in compulsory military service. On 17 February 1943 the commission's chair, Paul V. McNutt, urged Secretary of War Henry L. Stimson and Secretary of the Navy Frank Knox to increase the utilization of African Americans in the U.S. military. McNutt expounded, "The problem of induction of Negroes into the Army and the Navy is acute. Negroes constitute approximately ten percent of our population. They constitute less than six percent of our armed forces." Pointing out that the Selective Training and Service Act of 1940 "prohibits discrimination in the selection of men on account of race or color," McNutt feared that the military services ignored either the spirit or letter of the law. He explained, "The control of admission of Negroes into the armed forces has been exercised by severe limitations on the numbers permitted to enlist, and in Selective Service by the use of Negro and White calls. The use of Negro and White calls compels the local board to disregard the order numbers of registrants in order to fill White calls. It is estimated that approximately 300,000 Negroes have been passed over to fill White calls." McNutt claimed that such a military personnel policy "has been the cause of continuous and mounting criticism" and recalled that the issue was discussed multiple times in late January 1943. At that time, the War Manpower Commission recommended to the War and Navy Departments that "beginning April 1 calls contain no reference to Negroes or to Whites."[36]

Asserting the War Manpower Commission's civilian role over the War Department, McNutt ordered Stimson to act: "The practice of placing separate calls for white and colored registrants is a position which is not tenable, and it is now necessary to begin delivering men in accordance with their order number without regard to race or color."[37] Although McNutt clearly found separate induction calls against the spirit of the antidiscrimination provisions of the Selective Training and Service Act of 1940, he initially framed his argument as a practical move intended to smooth the operation of the Selective Service System. On 14 April 1943, Stimson pushed back; he furnished McNutt with an opinion by the judge advocate general of the army that upheld the necessity and legality of separate racial induction calls. Stimson refused to concede to McNutt's initial pressures and claimed that removing race as a factor in military service resulted in "serious impairment of the military effort."[38] Even more resolute, McNutt held firm and maintained, "After careful consideration of the matter contained in this document, I am still definitely of the opinion that the practice of placing separate calls for White and Negro troops is contrary to the proper interpretation of that Act." He sternly warned Stimson that the Selective Service System planned to "abandon the practice of filling separate calls for White and Negro inductees" after 1 January 1944.[39]

In this instance, civilian leaders in the War Manpower Commission and the Selective Service System pressured military leaders in the War Department to remove race as a factor in inductions. Stimson, representing the army, pushed back through utilization of his judge advocate general. Ultimately, McNutt and the War Manpower Commission refused to relent and ordered the army to remove race as a factor in inductions by 1 January 1944. In this case, an urgent situation dictated by the efficient operation of the Selective Service System during wartime forced a reconsideration of military service and removed race as a factor for inductions.

McNutt held the line and stated that equal ratios did not preclude racial discrimination; instead, he insisted that the Selective Service System tolerate no racial discrimination. Compulsion demanded that military service have no disparities that invited criticism; racial discrimination by the military services was one such disparity. Compulsion accentuated the issue far more sharply than voluntary military service had done previously. The testy exchange between McNutt and Stimson illustrated how civilian policy makers exerted pressure on the military establishment to change, even when military leaders clearly did not wish to do so. While McNutt listened to their concerns and their ultimate desire to keep inequitable racial divisions, he told them that the military had to change. McNutt's forceful oversight linked the antidiscrimination aspects of the Selective Training and Service Act of 1940 to military service generally and was an initial spur to redefine U.S. military service.[40]

World War II began to change not only the racial dynamics of American military service. As more and more American men served in the military during World War II, U.S. policy makers also sought ways to increase female participation in both industry and military service. Hershey perceived, "The greatest possible source to meet the replacements required as a result of this necessary continual shifting of men from one group to another, as well as the increased demand for the services of workers, is to be found in the employment of women." Though he cautioned, "There are many problems indeed involved in the maximum utilization of available womanpower," Hershey highlighted possibilities of "greater utilization of women for clerical and administrative, and even technical services in all of the armed forces."[41]

On 14 May 1942, Congress authorized that the Women's Army Auxiliary Corps (WAAC) was intended for "noncombatant service with the Army of the United States for the purpose of making available to the national defense when needed the knowledge, skill, and special training of the women of this Nation." Later that summer, on July 30, Congress rescinded restrictions on women serving in the naval reserve. The following year brought additional changes. On 1 July 1943, Congress converted the WAAC to the Women's Army Corps (WAC), simultaneously making the organization part of the regular army—but only temporarily. That same year Congress approved the U.S. Marine Corps Women's Reserve. Other women's organizations joined the fray, including the navy's Women Accepted for Voluntary Emergency Service (WAVES) and the U.S. Coast Guard Women's Reserve, known colloquially as SPARs from combining the Latin and English versions of the Coast Guard motto, *Semper Paratus*, Always Ready. These changes were significant. World War II increased demands for men in military service and in turn led to compounded requirements for women in industry; it also opened new opportunities for women to fill clerical, administrative, and technical positions in military service. Over the course of World War II, approximately 400,000 women served in the U.S. military. Some analysts estimate that more than 500 U.S. military women paid the ultimate sacrifice in military service, overwhelmingly due to noncombat causes, and that 84 became prisoners of war.[42]

A rapidly burgeoning military also impacted the American economy. From December 1941 to December 1942 the number of Americans in military service rose from approximately 2.1 million to 5.5 million. During the same time period, Americans working in war-related industry soared from roughly 6.9 million to 17.5 million. Other categories—such as agriculture, self-employed, unemployed, and non–war-related industry—shrunk, in some cases dramatically. Such huge shifts illustrated the intense competition for personnel between these various enterprises and illuminated the practical need for policy makers to find alternative sources to supply them.[43] Policy makers analyzed these changes and argued for two solutions. One was to utilize women more fully, primarily in industry but also in military service. The other was to transfer more men from non–war-related industry primarily into military service but also into war-related industry. Early in the war, the Selective Service System identified women moving into the labor force as a strategic reserve: "There are two principal ways of increasing the number of persons included in our manpower pool. The first is by adding to the labor force the women who have not been in the labor force or redirecting them from nonessential industry. This is our largest source of reserve." In addition, the Selective Service System sought to "increase our pool by redirecting men from nonessential civilian occupations into the armed forces or into war production."[44] During World War II the Selective Service System strove to increase the number of women entering industry to free up men for military service. Although this development's attendant expansion of women in military service was limited, it represented an important step that foreshadowed a development that occurred more widely in the late 1960s and early 1970s with the advent of the all-volunteer force.

As previously discussed, the initial public perception of the draft was extremely positive. It also remained fairly consistent throughout the war, although the public's views became less positive the longer the draft was in place. Throughout World War II the American Institute of Public Opinion conducted Gallup polls that measured American attitudes toward the draft. Not surprisingly, favorable survey responses declined the longer the draft operated. There was still, however, fairly broad public approval of the overall fairness of the draft throughout the war. When asked in May 1941, "Do you think the draft has been handled fairly in your community?," 93 percent of respondents answered yes. When asked the same question one year later, only 88 percent of respondents replied in the affirmative. In November 1942 the draft was characterized as fair by 82 percent of respondents. By January 1944 favorable responses dropped to 75 percent. Even so, in the worst statistical measurement there was still a 3-to-1 ratio of respondents who characterized the operation of the draft as fair compared to respondents who did not.[45]

Even though the draft maintained consistent and widespread support during World War II, it experienced many problems. There were complexities of classification and unique situations. When speaking at the University of Pennsylvania's Wharton School of Finance and Commerce in Philadelphia, Hershey relayed an often heard song that a local board clerk had composed known as "The Clerk's Lament":

> Ten little registrants standing in a line;
> One joined the Navy, then there were nine.
> Nine little registrants sitting on a gate;
> One broke a vertebra, then there were eight.
> Eight little registrants, talking 'bout heaven;
> One went conscientious, then there were seven.
> Seven little registrants, what a strange mix!
> One became a pilot, and then there were six.
> Six little registrants very much alive;
> One went and drowned, and then there were five.
> Five little registrants full of canny lore;
> One stole a pig, and then there were four.
> Four little registrants, spry as they can be;
> One became twenty-eight, then there were three.
> Three little registrants, all alone and blue;
> One fed his relatives, then there were two.
> Two little registrants, what can be done!
> One went to a psychiatrist, then there was one.

One little registrant classified 1-A;
Physically, mentally, morally okay.
One little registrant to tote a big gun;
He got married, and then there were NONE![46]

In an understatement, Hershey recounted that "it was necessary for the System to give special attention to certain groups of registrants." In addition to handling issues of race in the draft, policy makers had to consider how to handle unique situations such as conscientious objectors, prisoners, and undocumented immigrants. The Selective Service System euphemistically characterized such challenges as "special problems of mobilization." There was also the important question of how to enforce the draft with Americans who refused to register or declined to report for induction.[47]

Another problem was outright fraud. Some extreme examples were ludicrous enough to be humorous. One registrant, "aged 28, declared Mary Ann Sheridan as his dependent. Mary Ann Sheridan was a horse. His claim for dependency kept him out of the Army for 2 years." In another case, a "clerk of Yonkers, N.Y., spirited away her sweetheart's file and destroyed the file of her brother-in-law." Two Ohio brothers conspired together: "This Ohio youth, 24 years old, paid his 14-year-old brother $6.00 to report in his place for induction. The registrant went to jail. His brother would like to stay in the Army." In addition to individual fraud, there were commercial ventures to educate Americans on creative ways to evade the draft. In New York City, one conspiring entrepreneur ran a school "where selectees were taught to fake deafness, mental disorders, or heart ailments to avoid military service." Even though such deception to avoid military service was dramatic, overall abuse was quite low given the huge number of Americans involved. There were approximately 100,000 recorded delinquencies as of 7 December 1942, falling precipitously to roughly 30,000 by 30 June 1944. Authorities inducted or convicted some of these Americans, whereas other cases were simply administrative errors in that the individual in question was either already in military service, had multiple registrations, or was dead.[48]

Delinquencies did not go unnoticed. Many Americans anonymously reported others who they thought should be in military service but were not. In one anonymous letter sent to the Federal Bureau of Investigation (FBI) on 12 April 1943, the author requested an inquiry into the selective service status of a local resident and provided the suspect's full name, exact address, and contact information for his local draft board. The informant complained, "He is collector for Prudential insurance which don't help to win the war and he is in 4F because he claims he is blind in one eye. I think its money in 4F. There's something wrong somewhere. . . . Please investigate. P.S. I have my only two boys in service and this guy snickers because he don't [sic] go. He is in 4F. He is as fit as any one."[49] Many Americans sent anonymous letters to the Selective Service System and the FBI and requested officials to investigate neighbors who they felt abused the system. It often worked. In the case of the letter above, a handwritten memo on the letter recorded "CC Sent To PA 5/3/43" and indicated that the FBI notified the local draft board, so it could conduct its own investigation into the allegation. There were numerous similar cases wherein Americans reported others and requested probes into the legitimacy of their selective service status.[50]

Other Americans exuded patriotism and clamored to enter military service even when they fell outside of established parameters for it. In one instance, H. B. Batleman, founder and owner of a successful fur shop established in 1911 in Norfolk, Virginia, pleaded with President Roosevelt to allow him to enter military service: "As a citizen of the United States I would like to state my opinion on the Selective Service. It could be handled in a different manner from what it is now handled. Why not draft men of all ages without any obligations to families as in my own case. I am 48 yrs. and have two married children, no obligations as my wife can be taken care of by my earnings."[51] Americans reacted to the Selective Service System in myriad ways and expressed diverse opinions about military service. Millions served in the military, the majority of them through the draft. Some campaigned to get out of military service while others argued to be allowed to serve even when they did not have to. Certain Americans expressed a desire to expand the draft whereas others wanted to contract it.

During 1944 reliance on the draft waned as Allied forces advanced toward victory in World War II. Lewis Hershey observed, "The end of organized resistance changed the demand on Selective Service. Calls for induction were lowered to around 52,000 men per month." At the same time, demobilization became a priority. Hershey recalled, "Discharges from the Army and Navy rose to a peak of more than 1,500,000 monthly thus stepping up greatly the veterans' reemployment work of the System." Massive demobilization changed the demand for military personnel. The most immediate problem became reintegration of veterans into civil society rather than induction of additional Americans into military service, roughly on a scale of thirty to one. By mid-1944, Roosevelt and Hershey sensed a desire among Americans to return to normal. Such a dynamic challenged the Selective Service System and forced stricter military personnel policies. "After some 3 years of striving to make America 'the arsenal of democracy,' it is not surprising that by July 1944 nonagricultural industries were much interested in an early return to the production of civilian goods, the market for which was assuming tremendous proportions," remarked Hershey.[52]

The transition from wartime to demobilization was not without its own set of monumental challenges. Beginning on 16 December 1944, the Battle of the Bulge tested personnel policy in an unexpected way. Hershey argued that it "put a stop at least temporarily to the idea that the war was about over. President Roosevelt in his annual message to the Congress urged the immediate enactment of a National Service Act, a law for the drafting of nurses, and one for universal military training after the war." Roosevelt urged a National Service Act as a way to keep Americans focused on completing the war, but "All of this brought upon Selective Service new pressures for occupational deferments and work-or-fight policies and caused it to tighten deferment procedures during the period from the Battle of the Bulge to VE-day." With Victory in Europe Day, the U.S. military increased demobilization: "Immediately after VE-day, a point system for the demobilization of the Army was put into effect. Somewhat similar procedures were soon adopted by the other branches of the armed forces. It is not surprising then that in June 1945, the number of men separated to civil life, around 190,000, exceeded for the first time the monthly inductions which were 107,000. The number increased very rapidly each month thereafter and totaled more than 5,000,000 between VJ-day and the end of the year."[53] In just over one year, leaders dismantled the largest U.S. military ever mobilized.

As World War II climaxed and demobilization accelerated, U.S. policy makers retained the draft as a cautionary measure and proposed several policies related to military service, including national service. Although Roosevelt supported universal military training (UMT), he favored national service even more. Congress introduced other military personnel policies in rapid succession. On 17 January 1945, House Military Affairs Committee chair Andrew J. May (D-KY) urged "quick enactment of work-or-fight bill for men from 18–45." On 25 January 1945 high rejection rates spurred a Selective Service System survey that revealed "40.3 percent of the men called up for induction at age of 28 are rejected as physically unfit. At 34, the rejection rate is over 50 percent and at 38, 59.1 percent." On 8 March 1945 the U.S. Senate passed the "O'Mahoney-Kilgore bill, substitute for the May-Bailey bill, providing for limited national service."[54] Debates surrounding national service illustrated that military service was at its essence about the best usage of American youth. Military service early in life was less disruptive, and youth were also more physically fit. As a result, military service was (and is) directly related to the youth of America; it is at its core a youth question. This connection between military personnel policy and American youth permeated debates that intensified regarding the Selective Service System and national service. The same dynamic eventually characterized the campaign for (and against) UMT after the war that is discussed in detail in a later chapter.

"In anticipation of a general desire for greater vigor in the prosecution of the war both at home and abroad, and for more adequate postwar preparedness," President Roosevelt urged passage of an act requiring national service in his first message to the Seventy-Ninth Congress. His purpose was to achieve "the total mobilization of all our human resources," and in January Andrew J. May introduced such an act by way of an amendment to Section 5 of the Selective Training and Service Act of 1940. The National Service Act enjoyed fairly widespread approval and also garnered "the general support of the War and Navy Departments, the War Production Board, the War Manpower Commission, the War Food Administration, the American Farm Bureau Federation, and the Selective Service System." Although opposition to the act surfaced, primarily from labor unions, both the House and Senate passed versions of the act. While the two bodies worked out subtle differences, "the end of the war in Europe came before final action was taken."[55] The push for national service at the end of World War II demonstrated intimate linkages between national service and military service. National service was a broader mandate, engendered more resistance, and was more difficult to pass. It did, however, enjoy stronger support during wartime than peacetime.

After World War II ended, the Selective Service System conducted a rigorous and exhaustive analysis of military service during that war. The results were stunning. The Selective Service System reported, "All told, the Army and the Navy, including the Marine Corps and Coast Guard, attained the record-breaking peak strength of 12,314,000 on June 1, 1945, just after VE-day. This figure contained 275,000 women but did not include any personnel missing in action, captured or deceased. By December 31, 1945, as many as 15,000,000 men were then in the armed forces or had seen service at one time during the 5 years since the beginning of Selective Service in 1940. Of this total slightly more than 5,000,000 were non-registrant and registrant enlistees or officers, while the balance as indicated above were inductees." The rise in personnel during the course of World War II was meteoric. The U.S. military expanded from approximately a half-million personnel in July 1940 to 1.9 million Americans serving in the military by July 1941. Exactly one year later, the number stood at slightly more than 4 million Americans and by July 1943 was just under 9.5 million. In 1944 roughly 12 million Americans were under arms, and the strength of the U.S. military peaked at about 12,314,000 in June 1945. This was the largest mobilization in American history. The majority served as draftees, with voluntary enlistments and officers comprising roughly 40 percent of the total force. Such a situation illustrated how different the context of military service during World War II was from the present in both its vast scope and its steadfast reliance on conscription.[56]

On 12 April 1945, President Roosevelt died. As a result, Vice President Harry S. Truman took the oath of office as the thirty-second president. Less than two weeks later, Congress extended the Selective Training and Service Act until 15 May 1946. On 9 May 1945, President Truman signed the bill into law. The unusual situation was urgent and "had to be handled quickly by the Congress, for had none been taken, all inductions automatically would have stopped while the United States was still pursuing the war against Japan."[57] During the spring and summer of 1945, draft calls once again increased in preparation for Operation Olympic, set for 1 November 1945, and, if necessary, Operation Coronet, slated for 1 April 1946.[58] After Victory in Japan Day on 15 August 1945, however, pressure subsided. On 29 August, Truman issued Executive Order 9605 and thereby "restored voluntary enlistments in the armed forces for registrants in the age group acceptable for induction," reversing Roosevelt's previous order from December 1942. Almost immediately, the tension between voluntary and compulsory military service resurfaced: "The result of the order and the law was that Selective Service again faced the problem of filling monthly calls from a pool of men substantially reduced by those who had already enlisted before induction." The friction, however, faded as "the Army and Navy, after some pressure from the System, allowed credit against the call for enlistees of ages 18 through 25 which group constituted those acceptable for induction at that time." Such a dynamic was a stark reminder of the tension between draft-motivated volunteers and the draft. Draft-motivated volunteers contracted the available personnel pool and retained control over their assignment in military service. Assignments that were difficult to fill, such as infantry, remained understrength. The Selective Service System arranged to get "credit" for enlistees in the draft age, presumably because they were draft-motivated. Victory in Japan Day occurred on 15 August 1945, and shortly thereafter Congress approved an act to stimulate voluntary military service through "immediate and deferred monetary and other benefits."[59]

The end of World War II produced one final but significant episode in military personnel policy. On 4 October 1945, Secretary of War Robert P. Patterson established a board "to prepare a broad policy for utilization of Negro manpower in the military establishment." The members were three U.S. Army generals: Lieutenant General Alvan C. Gillem Jr. (chair), Major General Lewis A. Pick, and Brigadier General Winslow C. Morse. Brigadier General Aln D. Warnock served the board as recorder without a vote.[60] The board soon came to be known as the Gillem Board.

A little background on Gillem is instructive. His grandfather graduated from West Point with the class of 1851, attained the rank of major general, and served under the command of Ulysses S. Grant at Shiloh. Alvan Cullom Gillem Jr.'s military career was just as remarkable. He enlisted in the U.S. Army in 1910 as a private. He served in the Punitive Expedition from 1916 to 1917 and again in World War I. After the war, the army sent Gillem to Vladivostok, Siberia, and then to the Philippines, where he served on the staff of General Douglas MacArthur. Gillem commanded a tank brigade with the 2nd Armored Division under the command of General George S. Patton, commanded the 3rd Armored Division, and then served as a corps commander at Fort Knox. At the completion of his thirty-seven-year military career, Gillem was a lieutenant general and commanded the Third U.S. Army.[61]

The Gillem Board sifted through mountains of reports, data, and official materials provided by the War Department and heard from more than sixty military and civilian experts over the course of five months. The board concluded that World War II strained U.S. military personnel. The members admitted from the outset of their investigation that "the plan proposed is based upon the lessons of experience and envisions maximum efficiency in the use of all authorized manpower in the event of another emergency straining every resource of the nation." Gillem advocated an increased use of African Americans within the U.S. military: "The policies prepared by the War Department should be progressively flexible. They should envision the continued mental and physical improvement of all citizens. They should be implemented *promptly*. They *must* be objective in nature. They *must* eliminate, at the earliest practicable moment, any special consideration based on race. They should point towards the immediate objective of an evaluation of the Negro on the basis of individual merit and ability. They should point towards a long-range objective which visualizes, over a period of time, a still greater utilization of this manpower potential in the military machine of the nation."[62]

The board came to twenty-seven specific conclusions and issued eighteen explicit recommendations regarding the utilization of African Americans in the postwar military. It predicted that the proportion of African Americans in the army would certainly grow and "in case of another national emergency will no doubt exceed that of World War II." With proper planning, the board concluded, "A greater and more efficient use can be realized from this manpower in the military establishment of the future." Gillem highlighted the importance of leadership and advised, "Regardless of source of procurement and of racial antecedents all officers of all components of the Army should be accorded equal rights and opportunities for advancement and professional improvement as prescribed by law and regulation." He advocated timely progress: "The approval and promulgation of a constructive and progressive policy involving the utilization of this manpower potential should be effected without delay." The board also kept some views that proved problematic for expanding participation in the postwar military. It recommended that "the proportion of Negro to white manpower as exists in the civil population be the accepted ratio for creating a troop basis in the postwar Army." That ratio was 10 percent. The group also recommended "that groupings of Negro units with white units in composite organizations be continued in the postwar Army as a policy." Therefore, Gillem and his associates clung to a segregated army that had an upper limit on participation by African Americans. Even so, the board ended with a positive vision of expanded opportunity for African Americans within the military. It conceived that the "ultimate objective" was "the effective use of *all* manpower made available to the military establishment. . . . The manpower to be utilized, in the event of another major war, in the Army without regard to antecedents or race."[63]

Public reaction to the Gillem Board's report was mixed. *New York Times* correspondent Anthony Leviero characterized it as heralding "wider opportunities in service and advancement in the Army for Negroes." Although he lamented the elimination of African American combat divisions such as the Ninety-Second and Ninety-Third Infantry Divisions in place of smaller regiments, Leviero characterized the move "as a distinct gain, as recognition of their services in the war." Secretary of War Patterson proclaimed, "The report embodies an effort to profit by our experiences in the war. It represents a change in direction in Army policy. The ultimate objective is the employment of manpower in the Army on the basis of ability alone." In an understatement, Patterson admitted, "The recommendations in the report do not attempt to reach that objective immediately."[64] *The Plain Dealer*, an African American newspaper published in Kansas City, Kansas, reported, "Regardless of the directives and findings of army committees, the rank and file in the service do not want to see the provisions of the Gillem report successfully executed if what is reported transpiring at Fort Benning may be accepted as authentic." African American service members there reported meager efforts at integration, a lack of African American officers, and a location "surrounded by segregation" where "once they are off the army reservation, they are subjected to insult, arrest and even worse."[65]

Gillem extolled the virtues of the board's work several years later when he was commanding general of the U.S. Third Army. In a speech to the Command and General Staff College, Fort Leavenworth, Kansas, he affirmed: "During the period of this conflict, over 2,400,000 Negroes were called through the medium of the Selective Service. A maximum number of over 900,000 actually served under the colors. This large segment of the population contributed materially to the success attained by our military forces. In turn, many material and collateral advantages accrued to the men in service. The Negro enjoyed the privileges of citizenship and, in turn, willingly paid the premium by accepting service. In many instances, this payment was settled through the medium of the supreme sacrifice." Gillem related military service directly to changes in military personnel policy. As he recalled, "During the course of the war years, certain instructions were found necessary and promulgated. Most important, from a racial point of view, were Army Regulations 210-10, dated 20 December 1940, and War Department Memorandum 600-45, dated 14 June 1945. In these regulations the War Department enunciated a policy directed at lessening and ameliorating racial discrimination. This policy has been in effect over a period of years."[66]

The Gillem Board's report formed the basis for military personnel policy in the postwar army. On 27 April 1946 the War Department promulgated the findings of the Gillem Board as policy by means of War Department Circular Number 124, "Utilization of Negro Manpower in the

Postwar Army Policy." The stated purpose of the policy was "to effect the maximum efficient utilization of the authorized Negro manpower in the postwar period." The policy envisioned, "Negro manpower in the postwar Army will be utilized on a broader professional scale than has obtained heretofore. The development of leaders and specialists based on individual merit and ability, to meet effectively the requirements of an expanded war Army[,] will be accomplished through the medium of installations and organizations. Groupings of Negro units with white units in composite organizations will be accepted policy."[67]

It is important to note that during World War II the research branch of the War Department's Information and Education Division collected massive amounts of information regarding U.S. military service. While Major General Frederick H. Osborn directed the Information and Education Division, University of Chicago professor of sociology Samuel A. Stouffer led a team of social scientists in the research branch that surveyed the attitudes of approximately 500,000 American military personnel, analyzed the results, and in 1949 published them as a four-volume work entitled *The American Soldier*.[68] Historian Joseph W. Ryan characterized Stouffer as "a kind of circular conduit for soldiers—gathering their attitudes and then using the data to influence soldier policies."[69] Stouffer and the G.I. survey set the precedent for measuring attitudes on U.S. military service. Osborn revealed, "Never before had modern methods of social science been employed on so large a scale." Army Chief of Staff George C. Marshall and Head of Army Service Forces Brehon B. Somervell provided official sanction to the effort that over the course of the war issued more than 200 unique surveys; several studied as many as 100 separate items. *The American Soldier* highlighted how World War II and military personnel policy changed the military as a social organization: "For here one was looking at both the old Army and the new—the old Army as symbolized at the bottom by the traditional regular, the new Army as symbolized at the bottom by the new citizen-soldier drafted into uniform by Selective Service." Survey responses evidenced tension between "the old Army" and "the new Army." One draftee opined, "This new era in the Army brought about by the Selective Service Act should be dealt with accordingly. My First Sergeant knows the NCO's are not too intelligent—he admits this. He also admits that the SS men are, by far, more intelligent than the Army's regular NCO's. But he says there is nothing can be done about this. My advice is to run an IQ test and let the men who have the most knowledge be the bosses."[70]

The American Soldier also highlighted the racial discrimination of military personnel policy and observed, "When an Army was to be raised, Negroes were needed and were not excluded, but neither were they fully integrated or fully accepted." In March 1943 the group surveyed African American soldiers and asked, "If you could talk to the President of the United States, what are the three most important questions you would want to ask him about the war and your part in it?" A full 50 percent of African American soldiers listed "questions and protests about racial discrimination," whereas less than 0.5 percent of white respondents did likewise. One of the most common questions was "Will I as a Negro share this so-called democracy after the war?" *The American Soldier* concluded, "Their solution, on the whole, was not to ignore or resist the war, but to press harder for Negro rights in it: to agitate against discrimination in the Army and for opportunities to serve in elite and combat branches, and in general to win for themselves more of a feeling that the war was 'their affair.'" The survey results also conveyed "a feeling of many Negro soldiers that the contributions made by Negroes to winning the war would earn for them a moral claim to improved postwar conditions." African American soldiers displayed more than three times the support for military desegregation after the war than white soldiers. As one African American soldier responded, "Let's practice what we preach. All the colored Americans ask for is to be treated as citizens."[71]

The selective service idea dominated military personnel policy during World War II. It vaulted a woefully understrength military prior to the outbreak of war to the largest U.S. military ever mobilized. It did so through the institution of the first peacetime draft in American history that transitioned to a wartime draft that forbade voluntary enlistment less than one year into the war. As compulsion became law, the draft illuminated racial inequities within the nation's military service. Compulsion also allowed greater civilian oversight of the military services through civilian institutions such as the presidency, Congress, Selective Service System, and War Manpower Commission. First the McCloy Committee and later the Gillem Board reconsidered previous military personnel policy, specifically focusing on the role of African American males in military service. Women's roles expanded as well, although the emphasis in policy was on expanded opportunities for women first in industry and only secondarily in limited military service. Support for the draft began high and remained overwhelmingly positive, even though it decreased somewhat with time. Problems with the draft existed, although they remained relatively low proportionally. Demobilization came quickly and contracted the military from its peak at over 12 million Americans to only 5 million by the end of 1945. Peace overtook efforts to convert support for compulsory military service to obligatory national service, even while such efforts enjoyed broad support within the context of war. *The American Soldier* distilled Samuel A. Stouffer's G.I. survey and revealed soldiers' attitudes about military service during World War II. A war-weary Congress extended selective service easily, ushering in an uncertain and uneasy postwar era.

CHAPTER THREE

A SOUND AND DEMOCRATIC PRINCIPLE

In general, it may be said that a system of universal military training should provide that every young man will receive military or naval training—this on the sound and democratic principle that every man owes it to his country to undergo training which will enable him to defend it in a major emergency.[1]—James W. Wadsworth and Clifton A. Woodrum, 1945

Men from "both sides of the railroad tracks" will meet on common ground in the training camps, and the results should be a growing solidarity among Americans and the gradual effacement of such class distinctions and prejudices as exist today. Young men from the homes of working people will undergo the same drills, eat the same food, sleep in the same beds as boys from the homes of the well-to-do and the employer. Democracy will be genuinely at work, and the value of teamwork and cooperation will be a daily lesson.[2]—War Department, 5 May 1945

The man who built America's military might and who has laid the plans for America's future military strength is needed today to carry his plans into execution. That man is General of the Army George C. Marshall. His proposal—that universal military training be made the foundation of our national security—has now been formally indorsed by President Truman. It awaits decision by the Congress.[3]—*Washington Post*, 25 October 1945

The selective service idea transformed the U.S. military from an undersized force of less than 1 million Americans to the most powerful military the world ever witnessed, numbering more than 12 million strong. It also redefined military service from a voluntary expression of patriotism to a universal obligation for every American male. In the process, it illuminated race and many disparities between American ideals of democracy and unequal realities of American military service. With the fighting of World War II ended, a new arena of battle emerged. Policy makers, military leaders, and the American public considered, debated, and questioned the relationship between military service and the postwar environment. The leading proposed construct of U.S. military service after World War II was universal military training, or UMT.

The campaign for UMT after World War II began while war still raged. On 15 August 1944, Secretary of War Henry L. Stimson outlined the rational for UMT in a letter to Archibald G. Thacher, the chair of the Citizens' Committee for Universal Military Training. The Citizens' Committee was an advocacy group composed of influential civilians, many of whom were veterans. Stimson confided to Thacher, "The alternative to [UMT] would be a large standing Army. But it is traditional to our democracy to maintain a relatively small regular Army and in a major emergency to depend, in the main, on the citizen in arms. For the military policy to be effective, provision must be made whereby the armed forces can be expanded quickly to meet the military needs with trained and equipped manpower." Stimson further relayed that UMT was the solution to a speedy mobilization and benefited not only U.S. national security but also American society. He maintained, "This can only be done through a system of universal military training. By this I mean a system under which all of the physically fit young men of the nation would be given continuous training for one year and thus be prepared to defend their country. Certainly all Americans should accept the principle that every citizen who enjoys the protection of a free government, owes and should freely give his personal services to the defense of it. This means the system should be truly universal—all should be treated alike."[4] Stimson's advocacy of UMT as the ideal construct for military service in the postwar environment highlighted how strategic perceptions of time and geography had changed. Regarding time, military planners doubted that they would have a lengthy time to mobilize in case of a new conflict, as had previously been the case; regarding geography, such new developments as strategic bombing and atomic weapons lessened the perceived value of the Atlantic and Pacific oceans for U.S. defense. Stimson's advocacy also promoted the intimate connection between military service and citizenship by highlighting the universality of UMT.[5]

After several years of planning, the War Department settled on UMT as the basis of its postwar plans with War Department Circular Number 347, signed on 25 August 1944 by the army's chief of staff, George C. Marshall. With it, Marshall advocated UMT while making some significant—and eventually problematic—suppositions about Congress's ultimate acceptance of the plan. Marshall concluded, "It is also assumed, for purposes of planning, that the Congress will enact (as the essential foundation of an effective national military organization), that every able-bodied young American shall be trained to defend his country; and that for a reasonable period after his training (unless he volunteers for service in the regular establishment of the armed forces) he shall be incorporated in a reserve all, or any necessary part of which, shall be subject to active military duty in the event of an emergency requiring reinforcement of the Regular Army."[6] Marshall utilized War Department Circular Number 347 to summarize his conception of military service and promulgate his unwavering support of UMT. More important, he disseminated his model of military service throughout the War Department as official military personnel policy for the postwar era. Marshall defined crucial aspects of UMT, including a military focus on building an effective general reserve to speed mobilization, a universal application toward military training (and in case of war, military service) for all American males, and a strictly military rationale for UMT, albeit with important political, economic, and sociological nuances.

Other prominent civilian and military leaders joined Stimson and Marshall to advocate UMT. On 8 December 1944, Secretary of the Navy James V. Forrestal also lent Thacher his staunch support for UMT and explained his reasons for it. Forrestal encouraged Thacher to promote UMT broadly: "I hope you will continue and intensify your activities." Forrestal reasoned the world was a dangerous place and UMT mitigated risk, much like an insurance policy. He discussed the recent context of World War II, highlighted the surprise Japanese attack on Pearl Harbor, and underscored Germany's use of unrestricted submarine warfare. Forrestal concluded, "Whether we like it or not, we live in a world where we may have to fight—or be conquered." Forrestal also specifically asserted that strategic bombing changed the international security environment: "The enormous range of our aircraft carrier task forces and of our B-29's

can be hailed with the greatest satisfaction, but we must bear in mind that each such extension in the range of weapons brings about a corresponding foreshortening of our traditional immunity from attack. The airplane and the robot plane already have dried up the English Channel and they may also dry up the Atlantic and Pacific Oceans." After he outlined the strategic rationale behind UMT, Forrestal added his unwavering backing to the proposal and provided an unqualified endorsement of it: "Therefore, if we should ever again be plunged in war, I am sure that we would all prefer that our sons should have had a year's training which would fit them to take up promptly a citizen's responsibility for defending his country. Universal military training contemplates simply that. It is not advocated as the means of alleviating social or economic ills. It is not an attempt to undermine our democratic institutions because in other nations it has existed side by side with the democratic form of government for many years. It is simply a method of preparing a citizen for the responsibility of defending our country if circumstances ever make that responsibility paramount."[7] The consistent, widespread, and vocal support of such prominent civilian and military leaders as Stimson, Marshall, and Forrestal demonstrated the broad support UMT garnered in the immediate aftermath of World War II. Their extensive reasoning also clearly explained the strategic rationale for it as the basis for postwar military personnel policy. UMT had momentum, and its boosters pressed to enact it.

No individual was a more vocal proponent for UMT than George C. Marshall. In order to understand Marshall's ardent and unrelenting advocacy, one must first understand his close friendship with another army general, Brigadier General John M. Palmer.[8] Marshall and Palmer were lifelong friends.[9] They also held a profound respect for one another. Even though Marshall was senior in rank by the end of their careers, Palmer was older by more than ten years and had served in the army for a decade by the time Marshall received his commission. They met when Marshall was a first lieutenant and Palmer was a captain. Together, the two men led the Service Schools Branch of the Infantry Association at Fort Leavenworth; Palmer served as president, and Marshall served as secretary of the combat arms organization. Palmer reminisced with pride, "This little group of Infantry officers started something new in our service history when it . . . did some spade work on military policy which, ten years later, became the indispensable basis for all of the really constructive features in the National Defense Act of 1920."[10] Palmer fondly remembered the special relationship that he and Marshall nurtured for decades and privately confided to Marshall, "Since our Leavenworth days, I have always felt toward you as an elder brother feels toward a younger brother of whom he is very proud."[11] For many years, Palmer considered Marshall "the ablest officer in the Army" and sought to provide him sound counsel.[12] A self-described "old timer," Palmer succinctly characterized their relationship: "It is a fine thing for an old soldier, long past the retiring age, to be given a chance to help younger men in the completion of a task that he has worked on all his life. . . . I think we shall be able to prove the wisdom of the old proverb: 'Young men for action, old men for counsel.'"[13] Regarding UMT, both men accepted the notion that Palmer provided the counsel and Marshall provided the action.

Although George Marshall truly believed in universal military training and promoted it widely, John Palmer provided the intellectual conceptualization for it. Palmer possessed the zeal of a prophet when he related UMT to sociological foundations of a democratic society; his faith was unshakeable. He often used the analogy of concrete and steel in a building to represent the proper relationship between reserve and professional

George C. Marshall (right) and John M. Palmer in General Marshall's office. (U.S. Army Signal Corps, courtesy George C. Marshall Library)

forces, respectively: "With too little steel there would be a deficiency in tensile strength throughout the structure; with too much it would be unnecessarily expensive." Palmer related his analogy directly to the task of constructing U.S. military service. He urged, "We should go through the whole structure of national defense in much the same way. We should use professionals, with a liberal factor of safety, where professionals alone will serve the purpose. But we should not use more professionals than necessary and we should never employ expensive professionals to do things that can be done effectively and in time by less expensive but competent nonprofessionals." Palmer justified why in terms of fiscal responsibility, antimilitarism, and civil-military relations. He warned, "Whenever we maintain an officer or a man or a unit in any one of the regular establishments to do something that can be done effectively and in time by an officer or a man or a unit in the civilian components, we increase the national budget unduly, take a step toward militarism, depart from sound democratic tradition and reduce our ultimate capacity for national defense."[14] Much of Palmer's—and subsequently Marshall's—advocacy of UMT surfaced because they both envisioned it as the less expensive and less militaristic alternative to a large professional military. Therefore, it resulted in a more direct and more positive relationship between military service and American society.

Utilizing Palmer's detailed and original conception of universal military training, Marshall advocated it as the basis of postwar U.S. military service. In his final report as army chief of staff, entitled *For the Common Defense*, Marshall distilled his many previous exhortations into a comprehensive, detailed, and rousing proposal to enact UMT. He contended, "To those who consider the introduction of a system of universal military training an imposition on democracy, I would reply that in my opinion it would be the most democratic expression of our national life." In making his case, Marshall appealed directly to his interpretation of the military legacy of George Washington. He argued, "Whatever my limitations may be in judging this matter, I submit the evidence of the proposal of our first President." Marshall expounded his interpretation of Washington's intended military personnel policy: "Washington's program provided for universal training of all men arriving at the age of 17. The citizen-militia was to be divided into three classes, men from 17 to 21, known as the advance corps, men 21 to 46, known as the main corps, and men from 46 to 61, known as the reserve corps. All of the peacetime training would have been concentrated in the advance corps, but eventually all members of main and reserve corps would have been graduates of the training program." Marshall then clarified for the military establishment and by extension the American people what became of Washington's plan. He lamented, "The militia bill was first introduced in the Third Session of the First Congress. It was considered in the House on 5 March, 1792, and as finally enacted contained no element of any of Washington's recommendations. It was so emasculated when finally adopted that the representative who introduced the bill himself voted against its passage."[15] *For the Common Defense* distilled Marshall's decades-long conception of UMT and extolled its virtues and importance to military service. It also demonstrated Marshall's willingness to connect UMT to the nation's military history by way of George Washington.[16] Marshall urged that the best form of military service was found with the founder of the nation himself. As he contended, "President Washington answered that question in recommendations to the first Congress to convene under the United States Constitution. He proposed a program for the peacetime training of a citizen army."[17] Marshall connected UMT to Washington primarily through "Sentiments on a Peace Establishment," which Washington wrote to Alexander Hamilton. Marshall articulated his interpretation of Washington's views succinctly: "Washington's plan embraced a small regular standing army backed up by a well-organized militia."[18]

In response, Marshall asked a central question: "What then must we do to remain strong and still not bankrupt ourselves on military expenditures to maintain a prohibitively expensive professional army even if one could be recruited?" Marshall argued that universal military training benefited the nation in terms of cost. He reasoned that it allowed a small, and therefore inexpensive, professional army during peacetime. Marshall did not fear many things, but he dreaded the vicissitudes of the U.S. Congress. He bemoaned budget cuts after World War I that weakened the U.S. military during the interwar period. As a result, he remained wary of proposals that entailed a large, permanent, and professional military, because he maintained that such proposals always suffered under a parsimonious Congress. Instead, Marshall saw economic and political factors as benefits of UMT, namely its low cost relative to a large standing army and its independence from reliance on congressional largess. Marshall hoped that constructing U.S. military service in the form of UMT would avoid drastic cuts to a bloated army budget after World War II. He warned, "The determining factor in solving this problem will inevitably be the relation between the maintenance of military power and the cost in annual appropriations. No system, even if actually adopted in the near future, can survive the political pressure to reduce the military budget if the costs are high—and professional armies are very costly."[19]

Marshall urged universal military training throughout the military establishment. He also repeatedly presented his views to the U.S. Congress and American public. On 16 June 1945, at four o'clock on a Saturday afternoon before a crowded room, Marshall testified before the Select Committee on Post-War Military Policy of the House of Representatives, known informally as the Woodrum Committee after its chair, Clifton A. Woodrum (D-VA). Marshall pleaded for UMT. Before the watchful audience, he first situated military service within the context of a democracy. He expounded, "The decision regarding the military policy of the United States is directly related to the democratic processes of the Government, really meaning the reaction of the people to the services the individual citizen might be required to render the Government." Marshall included in these "democratic processes" the twin civic pillars of rendering individual military service and paying taxes to provide for the defense establishment. He railed against a large professional military establishment for three reasons: "Its cost would be prohibitive; the necessary men to fill its ranks could not be hired in time of peace; and it would be repugnant to the American people. Therefore some other solution must be found."[20]

Even given the inherent uncertainty of the postwar environment, Marshall refused to waffle and unequivocally declared that universal military training was that solution. He announced, "Until the settlement of the terms of the peace it will be impossible to determine the strength of the post-war military forces to be maintained on an active status. We shall not know until then just what our military obligations or requirements are to be. But it is clear to me that whatever the terms of peace, the fundamental basis of our defense must be universal military training." Marshall articulated three rationales: one political, one sociological, and one economic. First, Marshall argued that UMT demonstrated to the world the preparedness of the United States and thereby stabilized the postwar security environment. This was especially important given the nation's newfound role as a world superpower. Second, Marshall contended that UMT fit well with American democracy. A universal obligation for military training in peacetime and for military service in wartime wove military and society together in a close-knit relationship. Third, Marshall reasoned that UMT allowed a small professional army buttressed by a large general reserve; it was therefore economical.[21]

To Marshall, maintaining such a military was less costly than a large professional force and therefore was more viable under budget cuts that he anticipated Congress would pursue after the war. After outlining the rationale for universal military training, Marshall pleaded for congressional approval. He urged, "The acceptance at the present time of a general policy recognizing the necessity for universal military training would in my opinion have a far-reaching effect in obtaining a satisfactory international agreement for the terms of the peace." Marshall further explained why: "It would certainly be in keeping with the tragic lessons of our history. It would be a supremely democratic procedure, and would not involve the individual in military service except by further Act of Congress and approval of the President. It would be far more economical than any other method for maintaining military power." He concluded, "If we are to have an effective and economical transition from our vast war establishment to our peace establishment, we must now decide on the fundamental basis on which we are to proceed."[22] Marshall clarified that UMT was the best solution and pressed for its acceptance by civilian leaders; he received it from President Truman but never from a majority in Congress. Unfazed, Marshall persevered to make UMT the foundation of the postwar U.S. military establishment.

Marshall's initial efforts to achieve universal military training were successful and boded well as the campaign gained momentum. The Woodrum Committee endorsed adopting UMT. Specifically, the committee's final report recommended that it "should be universal and democratic, applicable to rich and poor alike, and with a minimum of exemptions and exceptions." The committee directly placed the onus on Congress and advised that "Congress give the subject of this report prompt and thorough consideration, with a view to determining what course of action should be followed in this particular. It is manifest that those who are charged with the responsibility of planning the composition of the Nation's military and naval establishments will be severely handicapped unless and until the Congress, by appropriate enactment, defines the future policy and thus lays the predicate for an orderly transition from the wartime to the peacetime military organizations."[23] The Woodrum Committee highlighted an important conundrum in American civil-military relations; even when military leaders, in this case the most revered one of his time, advocated strongly for a particular military personnel policy, they still needed civilian approval to achieve it.[24] Sometimes, such as in the case of UMT, this aspect of civilian control slowed, altered, or prevented changes in military personnel policy. After World War II most military leaders recommended UMT and for almost a decade planned the program. Even so, Congress neither approved it nor provided any substantive guidance on alternatives. Such a situation illustrates one challenge of American civil-military relations: civilian leaders failing to provide direction sufficient to allow for effective military planning. At other times in American history, as subsequent chapters will detail, the same dynamic worked in reverse to spur change that military leaders did not want and even openly resisted.[25]

After the momentum and publicity created by the Woodrum Committee, the War Department crafted a comprehensive plan for UMT after World War II. The plan developed over time, assumed various forms, and sparked many alternative versions offered by politicians, civilians, veterans' organizations, and even ordinary citizens. The War Department plan envisioned a small professional military, a large trained general reserve provided by universal military training, and shortened mobilization timeframes as a result. Army Ground Forces (AGF) Commanding General Jacob L. Devers relayed to all unit commanders within the AGF, "The War Department assumes that the peacetime professional Army will be no larger than necessary to discharge peacetime responsibilities. Therefore, in emergencies it must be reinforced promptly by previously trained reserves. In order to protect our nation and finally assure our national security, we must achieve a state of military preparedness which will enable us to take effective military action in the shortest possible time."[26]

Though universal military training experienced wide-ranging support within the U.S. government and from the American public during and immediately after World War II, its two biggest individual proponents were John M. Palmer and George C. Marshall. Working in tandem, Palmer provided the intellectual foundation for the plan, and Marshall added such nuanced practical points as maintaining a smaller active force and larger reserve component, thereby reducing costs and avoiding budgetary cuts from Congress. When Marshall's tenure as army chief of staff ended in 1945, however, the campaign lost impetus. Even though Marshall's support of UMT never wavered, his replacement, Dwight D. Eisenhower, never held the steadfast commitment to it that Marshall had exhibited. In fact, Eisenhower's views on UMT shifted slightly, yet perceptibly, over the course of the next five years.

In a private discussion with Eisenhower, Marshall revealed how his pending departure influenced his actions. Marshall disclosed that the military had asked for a large buildup in the postwar period, one he disagreed with but felt compelled not to fight publicly because he would not be in charge of the army after 1945. Marshall confided, "I find myself in a most difficult position in this matter due to the fact that I am not to continue in office and therefore will not have the responsibility for the future of the Army during the next three or four years, particularly its initial postwar basis." On 20 September 1945, Marshall regretted "the present hullabaloo over demobilization with the accusations that the Army is trying to conduct demobilization with a view to the maintenance of a force of 2,500,000 next July" and divulged to Eisenhower that such an enlargement of the military was "a course of action with which I am almost in complete disagreement." Ultimately, the quarrel centered on the War Department staff's desire to expand the army's active component to parry the enlargement of the navy and the pending detachment of the Army Air Forces on the one hand, and on the other hand Marshall's unwavering support of universal military training as a way to maintain a smaller active force and larger general reserve in the long term. Marshall concluded that the War Department staff's plan was "a course of action which I feel will not only ruin the confidence of the Congress in the War Department's wisdom but will defeat Universal Military Training." Marshall left no doubt that his 18 November 1945 departure changed everything: "Were I to continue as Chief of Staff I would have no hesitancy at all as to how to act but I am greatly embarrassed by reason of my complete disagreement with the Staff in this matter and my feeling that they do not properly evaluate the power and application of Universal Military Training to our military structure nor have they a proper appreciation of the dominant budgetary influence in time of peace."[27]

Marshall related this quandary directly to his experience with demobilization after World War I and feared that history was about to repeat itself: "I went through this business in a conspicuous position in 1920 and remained with General Pershing through the successive emasculations of the Army until 1924. I was on the Reorganization Board—the junior member—in June, 1920, with Fox Conner, Campbell King, George Simonds, General Lassiter, and others I have forgotten, and we interviewed the leading officers of the Army in this matter. In other words it is an old story to me which I find now about to be repeated—the matters to which they attached great importance which received no consideration whatsoever in the final make-up of the Army." Marshall considered a large buildup of the military counterproductive and even dangerous, as it created "a demand for annual appropriations which is wholly unreasonable in relation to the state of the world, assuming we have Universal Military Training."[28]

Even so, Marshall deferred to Eisenhower, agreeing to "suppress my views so as not to embarrass you" and to "endeavor to carry out your wishes." His deference to Eisenhower highlighted the fact that momentum for universal military training dissipated as Eisenhower's emphasis shifted toward selective service. Such a swing portended an increasing focus on selective service as the foundation for a large and expanded military establishment.[29]

For the moment, however, the thrust for universal military training continued. The War Department crafted detailed plans under the assumption that it would frame postwar military service. The UMT Experimental Unit, located at Fort Knox, Kentucky, was created to practice implementing the concept and to demonstrate its utility to the military and the American public. Before long, residents living near the base could hear

General Marshall (right) greets General Eisenhower at National Airport. 18 June 1945. (Courtesy George C. Marshall Library)

"Umtees," as observers colloquially referred to trainees in the unit, calling out the cadence "Marching along Together, Soldiers of the UMT":

> Marching along together
> Soldiers of the UMT
> Marching along together
> For people far and wide to see
> Guardians of the future
> Look to the morning sun
> Our basic training is Infantry
> But when the job is done
> We'll take our places in history
> With men behind the gun . . . Oh,
> Marching along together
> Soldiers of the UMT[30]

From its inception, the UMT Experimental Unit had a significant public relations function: "The PR mission is to publicize this demonstration

John M. Devine instructs a UMT Experimental Unit trainee. Circa May 1947. (Courtesy Harry S. Truman Library)

of UMT so as to win for the overall UMT program the hearty approval of the general public, organizations and individuals who influence public opinion, personnel of the Armed Services, [and] young men affected by the UMT program and their parents."[31] Due to its intimate connection to public relations, the main focus of the experimental unit quickly morphed into promoting the good behavior of trainees so as to prove the experience had a positive impact on American youth. The UMT Experimental Unit's commanding officer, Brigadier General John M. Devine, directly compared the experiment with the American education system. He demanded, "Our disciplinary record must compare favorably with that of any other unit. We must be able to go farther and claim that the language in our barracks, the behavior in our mess halls, [and] our venereal rate, will compare favorably with that of any college freshman class. This is the real test of discipline." Such a concern with behavior led to the establishment of a UMT Advisory Committee, composed of well-known civilians from the surrounding communities, and the issuance of a distinctive patch to all Umtees. Devine revealed that the unique insignia "also facilitated the identification of trainees in nearby towns by civilians whose active support in the entertainment and control of trainees on pass was encouraged."[32]

While Umtees paraded the grounds of Fort Knox, civilian leaders took an increasing interest in universal military training. President Truman, a longtime proponent of military service himself, repeatedly and aggres-

Chairman Karl T. Compton (second from left) gives President Harry S. Truman (seated) the Report of the President's Advisory Commission on Universal Training at the White House as other members of the commission look on. 29 May 1947. (Courtesy Harry S. Truman Library)

sively promoted it.[33] He formed a presidential commission of prominent civilians and tasked them to study the issue for almost six months. Between the fall of 1946 and spring of 1947, the President's Advisory Commission on Universal Training (PACUT) held numerous hearings that considered views from roughly 200 individuals and organizations for and against UMT. The commission also conducted extensive research on the historical context of military service; it examined the relationship of UMT to such issues as constitutionality, demography, technology, health care, education, youth, women, labor, and conscientious objection. In addition, the commission compared UMT to military service in other countries, including Great Britain, Switzerland, South Africa, Sweden, and the USSR.[34] After its arduous investigation, PACUT publicly and vigorously endorsed UMT. Amid much fanfare, it delivered its final report to President Truman on 29 May 1947, which said, in part, "Out of these studies we have come to a clear, unanimous, and strong conviction about the course which our country should follow in respect to universal training in the foreseeable future. We recommend this course as a wise and prudent investment in American security, liberty, and prosperity."[35]

Of the many issues that the commission considered in relation to universal military training, none was as significant as race. Dr. Ambrose Caliver from the Office of Education appeared before the members on 19 April 1947, along with representatives of the Federal Security Agency. Caliver, a specialist on race relations, presented four general assumptions, "the validity of which should not require any discussion." He stated that UMT was "only one phase of a national security program," that national security demanded "full and effective utilization of the total manpower of the nation," that African Americans possessed "the same potentialities for contributing to the national security as other groups of our citizens," and that "the United States's role of world leadership requires a full utilization of the potentialities of Negroes and their recognition as full, first-class citizens." Caliver then highlighted acute shortages of auto mechanics, carpenters, plumbers, draftsmen, machinists, and welders and finished by mourning the low morale created by racial discrimination in U.S. military service: "It is common knowledge that many factors often militate against the development and maintenance of high morale among Negro soldiers." Caliver specifically emphasized "the attitude of the officers," "discrimination in promotion practices," "discriminatory treatment by the civilian police," "inadequate transportation facilities to and from the community," and "discrimination by bus drivers." Overall, he relayed, "A frequent complaint heard among Negro service men was their inability to develop a 'sense of belonging,' sometimes due to their lack of opportunity to engage in combat, and often to the inconsistency between their treatment in the service, and the principles of democracy for which the war was fought."[36]

During the height of the postwar campaign for universal military training, the Selective Service System lapsed. A war scare with the Soviet Union propelled UMT forward, while simultaneously critics contended that heightened international tensions demonstrated the value of selective service in the short term. Ultimately, Congress reestablished the Selective Service Act on 24 June 1948.[37] As a result, Congress enacted selected service and sacrificed UMT in the process.

With the outbreak of the Korean War on 25 June 1950, debates over universal military training resurfaced. As they intensified, philosophical differences between Marshall and Eisenhower regarding UMT contrasted more and more. Marshall continually touted UMT as the best way to maintain a smaller active force supplemented by a larger reserve component, especially the general reserve composed of UMT graduates. In contrast, Eisenhower's focus on universal military service evidenced far more contentment with a large military establishment. Eisenhower's preference eventually demonstrated a decisive shift away from UMT toward selective service and a large military. The two generals' views presented a series of dichotomies: small versus large military; peacetime military training versus peacetime military service; and economy through reserve forces versus expenses through active forces.[38]

In spite of clear divergences between himself and Eisenhower, Marshall tirelessly advocated universal military training. On 23 October 1950 he conveyed to Eisenhower, "Furthermore, we feel that the former procedure would lend itself better to the adoption of some system for building up trained reserves. We are therefore of the opinion—and we are still working on the practicability of the proposition, that there should be an immediate adoption of a law authorizing some form of Universal Military Training in such a fashion that it could be gradually initiated as the urgent need for the Selective Service action decreased." While Marshall admitted that great uncertainty lie ahead, he ardently urged UMT as the best way to greet it. As he explained to Eisenhower, "Whether that would be within six months, a year or two years, I am not prepared now to hazard an estimate, but I am completely convinced that unless we get started on this thing, get it into the law, and get the thinking headed towards it, we will inevitably be back in the same predicament we were six months ago." Marshall urged getting some form of UMT in place and then slowly expanding it as the Korean War relented. No one, however, anticipated that the war would drag on, certainly not in the fall of 1950 when it looked as though Korea might be unified. Therefore, Marshall encountered a dynamic I previously characterized as "the paradox of preparedness": short-term and long-term national security goals often compete with each other and can even work at cross-purposes.[39]

Even with such high hopes for universal military training in the fall of 1950, Marshall admitted that significant challenges still lie ahead. He relayed to Eisenhower, "We seem to be heading for trouble in the house on our Universal Military Training and Service Bill, but have hopes that if we do not make out too badly there, we will be able to get the important things ironed out in conference." Such sentiments indicated that Marshall expected difficulties on passage of the bill, but he was still hopeful for the inclusion of UMT, as he always remained.[40]

The Korean War created disagreement among policy makers regarding the best way to construct U.S. military service. Whereas Marshall remained wedded to the long-term application of UMT, others throughout the Defense Department, especially Eisenhower, became progressively more comfortable with selective service as the Korean War intensified and military personnel requirements mounted. Describing a personal meeting with Marshall and requesting that it be considered "at least semiconfidential," James W. Wadsworth Jr. (R-NY) relayed to longtime confidant Archibald G. Thacher, "I learned that when Marshall took over the job of Secretary of Defense he found the Pentagon people pretty thoroughly persuaded that the only thing to do was to recruit through the draft as soon as possible a total military force of three million men and to go on with such a program as long as necessary—the Lord knows how long." Wadsworth relayed differences between such supporters of UMT as Marshall and deputy secretary of defense Robert A. Lovett and opponents within the Department of Defense seeking a large military through selective service: "Marshall has called a halt to this program and is insisting that these people look farther ahead and realize that their program is utterly impossible, both from the fiscal and democratic standpoint. Incidentally, Lovett is supporting him in his efforts." The key difference between the two constructs of military service at that time—universal military training and selective service—were universal application and time horizon: UMT was universal and long-term whereas selective service was discerning and short-term. Wadsworth further explained how Marshall and Lovett were "using all their powers of persuasion with the ultra-professional military people and are reminding them that while it is necessary to recruit an adequate force pretty quickly, the insertion of UMT as the only element which can bring a sound solution must be arranged, difficult though it may be." Wadsworth finished by explaining that Marshall's devotion to UMT was still as strong during the height of the Korean War as it had been at the end of World War II. Referring to War Department Circular Number 347, Wadsworth relayed, "As a matter of fact Marshall's present views are identical with those expressed in his famous directive issued to the army in the latter part of 1944."[41]

During the spring of 1951 a new Universal Military Training and Service (UMTS) bill made its way through Congress. Because the bill initially contained a provision for a UMT program, Marshall—who was then secretary of defense—strongly supported it. Marshall characterized it "as a basic step toward national security." He explained, "The proposed legislation would lower the minimum age for induction into the armed services from nineteen years to eighteen; it would extend the period of service for those inducted from twenty-one months to twenty-seven and it would add one year to the enlistment period of all men whose original enlistments were scheduled to expire during fiscal years 1952 or 1953." More important to Marshall, "the bill would make it the national obligation of all physically fit young men reaching the age of 18 to undergo military service and training and to follow that service with a specified term of duty in a reserve component." To counter criticism of the UMT component of the bill, Marshall reassured potential critics, "The bill authorizes the President to reduce the period of service whenever the national security permits. He could eventually withdraw the service requirement entirely but the obligation for training would remain so that young men would always be coming forward to build up a vigorous, strong reserve." Marshall characterized the bill as "in the best democratic tradition" and contended that it provided "the kind of basic protection we need to keep us strong with minimum drain on our productive energies."[42]

However, Marshall soon became concerned the Senate might eliminate the UMT provision contained in the bill. In response, he drafted a letter to all senators that Senator Lyndon B. Johnson (D-TX) delivered to them by hand. In his letter Marshall urged the senators to keep the UMT provision: "In my opinion this is not just another amendment, to be given hasty consideration. Scrapping the Universal Military Training provisions would cut the heart out of the bill. The distinctive contribution the bill makes to our national security would be removed. This single action would be sufficient to cancel the assurance that our defenses would have, for the first time, an enduring base that would guarantee us adequate military strength at a cost we could bear for the years of critical world tension that we now face." Even though the chances of his success seemed slim, Marshall pushed to keep UMT alive. As he demonstrated throughout his previous tenure as army chief of staff, it was the central piece of the legislation to him, not the selective service aspects. Marshall made clear to senators why this was the case: "Our past history is a fever chart of panicky mobilization in periods of crisis, followed by too hasty disarmament when the sense of urgency subsided."[43] He asserted that preparedness in general and UMT specifically were the answers to such a quandary.

One month later, Marshall became alarmed that the House of Representatives also appeared in favor of eliminating the universal military training provisions of the UMTS bill. He shared his apprehensions with

Speaker of the House Sam Rayburn (D-TX): "It is a matter of extreme concern to learn that there will be serious efforts in the House debate on this legislation to eliminate all sections relating to Universal Military Training or to emasculate the present proposal to permit its gradual introduction into the national system of defense."[44]

As a consequence of the Korean War, on 19 June 1951, Congress enacted the Universal Military Training and Service Act, which renewed the draft for four more years. The passage of the bill marked a pyrrhic victory for UMT supporters. The act enshrined the principle of UMT in its name, but did little else. Supporters hoped that with time such a seed would germinate into the full-fledged UMT program that they had campaigned for during much of the past decade. The initial reaction to the passage of the bill illustrated that such a hope was anything but certain. On 12 August 1951, *Washington Star* correspondent Quentin R. Mott pondered: "Whatever became of UMT? The answer is, it is still in the offing, but its approach is very slow, and not entirely sure. For the draft act signed by President Truman on June 19—which laid the groundwork for this unprecedented plan for universal training of our youth—also imposes a few hurdles for the project." The most important hindrance was the complex relationship between a potential UMT program and an already enacted and operational Selective Service System. Mott warned, "If UMT were to start taking the 18-year-olds, it would dip into the manpower pool from which Selective Service makes replacements."[45] That situation combined with congressional delays; mounting resistance to UMT by labor, religious, and special interest groups; and growing comfort with selective service among military leaders and policy makers to stymie further UMT efforts.[46] Mott exclaimed, "No matter how prompt the commissioners are, a combination of law and circumstances makes it highly improbable that UMT will be anything more than a paper program for some time to come."[47]

President Truman signed the UMTS bill on 19 June 1951. It established a draft of American males at least eighteen and one-half years of age for twenty-four months of military service, capped the overall size of the American military at 5 million service members, and enshrined the principle of UMT, although in its final form it had no provisions to convert such an idea into reality.[48] It also established a National Security Training Committee (NSTC) composed of prominent experts on national security, many of whom were long-time advocates of UMT. Members included Owen J. Roberts (national chair), Joseph Clark Grew, LaFell Dickinson,

Howard C. Petersen, John H. Wilson, and Arthur L. Williston.[49] The bill tasked the group with continuing efforts on UMT by honing plans to implement it.

The Korean War solidified the shift away from UMT toward selective service. James W. Wadsworth Jr., a long-time and ardent booster of universal military training, articulated to Lieutenant Barber B. Conable Jr., a young military officer in training at Fort Sill, Oklahoma, awaiting orders to Korea, how this would happen: "Our real trouble is the scarcity of available enlisted men in the reserve. True, many of them are being called up but there are not nearly enough of them. What we need most of all is riflemen—the slogging infantryman." Wadsworth lamented the failure of Congress to pass UMT for just such a situation: "Had we established UMT four or five years ago we would have had plenty. As it is we are employing the draft, a form of conscription, because we have no other machinery for getting men. And of course when the draftee comes forward he comes as a raw recruit. To train him and work him into tactical units of either of the military services consumes months of time. Moreover, he comes in merely to fill the rear ranks, as it were, of existing services with little opportunity to rise." Wadsworth concluded that such a failure was significant because the lack of UMT in peacetime forced reliance on selective service in wartime. He confessed, "We are guilty of a fundamental error in our military policy due, in my judgment, solely to the fact that, having failed to train all young men in time of peace, we are once more resorting to straight out conscription of raw recruits."[50]

The Korean War also demonstrated the final break between Marshall and Eisenhower regarding military service. Marshall's confidant, Assistant Secretary of Defense (Manpower and Personnel) Anna M. Rosenberg, challenged Eisenhower in a testy exchange during the summer of 1952. Claiming that she had become "sold" on UMT immediately after V-E Day during World War II, she commended Eisenhower for his own earlier support of it. "You were the one to convince me," she admitted to him.[51] Rosenberg then relayed to Eisenhower that newspapers quoted him as opposing UMT at a conference in Denver on 19 June 1952: "He believes that the country has more to fear from universal military training than from a small professional army when it comes to the threat of creating a militaristic state." It also had been reported that during a press conference at the Pentagon, "he doubted UMT and Selective Service could go hand in hand, however, as recently proposed in Congress." In response to these reports, Rosenberg challenged Eisenhower's commitment to UMT.

Assistant Secretary of Defense
(Manpower and Personnel)
Anna M. Rosenberg. 2
February 1951. (U.S. Army,
courtesy Harry S. Truman
Library)

She conceded, "I realize that excerpts taken out of context can be very mis-leading but, at face value, this statement supports the present position of UMT opponents, i.e., UMT and drafting for service can't operate together and since we can't wholly maintain the Armed Forces on a voluntary basis and must resort to the draft, we should delay action on UMT until we no longer require involuntary military service. That would mean for the next 5 or 10 years and probably *never!*" Rosenberg chafed at Eisenhower's apparent change of position and pointed out, "This alleged statement and the one referred to in the attached letter are, of course, contrary to what you've said in the past and I know do not reflect your position. However, I am afraid that the enemies of UMT may try to use them in the future." Rosenberg urged Eisenhower "to state in unmistakable language what UMT is, why you favor it and why it is necessary now."[52]

The following week, Eisenhower rebuffed Rosenberg and confirmed his clear break from UMT boosters. As he rebutted, "In talking about UMT in our present situation, I have frequently said that I do not see how we can manage—at one and the same time—selective service and any system of universal military training. I have also said that my expe-riences convinced me, at the end of World War II, that in justice to the

Secretary of Defense George C. Marshall with Anna M. Rosenberg during a conference in the Pentagon. 19 October 1950. (Courtesy George C. Marshall Library)

nation and to the individual we should then adopt some form of universal military *service.*" Eisenhower explained that his earlier perceived support of UMT was largely deference to Marshall: "I later became a supporter of universal military training, a system of training completely separated from the Army itself, because General Marshall and his civilian supporters convinced me that the pursuit of my own convictions would merely result in the defeat of everything."[53] Eisenhower made plain that the two esteemed generals now held vastly different conceptions of U.S. military service; Eisenhower promoted either selective or universal military service, whereas Marshall consistently promoted universal military training. The fact that Eisenhower went along with the campaign for UMT originally, even against "[his] own convictions," was a testament to Marshall's vast influence.

One week later Rosenberg dutifully informed her boss, Marshall, that Eisenhower had indeed split from the UMT camp and that there was now a clear and ever widening divide between Marshall and Eisenhower and between military training and military service. Referring to Eisenhower's new role as president of Columbia University, she bitterly complained, "I thought you might be interested in the answer I received from him today, which is difficult to understand. Evidently college professors have made a deeper impression on General Eisenhower than his life-long associates."[54] The cross altercation between Rosenberg and Eisenhower substantiated that as a result of the Korean War there was significant disagreement regarding the preferred construct of U.S. military service. Although Eisenhower previously articulated support of UMT, he was never a true believer in it like Marshall, Rosenberg, John M. Palmer, John J. McCloy, and others who led the campaign for it. With war raging on the Korean peninsula, Eisenhower and Congress found selective service increasingly appropriate and useful, whereas Marshall, Rosenberg, and their supporters saw selective service only as a temporary bridge toward the permanent enactment of UMT.

U.S. military service emerged from World War II with the potential for vast change. The selective service idea of World War II gave way to the hope of many civilian and military leaders that universal military training, or UMT, represented a sound and democratic principle upon which to build the postwar military. George C. Marshall, drawing inspiration from his deep respect for and lifelong friendship with John M. Palmer, led the charge, and many other prominent Americans followed. The Woodrum Committee made UMT an official goal of American postwar military personnel policy. The War Department crafted specific and detailed plans for instituting UMT as the basis for its postwar plan and established an experimental unit meant to both practice it and demonstrate its value to the nation. Politicians joined the fray, as President Truman created a commission of prominent civilians that unanimously and publicly advocated UMT. Hurdles mounted, however, as the issue of race surfaced and highlighted inequities that vividly contrasted with picturesque portrayals. In addition to questions of who served, how they served also created fissures. The diverging views of Marshall and Eisenhower were the most prominent example. The Korean War and the UMTS bill combined to ensure that the only victory UMT achieved was a pyrrhic one. Ultimately, the sound and democratic principle reverted once again to the selective service idea. Debates regarding how Americans served in the military were settled temporarily in favor of selective service but soon shifted to questions regarding who served, initially focusing on race.

CHAPTER FOUR

FREEDOM TO SERVE

The approach now is to determine the best possible military usage of the 10 percent of our population that may be a determining factor in any future war in which this country is engaged. The policies that will make for the best military usage will be supported by a nation united in the conviction that the burdens of military participation are being equitably distributed over all of our population and that the responsibilities of military service are being assigned on the basis of ability.[1]—Truman K. Gibson, 8 December 1945

As a result of reports by field commanders throughout the war and the exhaustive study undertaken in response to the recommendation of the Special Troop Policies Committee, the Army had also come to the conclusion by the fall of 1945 that its policy over a long period of years had not proved satisfactory and that changes must be made in the utilization of Negro troops in the postwar Army.[2]—Fahy Committee, 1950

The armed forces are one of our major status symbols; the fact that members of minority groups successfully bear arms in defense of the country, alongside other citizens, serves as a major basis for their claim to equality elsewhere. For the minority groups themselves discrimination in the armed forces seems more immoral and painful than elsewhere. The notion that not even in the defense of their country (which discriminates against them in many ways) can they fight, be wounded, or even killed on an equal basis with others, is infuriating.[3]—Robert K. Carr, 10 June 1947

The President should speak out fully on his Civil Rights record. He can refer to his votes in the Senate,

his support of the wartime FEPC [Fair Employment
Practices Committee], and his recent Executive Orders
to end discrimination in the Government and the
armed services. His record proves that he *acts* as well
as *talks* Civil Rights.[4]—Clark M. Clifford, 17 August 1948

Simultaneous with the campaign for universal
military training, debates intensified regarding eliminating racial discrimination that existed within U.S. military service and expanding
opportunities for African Americans throughout the military. African
American leaders such as Lester B. Granger, Walter White, Mary Mc-
Leod Bethune, Truman K. Gibson, Sadie T. M. Alexander, Channing Tobias, and many others led efforts to pressure civilian and military leaders
to alter military personnel policy. On 26 July 1948, President Truman
issued a landmark military personnel policy that began the desegregation of the U.S. military. The resulting Fahy Committee studied ways
to expand equality and opportunity in American military service. The
Korean War tested such rhetoric, and social scientists in Project Clear
urged full desegregation. Racial integration in military service finally
occurred during the later stages of the Korean War, but that conflict also
reinforced greater reliance on the draft.

Before, during, and after World War II, African American leaders
urged policy makers to eliminate military personnel policies that perpetu-
ated institutional racism. In the postwar environment, such efforts gained
momentum. On 26 April 1948, Secretary of Defense James V. Forrestal
convened the National Defense Conference on Negro Affairs. During the
pivotal event, sixteen prominent civil rights leaders conferred with military officials at the Pentagon on a Monday from nine in the morning until
four in the afternoon. Lester B. Granger, the executive secretary of the
National Urban League, chaired the conference. Among the participants
were Sadie T. M. Alexander, Mary McLeod Bethune, Truman K. Gibson,
Walter White, and Channing H. Tobias. Forrestal wanted the conference
to spur additional examinations of race in American military service. He
confided to the group, "I am in hopes that one outgrowth of the meeting
will be the setting up of an advisory panel to assist the Military Establishment in handling the many difficult problems facing the armed services
in the field of inter-racial relations."[5] The participants produced a detailed

President Harry S. Truman. Circa November 1945. (U.S. Army Signal Corps, courtesy Harry S. Truman Library)

report based on their intensive deliberations; contemporary observers colloquially referred to it as the Granger report after the group's chair.

Civil rights leaders attending the conference also had high hopes of improving opportunities for African Americans in military service. They argued that military service performed a unique function in a democracy: "The opinion of Negro Americans is united in the belief that racial segregation is especially intolerable when imposed by the federal government in any area of citizenship activity. It is even more outrageous when it is carried out in the armed forces, where a citizen stands ready to die, if necessary, for the protection of his country." The leadership gave military service a mixed appraisal on this metric. While they took some "encouragement in the policies of the Navy and the Air Service toward Negro personnel," they "were deeply disappointed, and indeed offended, by the general attitude assumed by some of the spokesmen for the armed forces, notably Secretary of the Army Royall." They further protested, "Mr. Royall declared at that time there was no prevailing opinion among Army leadership that racial segregation could or should be eliminated to any greater extent than provided for in current official policy." Civil rights leaders argued that the fundamental problem was that current army leadership misinterpreted the previous Gillem Board report and therefore shunned necessary changes to military personnel policy. They observed, "Reference was made repeatedly to the fact that although the Army constantly refers to the Gillem Board report as its accepted guide and as a reason for not raising present levels of policy and practice, even the Gillem Board report has not been followed. For, as one conferee pointed out, in summarizing and publicizing the report certain basic recommendations were either ignored or were misinterpreted." Granger insisted that such resistance to change military personnel policy on the part of army leaders revealed "the inadequacy of the nation's approach to the entire problem of training Negro youth for the armed forces." The solution to the group appeared simple; the army had to expand opportunities for African Americans in accordance with the ultimate intention and long-term recommendations of the Gillem Board. The conferees demanded, "The Army is obligated by its adoption of the original Gillem board report to implement it under its broadest rather than its narrowest construction."[6]

The Granger report made seven specific recommendations for ending discrimination in military service, including a "restudy" of the Gillem Board report, a "laboratory project" of integrated military units, "hearty and unqualified approval" for ending segregation in National Guard units, a "formal published policy" eliminating racial quotas in the military, ending racial restrictions for navy stewards, increasing African American officers in the navy, and focused recruiting to demonstrate to African American youths that the navy was a "self-respecting, secure and rewarding career."[7]

With the publication of the Granger report, pressure on President Truman to address segregation in the military mounted during the summer of 1948. Civil rights leaders Grant Reynolds and A. Philip Randolph repeatedly sought an audience with the president to urge long-overdue changes to military personnel policy. Referring to the selective service bill that had defeated UMT in the summer of 1948, the duo pleaded, "Because Congress enacted, and you have now signed, a Selective Service bill devoid of any safeguards for Negro youth, we should like to request, at your earliest convenience, a conference with you to discuss the issuance of an executive order abolishing all *segregation* and discrimination from the armed forces." Reynolds and Randolph explained why and threatened to launch a civil disobedience campaign against the draft if Truman ignored their plea:

> In the light of past official civil rights pronouncements, it is our belief that the President, as Commander-in-Chief, is morally obligated to issue such an order now. Unless this is done, Negro youth will have no alternative but to resist a law, the inevitable consequence of which would be to expose them to the un-American brutality so familiar during the last war. America must not subject one-tenth of its population to such treatment again. Knowing that you have it in your power to prevent this, we are seeking an opportunity to confer with you on implementing this essential part of your civil rights program.[8]

Others urged action as well, including citizens Mr. and Mrs. Irvin Dagen. They remonstrated: "As white residents of a city which is seething with Negro resentment at the possibility of having to serve in a Jim Crowed military force again, we wish to ask you to use all the power you have to abolish such undemocratic segregation of ANY kind in all of the branches of the armed services." The couple related military personnel policy directly to American values and expounded, "We feel that one of the most effective, firm, and noticeable ways in which we can show the rest of the world we believe in Democracy is to practice such a virtue in all possible places at home. We believe that this will still Russian propaganda against us for this gross injustice in our country. We commend you for your Civil Rights Report. And we ask you further to use your Presidential Power to declare that emergency exists and to hand down an Executive Order which will abolish such practices immediately and completely."[9]

As pressure mounted from both civil rights leaders and ordinary citizens to address racial discrimination in American military service, on 26 July 1948 President Truman issued Executive Order 9981. Its official title was "Establishing the President's Committee on Equality of Treatment and Opportunity in the Armed Services." The executive order conveyed to the military and American society both a broad purpose and a specific policy. The purpose declared that "it is essential that there be maintained in the armed services of the United States the highest standards of democracy, with equality of treatment and opportunity for all those who serve in our country's defense." To fulfill that broad purpose, Truman announced a new specific military personnel policy: "It is hereby declared to be the policy of the President that there shall be equality of treatment and opportunity for all persons in the armed services without regard to race, color, religion or national origin." President Truman ordered, "This policy shall be put into effect as rapidly as possible, having due regard to the time required to effectuate any necessary changes without impairing efficiency or morale."[10] The executive order also established a committee of seven members that Truman would appoint at a later date.

It is clear that at least part of Truman's goal was to use the executive order for political advantage in the 1948 election campaign. Presidential advisor Clark M. Clifford and attorney James Rowe specifically addressed such a motive in a confidential memorandum to Truman on 17 August 1948. They recommended, "The President should speak out fully on his Civil Rights record. He can refer to his votes in the Senate, his support of the wartime FEPC, and his recent Executive Orders to end discrimination in the Government and the armed services." Clifford and Rowe advised that doing so illuminated to the American public that Truman's "record proves that he *acts* as well as *talks* Civil Rights."[11]

James C. Evans, a Truman administration official, countered that Truman's issuance of Executive Order 9981 represented a principled stand for expanded opportunity in American military service. Evans served for roughly three decades within the military establishment, working primarily on military personnel policy. He served first as vice director to Truman K. Gibson and later as special assistant to the secretary of defense during the late 1940s, 1950s, and early 1960s. As a result, he witnessed the inner workings of military personnel policy debates, formulation, and changes during that expansive time frame. Evans later recalled, "I was in the Department before the end of the 30s, but not officially, and I came on board officially early in the 40s, so I was there for 30 years, from 1940 until 1970." He characterized the dynamic process of interaction between reformers within the military such as himself and reformers outside of the military as a "push-pull operation," wherein such outside forces as the NAACP and Urban League pushed and such insiders as William H. Hastie, Gibson, and himself pulled military personnel policy to create progress. Evans admitted that observers did not always appreciate this process and recalled, "What we were doing—advocating and doing all we could to include and involve Negroes, men and women in the uniform—was not always well received by the Negro press or by the organizations, for that matter." When asked in an oral history interview about Truman's motivation behind issuing his executive order, Evans answered, "I would say from what I knew of him—and I did know him quite well, I might say—that he was determined on justice first and the vote next. On more than one occasion I know he went out on terms of what he felt was right. And he was right when everybody thought he was wrong."[12] So while it is clear that there was some political motivation to Truman's order, Evans's characterization suggests that politics were secondary to Truman's primary intent to establish a principle of equality and opportunity in U.S. military service.

Of course, the reaction to Executive Order 9981 was not all positive. Joseph Beauharnais wrote to Secretary of Defense Louis A. Johnson and sent a copy of his letter to Harry S. Truman. In the letter, Beauharnais vented,

> Therefore, you will not be surprised to learn that we were all sickened and disgusted to learn from the press reports that you are an advocate of non-segregation in the armed forces of the United States, which in plain blunt language means that because of your military authority and high-ranking power, you feel that you can change or enforce long-standing social edicts and customs by issuing directives to white men who are in the majority in the armed forces that they must eat, sleep and work with negroes, without their consent and against their wills. I think your decree is outrageous and I would never voluntarily enlist now in any branch of the armed forces under any circumstances.[13]

On 18 September 1948, Truman appointed seven members to the President's Committee on Equality of Treatment and Opportunity in the Armed Forces. Charles H. Fahy, former U.S. solicitor general, would chair the committee. The remaining members were Alphonsus J. Donahue, president of A. J. Donahue Corporation; Lester Granger, executive secretary of the National Urban League; Charles Luckman, president of Lever Brothers; Dwight R. G. Palmer, president of General Cable Corporation; John H. Sengstacke, publisher of the *Chicago Defender*; and William E. Stevenson, president of Oberlin College.[14]

It is important to note that even the selection of the members of the Fahy Committee was controversial. One example portended significant

The Committee on Equality of Treatment and Opportunity in the Armed Services. Seated with President Truman are James V. Forrestal (left) and Alphonsus J. Donahue (right). Standing, left to right: Thomas R. Reid, General C. T. Lanham, John H. Sengstacke, William E. Stevenson, Kenneth Royall, Stuart Symington, Charles H. Fahy, committee chair, and some other unidentified people in a White House office. 13 January 1949 (Courtesy Harry S. Truman Library)

resistance among some army leaders who opposed military integration. The day before Truman made public his selections for the Fahy Committee, Secretary of the Army Kenneth C. Royall pleaded against the selection of Lester Granger. Royall informed Truman, "It has come to my attention that a number of the men being considered for appointment on the President's Committee on Equality of Treatment and Opportunity in the Armed Services have publicly expressed their opinion in favor of abolishing segregation in the Armed Services. At least one of them, Lester Granger, has been critical both of the Army and of me personally on this particular matter." Royall made an impassioned plea for Truman to exclude Granger from the committee. As he contended, "I feel strongly that no person should serve on this Committee who has formed a fixed opinion on this subject on either side, certainly no person who had made a public pronouncement of such opinion. Otherwise the Committee could not give fair consideration to the subject."[15] Granger's selection the following day and his continued service on the committee throughout its work demonstrated that President Truman disagreed with Royall's assessment; Royall's unrelenting resistance to the work of the Fahy Committee demonstrated that his quarrel was not only with Granger's selection, but with the very issue of military integration.

Early in 1949, President Truman convened a meeting between the four military service secretaries and the Fahy Committee. The meeting was held in the Cabinet Room of the White House at 12:15 p.m. on 12 January 1949. Attendees were Secretary of Defense James V. Forrestal, Secretary of the Army Kenneth C. Royall, Secretary of the Navy John L. Sullivan, Secretary of the Air Force Stuart Symington, Donald S. Dawson (administrative assistant to President Truman), and all Fahy Committee members except Charles Luckman, who was absent. Many members of the Office of the Secretary of Defense staff were also in attendance.

Truman disclosed to the group his intention to use Executive Order 9981 as a wedge to increase participation across the whole of government and society beyond just the military. After exchanging pleasantries, Truman informed his guests: "I want this rounded out a little bit. I want the Department of the Interior, the Commerce Department, the Treasury Department, interviewed on the subject why you are in existence, and let's make it a Government proposition, as well as an Armed Services." Truman revealed one interesting aspect of civil-military relations related to military personnel policy: he explained that the malleability of the military allowed it to be used as a lever for further change. Truman divulged to the group,

> As Commander in Chief, I can issue orders to the Armed Services, and, if there is some legal approach in all the rest of the branches of the Government, we might as well make a complete program out of it while we are at it, and not limit it to just one branch of the Government. That's what I have in mind all the way down the line. Not only that, I think that we've got to go further—not at this time, but later—and see that the state and local governments carry out the spirit of the laws which we hope to get on the books down here during this session of Congress.[16]

Truman made clear that he saw service in the armed forces as a leading edge to broaden participation in civil society. He also hinted at the ironic importance of adherence to orders and strict vertical hierarchy as key organizational characteristics that allowed civilian leaders to prompt change in a typically conservative and traditional organization such as the military.

Throughout the spring of 1949, Secretary Royall mounted a vicious assault on the efforts of the Fahy Committee utilizing an array of tactics; he stalled, obfuscated, and countered. The Fahy Committee relentlessly responded move for move and refused to negotiate on its fundamental goals. On 27 April 1949, Royall resigned amid mounting pressure. Gordon Gray replaced him, and throughout the summer Gray steered the army's plan to implement Executive Order 9981 closer to Truman's original intent. Even though Secretary of Defense Louis A. Johnson accepted the army's revised plan on 30 September 1949, Fahy remained unsatisfied. On 6 October 1949, the committee submitted an interim report to President Truman and demanded, "The program announced September 30, 1949, should now be supplemented so as to make clear that all personnel to whom under the new policy all Military Occupational Specialties are open and to whom all Army School courses are open, both without regard to race or color, shall also be assigned according to their qualifications without regard to race or color." The group also insisted, "The Committee's consideration with the Army of the quota enlistment and other problems should be continued."[17]

Fahy reminded Truman, "Your Committee had recommended to the Army a four point program toward achieving equality of treatment and opportunity." Such a program included opening "all Army school courses," releasing "all Army military occupational specialties," and assigning "school-trained individuals to duty on the basis of qualification without regard to race or color." It also required abolishing "the racial quota system for enlistment." Fahy confided to Truman, "With respect to the question of the 10 per cent Negro quota, the Army and the Committee are continuing discussions."[18]

As the new year of 1950 rang in, members of the Fahy Committee displayed justifiable pride regarding their impact on military personnel policy. The group had forced concessions from the military services, especially the army, and paved the way for the racial integration of the military that would occur during the last two years of the Korean War. In an address before the St. Louis Urban League's annual dinner on 23 January 1950, Oberlin College president and Fahy Committee member William Stevenson contemplated "The Road to Democracy." Stevenson boasted an impressive record. He graduated from Princeton University, was a Rhodes Scholar, and was a previous member of the U.S. Olympic team. He also led American Red Cross efforts in England, North Africa, Sicily, and Italy during World War II. With these prestigious credentials, Stevenson assailed inequality within American military service: "That the tide is running rapidly in the direction of equality of treatment and opportunity for peoples of all races is dramatically demonstrated by what has taken place in our Armed Services in the past ten years. Before this last war began there were no Negroes in the Marines, none in the Navy outside of mess attendants and the few in the Army were limited to jobs of a menial nature and in only a very few types of units." Stevenson explained the impact of World War II on military personnel policy: "As we all know, the demand for qualified manpower during the Second World War forced a change in the thinking of our high ranking procurement officers, and by the time the war was over Negroes had been admitted to the Marines, to many new jobs in the Navy, and in a wide variety of positions in the Army. Thanks to the education which such war experiences brought about, these gains, far from having been lost, have been consolidated and even far greater gains have now been made." Stevenson highlighted some of these gains: "For many months now, the Navy has been functioning under a policy of complete abandonment of any racial discrimination. . . . The same improved attitude obtains in the Marines and in the Air Force, the latter having abolished segregation about a year or so ago and having disbanded its all-Negro fighter unit and assigned its personnel to serve with various units, which previously had been all white." Stevenson concluded by pointing out that even the army had made some progress: "Only a week ago, the Army, which hitherto had moved forward more slowly than had the other branches of the Department of Defense, adopted a policy of historic significance, so far as race relations are concerned."[19]

The Fahy Committee interpreted its mission in the broadest sense. As its executive secretary, E. W. Kenworthy, explained, "The Committee has spent most of its time examining into the policies, practices and procedures of the armed services in an endeavor to determine how those practices and procedures might be changed to secure equal opportunity for minorities."[20] At noon on 22 May 1950 the Fahy Committee publicly released its conclusions, recommendations, and final report, entitled *Freedom to Serve*. After extensive research into military service, the committee determined, "The historical experience of the services . . . showed that these policies had deprived the services of the talents of many highly qualified Negroes whose individual skills could not find a place in segregated units." *Freedom to Serve* also highlighted the dynamic that military desegregation did not impact military readiness. The group affirmed, "The Navy and Air Force had proved, under their new policies, that when Negroes were trained and assigned on the basis of individual capacity rather than race, more effective manpower utilization resulted. Neither the Navy nor the Air Force had experienced any difficulty from the assignment of whites and Negroes to the same ships and units." As a result, the Fahy Committee concluded, "New programs for equal treatment and opportunity were not only 'right and just' but would 'strengthen the nation.'"[21]

The Fahy Committee provides an excellent historical case study illuminating the unique nature of American civil-military relations. Spurred on by civil rights activists, President Truman challenged military leaders to abandon personnel policies of segregation and racial discrimination. Although met with fierce resistance by military leaders and large segments of American society, the Fahy Committee persevered and carried Truman's intent forward. The group forced constant negotiation and concessions on the part of military leaders, especially Secretary of the Army Royall. As a result, the committee illuminated a key strength of American civil-military relations: civilian control of the military. While this dynamic is most often situated in the context of strategic decision making, the Fahy Committee demonstrated its value in ensuring "the highest standards of democracy" are enshrined in military personnel policy as well.

Few Americans in the spring of 1950 would have guessed that by summer, battlefields on the Korean peninsula would immediately test the lofty rhetoric of the Fahy Committee. With the outbreak of the Korean War on 25 June 1950, most attention shifted from debates regarding peacetime military service to the impact of war. Military integration was the most visible issue at the time, and it most directly impacted the army. One reason for this impact was simple numbers. At the end of 1950 the army had 972,908 enlisted male personnel, of whom 113,908 (11.7 percent) were African American. Air force enlisted male personnel numbered 489,428, of whom 30,169 (6.2 percent) were African American. The navy counted 477,898 enlisted male personnel, of whom 17,588 (3.7 percent) were African American. The marine corps counted 173,083 enlisted male personnel, of whom 2,077 (1.2 percent) were African American. This snapshot of personnel in U.S. military service at the end of 1950 demonstrated the significance of race in the army, because the army number of enlisted male African Americans was roughly twice that of the navy and air force in both real terms and as a percentage of the organization.[22]

At the same time, navy and air force efforts on military integration advanced beyond those of the army. In a memorandum to Army Chief of Staff J. Lawton Collins, Assistant Chief of Staff G-1 (Personnel) Lieutenant General Edward H. Brooks characterized navy efforts as "complete integration" since 1945, including no racial designations and no racial considerations in duty assignments. Brooks also highlighted the lack of segregation in the navy in both duty and mess facilities, including bunk assignments based on duty without racial segregation. Air force policy was less standardized, with "no reference" to race regarding recreational facilities because commanders retained the right to determine local practices. In contrast, Brooks reported that the army had achieved "complete integration" in only seven out of nine training divisions and that those two were "changing over." Brooks observed that in the army most "units are racially designated and assignment of personnel to such units is generally made accordingly." Navy and air force efforts on military desegregation quickly outpaced those of the army, in part because the overall issue was smaller and therefore easier for those services to sort out.[23]

Executive Order 9981 spurred momentum for change; combat accelerated it. In addition to higher percentages of young Americans serving in the military during the Korean War, the outbreak of hostilities spurred progress on racial integration within the military.[24] Stan Swinton, a reporter for the *Negro Star* serving with the Twenty-Fifth Division in Korea, reported, "Limited numbers of Negro infantry replacements are being fed into what were all-white infantry combat units here." In addition, Swinton narrated the reverse dynamic: "South Korean squads, under white American noncommissioned officers, also are being incorporated into one Negro regiment which never before had white enlisted personnel." After acknowledging the time lag between Executive Order 9981 and actual integration in the field, Swinton commented, "The new move in Korea puts individual Negro soldiers shoulder-to-shoulder with white enlisted men in the same units, including one of the most famous regiments of the U.S. army."[25]

Secretary of the Army Frank Pace Jr. indicated to the Truman administration that progress in expanding opportunity for African Americans in the army had occurred. He stated to David K. Niles, political advisor to President Truman, "That this has been so is clearly indicated by the rise in percentage of enlisted negroes in the Army from approximately 10% to a current 14% in the Regular Army—12% in the Army overall. This contrasts with approximately 4% overall in the Navy and 6% overall in the Air Force."[26] Even with such claims of progress emanating from army officials in Washington, what really spurred change was the combination of military personnel policy changes forced by civilian leaders and the

Frank Pace Jr. (right) is sworn into office as the new secretary of the army by Chief Justice Fred M. Vinson (left), as witnessed by Secretary of the Treasury John W. Snyder, Secretary of Defense Louis Johnson, former secretary of the army Gordon Gray, and Secretary of State Dean Acheson (barely visible). 12 April 1950. (Courtesy Harry S. Truman Library)

necessity for large numbers of personnel driven by battlefield conditions during the Korean War.

As the Korean War raged, Major General Ward H. Maris, deputy assistant chief of staff of the army for research and development, requested on 29 March 1951 that Johns Hopkins University's Operations Research Office "initiate a project to determine how best to utilize Negro personnel within the Army." Thus began Project Clear, a secret effort to conduct social research on the U.S. Army during the Korean War. There were archetypes for such an undertaking. Samuel A. Stouffer's groundbreaking soldier surveys and the extensive work of the U.S. Army's Research Branch during World War II set a precedent for Project Clear during the Korean War. Leo Bogart, the person tasked to lead the effort, referred to Stouffer's earlier work as "the significant forerunners of *Clear*." He also highlighted crucial differences: "Whereas they ranged broadly over a great variety of subjects of interest to military leadership, *Clear* was narrowly focused. And whereas the surveys made for *Clear* underwent only minor

This machine gun crew of African American soldiers in the Korean War beat off a fierce night attack with their accurate firing. Circa 1950. (Courtesy Harry S. Truman Library)

secondary analysis of the original data, Stouffer's landmark volumes on *The American Soldier* are a complete reanalysis, reprocessing and rethinking of a whole series of individual earlier studies made at different times, under diverse conditions and for varying motives."[27]

The study carried out by the Operations Research Office during the Korean War became one of the major confirmations that military desegregation did not harm military effectiveness. It indicated two key conclusions: that "integration has been working in sufficiently varied circumstances to justify expansion to entire AR [area of responsibility]" and that "performance of unit in combat or garrison is not adversely affected when integration is carried out."[28] As a result, Project Clear substantiated that racial integration and military readiness strengthened one another and therefore recommended expanding desegregation throughout the military. Efforts in the field developed in response to both policy changes in Washington and national security realities in Korea.

The Operations Research Office contracted New York research firm International Public Opinion Research (IPOR) to conduct field surveys of soldiers within the Far East Command. IPOR president Elmo C. Wilson had led the Office of War Information's survey research efforts in Europe during World War II, and he assigned Leo Bogart to lead IPOR's efforts on Project Clear during the Korean War. It included two exhaustive troop opinion surveys that Bogart characterized as "the heart of the project." Project Clear also included such other social research as "reviews of military history, troop performance records and incidents of racial conflict." Project Clear validated racial integration of the American military and based that endorsement upon concrete and exhaustive evidence obtained from soldiers themselves. Although there were some flaws with the surveys, such as Bogart's admission that "a case of whiskey was smuggled into Korea, labelled 'interview-inducing material,'" the breadth, scope, circumstances, and ultimate outcome of the surveys demonstrated that Project Clear (in addition to the World War II G.I. surveys that preceded it and "Don't Ask, Don't Tell" surveys that followed it) was a significant historical example of the interaction between social science, military service, and military personnel policy. As Bogart concluded, "*Clear* said clearly what is by hindsight obvious: racial integration 'worked.'"[29]

From 7 May to 15 June 1951 the team of social scientists queried numerous soldiers in Korea regarding race, military integration, and the impact of those two factors on military service. The team personally interviewed 600 officers and soldiers, surveyed more than 3,000 others, and specifically targeted combat units: "The bulk of the questionnaires were administered to men in infantry companies on the Korean Front." The continental United States study was even more robust, with roughly 9,200 interviews and questionnaires conducted from 8 July to 31 August 1951 at ten military installations located throughout the country.[30]

After conducting extensive soldier interviews and compiling a classified report, Bogart and his team briefed senior military leaders in Washington, first Army Vice Chief of Staff Wade H. Haislip on 13 July, then Army Chief of Staff J. Lawton Collins and Secretary of Defense George C. Marshall on 23 July 1951. Bogart recalled, "At the latter meeting, the conclusions were officially accepted and the Army initiated a policy of integration for the Far East Command." The results were significant enough to spark an extension of the original line of inquiry from the Far East Command to the Zone of the Interior. Bogart later remembered, "It was also directed to investigate more closely the combat performance in Korea of infantry squads with various levels of integration."[31]

Project Clear's two distinct survey efforts, those in the Far East Command and those in the Zone of the Interior, supported the same conclusion; military integration did not detract from military readiness. As Bogart recollected, "The two studies differed not only in the contrast between combat and garrison and between a primarily military society and one embedded in the civilian structure; they also differed in time." As Bogart further clarified, "The few months' interval between the Korean and U.S. studies had been sufficient to create within the Army itself an awareness of change in the official policy on Negro troops. This time dimension might even have been apparent within the weeks of U.S. fieldwork, had the data been analyzed according to the date of the interview rather than as though they all reflected the same moment in time." Bogart concluded, "In general, the Continental U.S. findings completely supported and recapitulated those obtained in the Far East Command, though the second study lacked the poignancy, excitement, and intensity of the original effort."[32]

Project Clear also revealed the significant transition that occurred regarding military personnel policy. After a thorough examination of Eighth Army military personnel policy in Korea, the Project Clear team observed, "As early as January 1951, it was recognized by personnel officers at Eighth Army Headquarters that, since Negro units would soon reach their fully authorized strength, two courses of action offered themselves: (1) To discontinue the flow of Negro replacements to Korea when the full quota in Class II units was reached; (2) To continue to receive all available Negro replacements and to assign Negro personnel to white units." The group further illuminated how the urgency of combat impacted military personnel policy: "It was felt that to request discontinuance of the flow of Negro replacements to Korea would reduce the amount of available manpower and thereby reduce the combat effectiveness of the command." The Project Clear team relayed the ultimate outcome: "Accordingly, official Eighth Army policy became one of assigning Negroes to units in Korea, white or Negro, that were below authorized strength. This policy was adopted in spite of the objections of a number of divisional commanders to any further assignment of Negro personnel to their divisions. These objections have lost their force in the intervening period." Overall, one of the main conclusions of Project Clear was that "integration of Negro and white personnel in Korea has been successful to the extent that it has been put into effect." There were caveats, however, including "widely varying interpretations by troop commanders in the field," a "lack of agreement among both officers and men as to what Army policy actually is," and the angst that "integration in the Zone of the Interior would bring with it problems which have not arisen in the Korean War." Despite these stipulations, Project Clear boldly recommended, "Integration of Negro and white personnel, which has been successfully undertaken in the Far East Command, should be carried through to completion on an Army-wide basis as quickly as possible through normal replacement procedures."[33]

Project Clear also benefited from fortuitous timing. Although the research was designed with military segregation as a given, the demands of the Korean War quickly and quietly altered the status quo. As Bogart described, "The research was designed with the assumption that segregation was still in effect among all the divisions in Korea—as in fact it was. By the time the first members of the survey team arrived in Japan, blacks had already entered many white units, as the report describes, but this fact was unknown in military circles in Tokyo and was discovered only after the team arrived at Eighth Army headquarters in Taegu, Korea." As a result, Project Clear commenced at the same time that the Korean War spurred momentum, albeit in great variation and to some degree of confusion, toward military integration. Bogart clarified, "The opportunity to manipulate circumstances was occasioned by the revolutionary changes taking place within the Far East Command at the very time the study was instituted, since there were, at that time, troop units with comparable assignments but with every conceivable racial balance."[34]

During the Korean War, Project Clear specifically and racial integration generally also demonstrated the impact that military personnel policy had on American society at large. The contested arena within which military integration occurred became a beacon of hope for expanded opportunity in other areas of American society. Bogart concluded: "In the decades of revolutionary changes that followed this study, the armed forces, and especially the Army, were often presented as models of the successful integration of blacks and whites in a formerly segregated institution. The military experience was repeatedly held up to doubting Thomases contemplating proposed desegregation measures in education and housing." In fact, because of its relevance to segregation in civilian society, Leo Bogart repeatedly attempted to have Project Clear declassified, only to be subject to "Kafkaesque evasions." He recalled, "Letters went unanswered; phone calls and telegrams were ignored." Army officials repeatedly denied him, insisting that the "obscene language" contained in many of the surveys was their primary reason. Bogart provided another, more likely, alternative: "The most obvious political sensitivities involved were those which surrounded the National Guard divisions, particularly those from the Deep South." As Bogart further clarified, "These divisions, which had been mobilized during the Korean War, remained lily white even after they were federalized, whereas the rest of the Army, including both the training divisions and the regular units, underwent desegregation after the Defense Department's acceptance of *Clear's* conclusions." The implication was straightforward. Bogart revealed, "Since these divisions siphoned off a disproportionate number of the young Southern white men of military age who might otherwise have gone into the regular Army, they were in part responsible for the relatively high proportion of black enlisted men in the Army in the years that followed." The military eventually declassified Project Clear on 7 November 1966.[35]

Bogart emphasized the relevance of Project Clear and military integration to American society: "Long before the era of affirmative action, years before the Supreme Court decision (in *Oliver Brown et al. vs. Board of Education of Topeka*) that struck down the longstanding 'separate but equal' doctrine that had prevailed since post–Civil War reconstruction, the American military moved to abolish racial segregation. This study provided the final push. Conducted at the height of the Korean War, it was a hastily organized and executed field investigation to find out how the Army could best use its black soldiers."[36] In this particular debate regarding American military service, civilian leaders forced military personnel policy to change ahead of the practice of American society. President Truman's Executive Order 9981 was the opening salvo, but Project Clear provided "the final push."

Leo Bogart repeatedly called on James Evans for assistance, something that Bogart acknowledged in the Project Clear report. In his oral history interview with Evans, Major Alan Gropman from the Office of Air Force History discussed Project Clear and its significance. Evans's analysis was especially valuable because he served continuously from 1940–1970 in the Department of Defense in a variety of roles focused on equal opportunity, mostly as special assistant to the secretary of defense. Gropman relayed to Evans, "Something that I am reading at night when I am not interviewing people is the Project Clear Report. A lot in the published material on this subject indicates that Project Clear was sort of a break-even point, the watershed point of it all, that Project Clear convinced the unconvinceables [sic] that integration would work and that the attitudes of the power structure would change, that the whites and blacks would get along in combat units, that blacks served better in combat units with whites than they did in segregated units." Gropman then asked Evans for his assessment of this general conclusion: "Has that been misplaced? Do you figure that Project Clear really had that kind of an impact, or was it misplaced?" Gropman felt that Project Clear was a pivotal event in the campaign for military desegregation, but he wanted Evans's confirmation since Evans had been a key participant throughout the campaign. Evans responded that Gropman's assessment was correct and even hinted that such a conclusion was one reason why the army did not publicize either Project Clear or the subsequent report that detailed it. As Evans responded, "I think that's right. If you read along with that type of thing why Project Clear was kept under wraps for so long. It was too good to be true, but it was true, and I was a party to that. When everybody else had given up the ghost I was still writing and agitating to get it declassified and brought out, where it could be used. We were talking about it at lunch today. It should be used by everybody, not just the military." Evans distilled Project Clear to a simple lesson; combat during the Korean War lessened to policy makers the relevance of race within military service. Evans compared his role to that of Leo Bogart and commented, "He persisted on the outside while I was persisting on the inside. There is nothing that Project Clear says except that as you get closer and closer to the battlefront the racial lines fade more and more, until when you finally get up there there are no racial lines." Evans concluded that Project Clear cemented what had been a continuous process of improvement toward expanded opportunity within U.S. military service. He boasted, "Our operation has rather been to improve, improve, improve on *this* design, and I think we are on the way. The great contribution which the Negro military man has made to me has been to exemplify democracy with complete, total, unlimited racial integration."[37]

In addition to Project Clear, combat during the Korean War accelerated the pace of military integration. After a trip throughout the Far East Command (FECOM) theater of operations, Assistant Chief of Staff G-3 (Operations) Maxwell D. Taylor provided Henry S. Aurand on 10 May 1951 "the draft of the recommendations relating to the use of negro troops in FECOM. It is my understanding that General Ridgway has not approved the paper, but in conversations he indicated his general agreement." As Taylor confided to Aurand, "All the commanders with whom I talked believe that complete integration up to about 12% is the only solution to the use of negroes. The Eighth Army is most anxious to break up all negro units and re-form them as integrated units. We should check to see whether this is possible in the case of the 24th Infantry, which I believe was established as a colored regiment by act of Congress." Taylor comprehended that the combat situation in Korea, notably understrength white units and overstrength African American units, presented a practical reason that sped military integration, with far-reaching consequences. He relayed: "The recommendations which are originating out of FECOM make it imperative for the Department of the Army to review its army-wide policy. It seems to me impossible to retain segregation in the Army if experience on the battlefield indicates it to be unsound. Certainly it would be difficult to resist pressure against segregation if we go for integration in the Far East."[38] Taylor's assessment of the relationship between battlefield necessity and overall military personnel policy was critical. It demonstrated that developments on the ground during the Korean War obliterated many of the remaining barriers to desegregation. As a result, military requirements combined with social and political pressures to speed the process. This happened in military and not civil society partly because witnessing someone risk their life and even die in military service was a dynamic rarely replicated in civilian society. There was inevitably a certain amount of respect that accrued and softened long-held assumptions. The other issue was that the military was ultimately a practical organization; it was (and is) mission-driven. Military leaders had to solve practical problems, in this case personnel shortages in white units while there were simultaneously overstrengths in African American units due to segregation. Initially forced to change policy by civilian leaders, combat conditions added to the momentum toward military integration. There was simply no equivalent in civil society.

In July 1951, George C. Marshall summarized for senators Herbert H. Lehman (D-NY) and Hubert H. Humphrey (D-MN) the military's efforts at desegregation throughout the first year of the war. Marshall conveyed "in some detail the present status of Army plans for the integration of Negro personnel." He outlined the Pentagon's efforts on integration and provided specifics on the influence of the Korean War on those endeavors. He confided, "For the past several months the Department of the Army has been conducting an intensive study in Korea directed toward improved employment of Negro manpower, particularly in combat units." The study included surveys and interviews of hundreds of military service personnel from all races; Marshall characterized it as shifting army policy toward integration: "The following planned action is based upon

An informal portrait of U.S. Army Brigadier General Anthony C. McAuliffe, who commanded the 101st Airborne Division, at Bastogne, Belgium. 5 January 1945. (U.S. Army, courtesy Harry S. Truman Library)

the findings of this study." Marshall reported that "Far East Command has been directed to inactivate the Negro 24th Infantry Regiment and to replace it with an integrated infantry regiment. Further, general integration has been ordered in the Eighth Army in Korea and in units in Japan of both combat and service type." As he also confided, "Secretary Pace, General Collins, and General Ridgway are giving the above plan their full support." Marshall indicated that FECOM planned to release on 1 August 1951 a public statement detailing the transition and that senior military leaders "propose to give equally careful consideration to other areas."[39]

Expansion to other areas proceeded rapidly. By the end of 1951, Lieutenant General Anthony C. McAuliffe, assistant chief of staff, G-1 (personnel), finished a thorough review of military desegregation efforts during the first eighteen months of the Korean War. In his detailed analysis, McAuliffe summarized military desegregation efforts during the early 1950s. He recorded that the number of African Americans in military service "has steadily increased since start of Korean War" and represented an increase from 10.9 percent on 30 June 1950 to 12.6 percent on 30 August 1951. McAuliffe predicted that this would rise to 13.5 percent by 30 June 1952. He revealed that such a situation within the context of segregation "has resulted in an over-strength in most Negro units." On 3 April 1951, Assistant Secretary of the Army Earl D. Johnson recommended to Secretary of the Army Pace that "excess Negro strength in segregated units be distributed among other units; implementation would eliminate segregated units" and recorded that "integration in FEC has been authorized to improve theater effectiveness."[40]

One excellent case study of the fluid relationship between integration and military service was the U.S. Sixth Army, based in San Francisco, California. Commanding General Joseph M. Swing explained his army's situation to senior military leaders at the Pentagon. Swing was surprised that officials there feared a public backlash resulting from military desegregation within his army: "I realize that the press reaction you worry about is probably one which compares Army areas and might force untimely action in the southern Army areas; and I also realize that the force and probability of this reaction can only be estimated in the Department of the Army. However, the concern shown by you over the press reaction to integrating these men into white units causes me to guess that your people may not realize the extent to which integration has already progressed—at least in the Sixth Army." Swing characterized the situation as one that had progressed far beyond the Pentagon's control and even awareness: "And, to show that it's really six of one and a half a dozen of the other in the Army area, I will cite finally the integration of white and colored WAC's here and at Stoneman. Almost without exception, integration is the accepted and expected thing here, and has been for some time prior to my arrival."[41] Swing demonstrated that Pentagon officials were unaware of the extent of integration that had already occurred and questioned how they could be worried about his army's integration efforts when integration had already occurred. It had already happened, and Pentagon officials were voicing concern that it *might* happen.

The following week, McAuliffe responded, "The whole problem is a very touchy one, the solution of which I must agree is integration. The difficulty is that my superiors are not prepared to admit that we are already launched on a progressive integration program." McAuliffe admitted that practical integration resulted from the Korean War and outpaced formal direction from the Pentagon. Referencing the Operations Research Office study already discussed, McAuliffe commented, "I am familiar with the present status of integration which, as you point out, is fairly widespread and has been accomplished without the dire results that were predicted by its opponents. The important fact to me is that we have over-strengths in colored units totaling 34,000 approximately. To me a costly and needless waste of manpower."[42] That the commanding general of the U.S. Sixth Army wrote the assistant chief of staff, G-1 (personnel) and highlighted how desegregation had already occurred in his army illustrated that integration had outpaced military officials in Washington. Pentagon leadership clearly was not ready for complete racial integration in the U.S. military, but events passed them by. Shortages of personnel drove a search for alternative sources. The structural lack of opportunity for African Americans due to segregation resulted in limited units for them to serve in, and that resulted in overstrengths in those units. Eventually, especially when combat conditions in Korea became dire, those overstrengths represented a critical source of available personnel that military leaders could not ignore. Military efficiency influenced events in a way that it did not in civilian society.

In the fall of 1952, Assistant Secretary of the Army (M&RA) Fred Korth provided a comprehensive "Progress Report on Elimination of Segregation in the Army," partly in response to a request from Senator Humphrey. Korth relayed, "Since March 1951 integration has been accomplished in all training divisions and in Replacement Training Centers throughout the United States. In May 1952 the Far East Command completed the process of integration, including the discontinuance of racial designations previously applicable to certain units." Korth also indicated that events in FECOM slowly expanded to other geographical areas: "In the Alaskan, Austrian and European Commands programs of gradual integration have been initiated and are being progressively implemented. The procedures followed in this regard are comparable to those used successfully in the Far East Command." Korth indicated that military integration in the continental United States also neared completion. He reported, "In the continental United States integration is nearing completion in the three Regular Army divisions and many non-division units regardless of geographical location."[43] Regarding military desegregation, the Far East Command set the precedent due to its involvement in the Korean War. Military desegregation also progressed more rapidly overseas because there was less contact with local American communities. The slowest progress was in the continental United States due to the oftentimes contentious relationship between military bases and local communities, especially in the South.

Progress on racial integration in the army proceeded quickly during the Korean War. The Far East Command saw the most rapid advance due to the exigency of the Korean War. Ridgway recommended integrating FECOM on 14 May 1951, and Army Chief of Staff J. Lawton Collins approved the change on 1 July 1951. In making his case for the integration of FECOM, Ridgway emphasized that "11 months experience in Korea had proved the advisability of such a move." Korth also underscored the direct connection between increased personnel requirements during war and enhanced willingness among military leaders to abandon segregation in military service: "Faced with personnel shortages in their white units and heavy personnel over-strengths in Negro units, local Commanders began a piecemeal integration in Korea. Some observers have estimated that approximately 60% of the units in Korea were integrated to some extent by Jan 1951." Even with the majority of military units in the Korean War integrated by that time, the following month Collins ordered an extensive review: "The Chamberlin Board reported itself opposed to integration; it concluded that racial quotas should be reinstated and segregated units should be maintained. Secretary Pace, however, refused to re-impose the quota, and integration continued to spread in Korea." The following month, "the Army called in a team of social scientists to study the effects of this unofficial integration. This undertaking was known by the code word Project CLEAR. At the time the Staff was considering General Ridgway's request, the social scientists submitted a preliminary report proclaiming integration to be an unqualified success and recommending that it be extended Army-wide." On 26 July 1951, "the Army announced publicly that integration would be completed in about six months in Japan, Korea, and Okinawa, and that the all-Negro 24th Infantry was being disbanded."[44]

As military integration proceeded within the Far East Command, ripples spread to other commands. Regarding the Zone of the Interior, Korth relayed, "Integration of the Army in the United States began in the training divisions in the spring of 1951. The Army announced on 18 March the integration of all basic training within the United States. As it had in FECOM, integration began in the United States unofficially as local commanders, on their own initiative, solved the problem of over-strength Negro units by integrating the excess colored soldiers into white units that were generally understrength." Military leaders interpreted initial results from such military personnel policy changes as positive in that "no racial conflicts developed from these moves, and several commanders urged the Department to allow them to adopt an official policy of complete integration." As previously discussed, Project Clear provided additional momentum for changes in military personnel policy: "The Department decided to wait until the final report from Project CLEAR was published in November. Armed with the strong recommendation from Project CLEAR to integrate, the Chief of Staff called a conference in December, 1951 and ordered the United States and ALCOM commanders to proceed with the orderly integration of all units under their command; no timetable was set, but they were informed that it was the Secretary's desire that integration should be completed within the next few years. By the end of 1951 the only major Army command not pursuing an active policy of integration was EUCOM."[45]

In the European Command (EUCOM), military integration proceeded intermittently and with delays. Korth revealed, "Faced with a certain amount of reluctance among commanders in Europe to integrate Negroes into white units, CSA [chief of staff of the army] visited Germany in the fall of 1951, and discussed the problem with the commanders. Shortly after returning to Washington, General Collins requested General Handy's integration plan." After repeated delays, EUCOM eventually submitted its proposal in December 1951, "but the plan contained several provisions considered unsatisfactory in the Pentagon. EUCOM wanted to limit integration to combat units, ignoring the service units where the great majority of Negroes served. The Staff said that service units must also be integrated, and made several other suggestions that had the effect of liberalizing General Handy's plan." As a result, "integration began in Europe 1 April 1952."[46]

The Korean War greatly amplified the need for military personnel. In his State of the Union address on 9 January 1952, President Truman detailed how much this was the case. He stated, "During this past year we added more than a million men and women to our Armed Forces. The total is now nearly 3½ million."[47] In part due to the demand created by such expansion during the Korean War, military desegregation eventually became a reality. By 1953 many observers considered racial integration within the military to be largely complete. *Detroit Michigan Free Press* reporter Collins George compared the progress toward racial integration that occurred during the Korean War to the important relationship between compulsion and the antidiscrimination proviso of the Selective Training and Service Act of 1940: "With the draft act of 1940, the Army was forced to use Negroes in more varied ways than ever before." As a result, the compulsion of selective service forced additional safeguards such as the antidiscrimination proviso. George compared an African American soldier stationed stateside (who still witnessed numerous vestiges of discrimination) to one sent to Korea (who by comparison saw less discrimination). There, combat and personnel shortages dealt a heavy blow to segregation: "If he were to be sent to Korea to fight, the situation was different. For by 1951 all combat units in that 'police action' had, by sheer force of military necessity, been completely integrated." Even in the army, historically the branch most resistant toward racial desegregation, such a dynamic had a palpable effect. George concluded, "Of all the military services, the Army can be accused most of having dragged its feet in the matter of racial integration. Yet integration in the Army now is nearly 90 per cent complete and has been achieved in less than five years under conditions which no other branch of the service had to face."[48] Such contemporary sentiments illustrated the fact that during the Korean War de facto desegregation followed the de jure desegregation that began in 1948. Military personnel policy changes combined with national security requirements to crumble stubborn barriers to expanded participation that had proven far more durable during peacetime.

The army lagged behind other military services on racial integration prior to the outbreak of the Korean War: "The Army, which took small steps toward integration starting with unsegregated training of officers at the beginning of World War II, put into operation a real breakdown of its color lines when the Korean war broke out four years ago." By the summer of 1954, however, the army and by extension the U.S. military completed integration. Reports indicated that upwards of 98 percent of the army was racially integrated, with "no more than fifteen" small specialist units composed exclusively of African Americans due to above average time to reassign these specialized personnel to other units. This milestone did not go unnoticed by others in American society: "The Justice Department, in its brief to the Supreme Court last fall supporting moves to declare public school segregation unconstitutional, cited the military's successful racial integration as one proof that school segregation could be ended without stress."[49] With military integration largely completed by 1954, the military became a model of success for other American institutions on the path toward desegregation. Leo Bogart considered military integration to have cascading effects: "Had there been no Korean War and had the process of integration in the Army then been temporized or postponed, as it might well have been, an important precedent by which to demonstrate that 'it works' would have been missing when the Supreme Court met to decide *Brown* in 1954."[50]

Of course, not all of the reaction to military integration was positive. Some well-known military leaders sounded off against military integration in the years that followed. On 28 April 1956, Mark W. Clark, former supreme commander of UN forces in the Far East, publicly voiced his opposition to integration "from the military point of view." Other dissenters joined in. A former commanding general of the 92nd Infantry Division, Edward M. Almond, immediately supported Clark's comments "100 per cent." Almond explained why: "I have always been opposed to integration of white troops and Negro troops. . . . When the Secretary of the Army, Mr. Frank Pace, and the Chief of Staff, Gen. J. Lawton Collins, visited my command post, the 10th Corps, in the spring of 1951, I told them this." Almond contended that the two senior leaders "ignored [his advice] completely."[51]

As military integration neared completion, military service continued to provide a litmus test for American values, extending into civilian society as well. One example during the late 1950s of a clash between military and civilian society regarding race in American military service was the 1957 Army-Tulane football game. The controversy was significant enough to warrant a specific memorandum on the subject from Secretary of the Army Wilber M. Brucker to President Dwight D. Eisenhower. Brucker mentioned, "On 15 June 1954 the Army Athletic Association contracted for one football game with Tulane University. The site and date are Tulane Stadium, New Orleans, Louisiana and 16 November 1957." Brucker explained to Eisenhower that on 16 July 1956 "a player segregation law was passed by Louisiana. This prohibited non-white participation in athletic contests in Louisiana." After remarking that at that time there was not an African American currently on the army varsity football team, Brucker insisted, "However, if one should become a member, he would be expected to participate on the same basis as Caucasians. Tulane University was advised of this on 8 March 1957, and of cancellation of the game in such an instance if a Negro were denied participation." Brucker's steadfast stance on the Army-Tulane game demonstrated that military personnel policy was ahead of certain segments of society regarding racial integration. The military had been integrated for several years at that time, in both the de jure and de facto sense, while the Louisiana stance demonstrated that certain civilian segments of society still resisted both in the late 1950s. Brucker's proposal also indicated that the army was willing to cancel the game if necessary to ensure equal opportunity. As Brucker concluded, "I have given serious thought to whether or not the game should be played" at all.[52] The controversy also attracted the attention of civil rights leaders as a litmus test for American values. Executive Secretary of the NAACP Roy Wilkins stated that the game "would be a conspicuous endorsement of racial segregation because the armed services' policy of no segregation would be violated." Wilkins's determined position illustrated that civil rights leaders often used military personnel policy as leverage against civilian segments of society (Tulane University and Louisiana in this case) to draw attention to discrimination throughout broader American society.[53]

The Korean War impacted military personnel policy in two major ways. First, it converted the de jure military desegregation that began with President Truman's issuance of Executive Order 9981 into de facto integration. Second, it cemented the place of the draft in American society during the Cold War. Between the end of World War II and the start of the Korean War, military leaders barely used the draft: "Only 30,000 men were inducted during the period from June, 1948, until the outbreak of the Korean War." With the communist invasion of South Korea on 25 June 1950, military personnel requirements soared, and the draft became a much more active mechanism to meet them. As a result, it provided a larger portion of military personnel than was previously the case. In fact, throughout the Korean War, "the draft provided 27 percent of those in uniform."[54]

After the Korean War resulted first in a stalemate and then an armistice, Congress subsequently renewed the draft in 1955, 1959, and 1963 with little controversy. The American population grew comfortable with the draft as military personnel requirements remained steady. This period was significant, however, because it "completed the evolution of the draft into a permanent part of the military manpower procurement structure, even though the nation was not fighting either a major or a declared war."[55] As the draft's place in American society solidified, the military remained quite large, even though the nation was at peace. The menace of communism loomed large during the Cold War, ensuring that peace was never truly peace and potential war was omnipresent: "The longest peacetime draft, however, was the one between the Korean and Vietnam Wars, when the threat from the Soviet Union prompted the United States to raise the largest peacetime force in its history. During that period, 1953 to 1964, total end strength in the military averaged 2.8 million officers and enlisted personnel. . . . That force was roughly 10 times the average size of the military in the 1920s and 1930s and about twice the size of the current force."[56] With such a large force, the impact remained significant, although not controversial due to perceived equity. On average, the draft called 193,000 Americans to military service per calendar year from 1952 to 1967. During this same time period, the active force strength of the military averaged 2.5 million Americans. By 1960 it had gradually dropped to about 2 million Americans. The Kennedy administration's subsequent buildup inaugurated a dramatic increase that led to hitting a peak of 3.55 million Americans in 1968.[57]

The Korean War era witnessed major changes in military personnel policy. With the defeat of universal military training and the ascendancy of selective service in 1948, the draft sparked major debates in American society. Similar to earlier dialogues regarding UMT, race figured prominently. Civil rights leaders applied steady pressure for progress, demonstrated by the National Defense Conference on Negro Affairs and the resulting Granger report. President Truman's Executive Order 9981 followed shortly thereafter, implicitly calling for the eventual desegregation of the military. The subsequent Fahy Committee analyzed race and military service and forced the military services, especially the army, to alter their personnel policies. The demands of the Korean War converted initial efforts toward racial integration into reality, aided significantly by Project Clear and the difficulties of fielding sufficient combat forces. By the armistice of the Korean War, military integration largely existed, albeit not without much resistance and criticism, even by such senior military leaders as Mark Clark and Edward Almond. The successful integration of the U.S. military served as an example touted by civilian leaders to spur further change in American society. The Korean War also reinforced the draft in society by increasing draft calls from roughly 15,000 per year in 1948–1950 to approximately 193,000 annually in 1952–1967. Such a dramatic increase in the use of the draft shifted debates regarding military service toward the issue of equity, because the nation's population growth ensured that even such large numbers of inductees were a progressively smaller fraction of American society. This situation combined with the shrinking number of active duty personnel during the last years of the Eisenhower administration to reframe conversations regarding military service. Debates about the freedom to serve shifted to questions regarding the matter of who serves when not all serve.

CHAPTER FIVE

WHO SERVES WHEN NOT ALL SERVE?

Discriminatory practices are morally wrong wherever they occur—they are especially inequitable and iniquitous when they inconvenience and embarrass those serving in the Armed Services and their families.[1]—John F. Kennedy, 24 July 1963

The mounting percentage of the military manpower being fed into Vietnam has so strained the official definition of a "limited" war, and increased the range of inequities of the present draft, that much support has developed in Congress for a restoration of the lottery method as the least discriminatory in effect.[2]—Arthur Krock, 23 June 1966

Who serves when not all serve? It is an enduring problem, but floodlighted today by the war in Vietnam. The echo of American battle fire impels, as it always should, the hard probe for better solutions.[3]—National Advisory Commission on Selective Service, February 1967

The 1960s witnessed many debates regarding military service and resulting changes to U.S. military personnel policy. The Gilpatric memorandum, a Department of Defense directive, sought to extend outward the equal opportunity that had been established within the military, influencing treatment of military service members and their families in surrounding civilian communities. The Gesell committee established by President John F. Kennedy wanted to accomplish many of the same objectives. The Vietnam War intensely fueled military personnel requirements that the draft provided to a greater extent. Such a dynamic progressively highlighted inequities within the draft and led to calls for its reform or outright abolition. The army scrutinized implications of ending the draft and concluded that the draft was essential. The Department of Defense conducted its own evaluation and determined the draft to be indispensable. Policy makers deemed utilizing a wholly volunteer construct for military service unrealistic, primarily due to higher costs and the inability to maintain necessary force levels. President Lyndon B. Johnson created the Marshall Commission to investigate inequities of the draft. In many ways, it epitomized the context for military service during the 1960s. Concurrently, the Department of Defense experimented with alternative sources of military personnel and launched Project 100,000, which sought to utilize men previously disqualified from military service. Compounded military personnel requirements continued throughout the Vietnam War and resulted in nearly 300,000 draft calls in 1968 alone.

On 19 June 1961, Deputy Secretary of Defense Roswell Gilpatric issued a directive to all branches of military service; he declared two main points. First, Gilpatric confidently claimed, "The policy of equal treatment for all members of the Armed Forces without regard to race, creed or color is firmly established within the Department of Defense." While convinced that equal opportunity existed on the military bases, Gilpatric perceived remaining difficulties off them. He explained that "in those areas where unsegregated facilities are not readily available to members of the Armed Forces in adjacent or surrounding communities, it is the policy of the Department of Defense to provide such facilities on military installations to the extent possible." Gilpatric went further, however, and ordered military commanders to take external measures to extend equality outward: "In addition, local commanders are expected to make every effort to obtain such facilities off base for members of the Armed Forces through command-community relations committees." Until the 1960s civilian leaders pressured military leaders to eliminate discrimination within the military; that meant on the bases themselves. As the preceding chapters have illustrated, there was plenty of work to accomplish in this regard. Progress was often far too slow, and military leaders repeatedly resisted such efforts, sometimes vehemently. By the 1960s, however, civilian leaders had made some progress on expanding equality and opportunity within military service; the off-base situation, therefore, took center stage. Such circumstances recognized significant problems of off-base discrimination and attempted to overturn them. Once again the ideal of military service served as a litmus test for American values and figured prominently in the rationale for taking a more proactive approach: "The Armed Forces are an ever-present symbol of our democracy. Both at home and abroad, they must be leaders rather than followers in establishing equal oppor-tunity. To the extent they practice and preach equality without regard to race, creed, color or national origin, they provide a standard by which communities at home may measure their own conduct and against which citizens of other lands may judge our adherence to the principles of equal-ity we advocate."[4] Gilpatric's efforts illustrated how military service served an important function relative to American society: it held both symbolic and social value. As before, increased national security demands broad-ened this dynamic and expanded opportunities for participation in mili-tary service for previously excluded groups. Once someone participated in military service, it became more difficult to deny him or her equal oppor-tunity in civil society. This theme first manifested itself in the military and subsequently extended beyond the military to American society. Such was the case because the military as an organization was never wholly sepa-rated from civil society. Even in times of war, the majority of the military usually resided within the United States and did not exist in a vacuum; it maintained linkages with surrounding civilian communities.

In June 1962, President Kennedy appointed a special committee to consider the progress of equal opportunity within military service. The members of the committee were attorney Gerhard A. Gesell (chair), NAACP leader Nathaniel S. Colley, former undersecretary of the inte-rior Abe Fortas, previous member of the Civil Aeronautics Board Louis J. Hector, former member of the Virginia Senate Benjamin Muse, *Chicago Defender* publisher John H. Sengstacke, and the executive director of the National Urban League, Whitney M. Young Jr. On 22 June 1962, Kennedy asked the members to consider two important questions. Kennedy first inquired, "What measures should be taken to improve the effectiveness of current policies and procedures in the Armed Forces with regard to equality of treatment and opportunity for persons in the Armed Forces?" Kennedy then directed their attention toward another related question: "What measures should be employed to improve equality of opportunity for members of the Armed Forces and their dependents in the civilian community, particularly with respect to housing, education, transporta-tion, recreational facilities, community events, programs and activities?"[5]

Throughout the course of the next year, the Gesell Committee emerged as the first significant attempt to analyze military personnel policy and its implications since the Fahy Committee issued its momentous final report in 1950. The committee met regularly and "held frequent sessions of two to three days' duration. During these sessions discussions were held with installation and other commanders, representatives of the Department of Defense and the Services, officials of interested Federal agencies, and others."[6]

On 13 June 1963 the committee released its initial report, entitled "Equality of Treatment and Opportunity for Negro Military Personnel Stationed within the United States." This report distilled a year of intensive deliberations and made recommendations for expanding equal opportunity in military service. Members emphasized to President Kennedy, "This report considers problems of equal opportunity affecting Negro military personnel on and off base within the United States. The recommendations emphasize matters which the Committee believes should receive the immediate attention of the Secretary of Defense."[7]

Gesell reported that much had changed regarding military service since 1948 and underscored the fact that "prior to 1948, the Negro had little or no opportunity in the Armed Forces. His skills and even his ability were a matter of debate. He was officially segregated, if not excluded; his duties were limited and his ability to serve his country in time of need was minimized or ignored." Gesell contrasted that situation with military personnel policy after 1948: "Such official policies no longer exist, and, in the main, the conditions which accompanied them have disappeared. Negroes have made military service their career in increasing numbers. They are formally integrated and have served well in both officer and enlisted ranks in times of war and peace."[8] Throughout its deliberations and in its resulting report the Gesell Committee linked itself to the legacy of the Fahy Committee that preceded it; it also directly connected resulting changes in military personnel policy to events begun in 1948 with Executive Order 9981.

The Gesell Committee highlighted the advances in military personnel policy that had occurred since World War II. Its report stressed, "There are no quotas or other forms of limitations on the recruiting of Negroes or on their assignment to career fields. All written policies governing advancement and promotion through both enlisted and commissioned ranks are non-discriminatory in character."[9] The absence of discriminatory policy was a significant difference from 1948 and even from 1951. Although such a shift did not mean that there was no discrimination or racism—these certainly existed—it presented a stark contrast to only fifteen years earlier, when there were many official discriminatory military personnel policies.

Even though the Gesell Committee found that significant progress had occurred, it pushed for expanding equal opportunity within U.S. military service. The committee argued, "While steps taken pursuant to President Truman's Executive Order were essential first ones in dealing with racial problems in the Armed Forces, it is wholly appropriate now to consider what further must be done to assure equality of treatment and opportunity for all qualified military personnel in the light of present day conditions."[10]

One of the conditions that the Gesell Committee highlighted was the striking growth in the size of the military in the post–World War II era. Such a massive peacetime force starkly contrasted with the undersized military of the interwar period. The committee mentioned, "Any consideration of problems pertaining to equality of treatment and opportunity for Negroes in the Armed Forces must emphasize the vast scope and complexity of the military establishment. As of September 30, 1962, there were 2,674,000 men in uniform stationed at home and abroad. Of these, approximately 1,900,000 were stationed in the United States."[11] It is important to remember that the postwar military was unprecedented in size. Staffing it was a far greater dilemma than had been the case prior to World War II. Massive personnel requirements often led to shortages that in turn created pressure to find alternative sources of personnel or to expand opportunities for previously underutilized groups. It was a slow-moving process that required pressure from above, but one that still occurred.

Even within a military of such large size, African Americans were still underrepresented in all the services except the army at the enlisted ranks and vastly underrepresented in all the services at the officer ranks. The committee noted, "The number of Negroes in the Armed Forces has increased since President Truman's Executive Order was issued in 1948. Nevertheless, while about 11 percent of our population is Negro, it is significant that only 8.2 percent of all military personnel is Negro." In 1962 the percentage of African Americans in the national population was indeed approximately 11 percent. In its enlisted ranks, the army remained consistently above that mark, with 12.4 percent in 1949, 13.7 percent in 1954, and 12.2 percent in 1962. All of the other services fell below that mark in their enlisted ranks, although the air force and marine corps exhibited significant increases after 1949. The air force rose from 5.1 percent in 1949 to 8.6 percent in 1954 and to 9.1 percent in 1962. The marine corps rose from 2.1 percent in 1949 to 6.5 percent in 1954 and to 7.7 percent in 1962. All the military services exhibited a dismal record regarding opportunities for African American officers, with only the army and air force having over 1 percent by 1962.[12] Such a situation illustrated why race was a special challenge for the army and also demonstrated the very poor record of all the services in promoting African American officers, although due to its size the army had the largest numbers and highest percentage of African American officers.

Even though the military services still lacked representativeness by 1962, military personnel policy had changed significantly since World War II. The Gesell Committee revealed, "The Armed Forces have made an intelligent and far-reaching advance toward complete integration, and, with some variations from Service to Service, substantial progress toward equality of treatment and opportunity." The committee detailed examples that it considered progress: "By and large, military bases reflect a clear pattern of integration. Segregation or exclusion of Negroes from barracks or other on-base housing facilities is not allowed. Military messes and all other on-base facilities are open to all personnel without regard to race. Negro personnel serve with whites in almost all types of units and at all unit levels. Negroes command white and Negro troops. Although the distribution is quite uneven, as will appear, Negroes have been placed in virtually all of the numerous job specialties and career fields which exist in the various Services."[13]

The committee proposed specific areas of needed reform, recommended changes in policy to address them, and declared that "the urgency of the remaining problems faced by Negro military personnel requires that this initial report be rendered at this time, so that corrective action may begin without delay. The headlines of recent weeks highlight this urgency. The great progress made is not enough." While lauding the progress that the military services had made, the committee urged military leaders to encourage additional improvements in civilian communities that surrounded military bases. It professed,

> Negro military personnel and their families are daily suffering humiliation and degradation in communities near the bases at which they are compelled to serve, and a vigorous, new program of action is needed to relieve the situation. In addition, remaining problems of equality of treatment and opportunity, both service-wide and at particular bases, call for correction. National policy requires prompt action to eliminate all these conditions. Equal opportunity for the Negro will exist only when it is possible for him to enter upon a career of military service

with assurance that his acceptance and his progress will be in no way impeded by reason of his color. Clearly, distinctions based on race prevent full utilization of Negro military personnel and are inconsistent with the objectives of our democratic society.[14]

The Gesell committee's report praised the significant progress that the military services had made, but it admitted that many problems still frequently occurred in local civilian communities. Civilian leaders adapted the military as a social organization largely due to its inherent hierarchy, detailed organization, and deference to command. In a vacuum, these organizational characteristics created a conservative and hidebound character. Under the control of civilian leaders, however, they created a malleability that enabled change to be instituted from above and extended in an orderly fashion. Civilian leaders used this dynamic to great effect to change military service for the better. Military leaders did not have the luxury to remain static; although they resisted, delayed, obfuscated, and complained, they ultimately obeyed orders, expanded opportunities, and ensured military effectiveness.

The starkest example of a lack of progress was the woeful underrepresentation of African Americans in the officer ranks of the U.S. military in 1963. In an understatement, the Gesell Committee admitted, "The slight Negro participation in higher non-commissioned and commissioned ranks . . . suggests strongly that Negroes, at least in the past, have not enjoyed equality of treatment and opportunity in the Armed Forces. In any event, this pattern acts to deter other Negroes from choosing the Armed Forces as a career." Even though the representation of African Americans had improved from World War II to the early 1960s, promotion remained slow and wholly inadequate. The measly record of promotion within officer ranks was a clear deterrent to African American enlistment in military service: "The ability of competent Negroes to succeed is all-important. Nothing will do more to encourage the able Negro to enter military service as a career than tangible proof, as yet almost entirely lacking, that Negro officers can receive equal recognition and opportunity for advancement with whites. Actual examples of Negroes who have achieved major positions of responsibility in the Armed Forces will be worth thousands of words devoted to claims that no barriers exist."[15] The issue of leadership remained unsolved. This was only partly because of the nature of military promotion. Changes in leadership within the military were (and continue to be) a slow, even glacial, process; it took approximately two or three decades to promote a colonel or general because there were no lateral promotions allowed from outside the military.

Social clubs also presented major difficulties: "One of the principal sources of difficulty arises in connection with the operation of on-base Service and NCO clubs. . . . At some bases, due to pressures brought by white personnel or other factors, forms of segregated Service clubs have developed in practice." The Gesell Committee recommended immediately remedying the situation and remarked, "These problems are not necessary and should be eliminated without delay. To do this, commanders should take affirmative action to insure that there is no *de facto* segregation or discrimination at any of these club facilities."[16] In addition, segregation of public facilities in communities adjacent to military installations was common. Military facilities tended to be sparse, especially for such a large military force as existed after World War II: "At many bases there is relatively little on-base housing. Therefore, it is quite usual for many of the married personnel to live off base. Statistics from the Department of Defense indicate that there are within the United States approximately 405,000 families residing in various types of off-base community housing, in communities near the service members' places of duty. As far as schools are concerned, the overwhelming majority of school-age dependents of military personnel use the local public school system, whether they live on or off base." Such a situation highlighted the intertwined relationship between military bases and local communities, in that the two entities never existed in complete isolation. Military personnel needed housing, school, transportation, and social venues located within the community; military personnel policy on base, however, did not always transfer off base. The Department of Defense conducted an expansive survey regarding segregation of public facilities in communities adjacent to military installations. The survey analyzed segregation in public schools, restaurants and bars, theaters, swimming pools, golf courses, beaches, bowling alleys, libraries, public transportation, hotels and motels, and churches at 760 installations that each had 100 or more military personnel assigned to it. Significant segregation existed within many of the communities surrounding these military installations. For example, 24 percent of the surveyed army installations and 25 percent of navy ones experienced segregated public schools off-base. An estimated 34 percent of the surveyed army installations and 43 percent of navy ones endured off-base segregated restaurants and bars. Roughly 31 percent of those army installations and 40 percent of navy ones suffered segregated theaters off-base. Such a prevalence of segregated public facilities off-base illustrated the many significant challenges that military personnel encountered in local communities around military bases and the difficulty of transferring military personnel policy into surrounding civilian communities.[17]

By the mid-1960s the Vietnam War surged the demand for military personnel. Draft calls significantly intensified in 1965, rising from only 5,000–10,000 per month previously to roughly 20,000–30,000 per month. The average age of inductees dropped sharply, from twenty-three to nineteen years. As a result of the greatly enlarged need for military personnel and corresponding escalation in the number of inductees, the draft again took center stage in American society. Draftees as a percentage of military personnel spiked, representing a full 25 percent of the approximately 9 million Americans who served in the military during the Vietnam War.[18] Draft-motivated volunteers comprised a large portion of the remaining 75 percent.

Partly in response to the heightened criticism that the draft engendered, the army studied the feasibility of eliminating it. The deputy chief of staff (personnel) sought "to determine the probable impact that elimination of the UMT&S Act would have on the Army's ability to meet projected manpower requirements." After intensive review, he concluded, "The United States Army has been unable to maintain its authorized enlisted strength without relying on the draft for the past sixteen (16) consecutive years ending 30 June 1964." One reason for this was the issue of draft-motivated volunteers: "Ten to thirty-five percent of all voluntary enlistments in the five services are draft motivated."[19]

In April 1964 the Department of Defense launched an extensive analysis of the draft. The objective was "to assess the possibility of meeting our military manpower requirements on an entirely voluntary basis in the coming decade." The scope of the study was vast. It included the military departments, the Selective Service System, Bureau of Census, Department of Labor, and Department of Health, Education, and Welfare (HEW). It evaluated data on "several hundred thousand men" and after two years of inquiry concluded that the draft was indispensable, especially for the army. Assistant Secretary of Defense (Manpower) Thomas Morris declared, "The Navy, Marine Corps and Air Force have—with limited exceptions—depended entirely upon volunteers. The Army, in most recent years, has obtained over half of its personnel through enlistments and its enlistment totals have exceeded those of any other Service. Nonetheless, our studies fully confirm the essentiality of the draft, both to supply the residual number of men needed to man our forces, and to encourage a larger number of volunteers." Department of Defense officials reminded Congress that the draft had been a significant part of military manpower policy since World War II but especially since the Korean War. Morris reiterated that between September 1950 and June 1966 there had been "188 draft calls placed with the Selective Service System—one in every month except May and June 1961. During this period, 11.3 million men have entered or been called to active service as enlisted men, of whom 3.5 million—nearly one in three—were draftees. This has meant an average monthly rate of inductions of about 18,600." In addition to the draft's ability to provide large numbers of service members, Morris praised its elasticity. He maintained, "The draft has proven to be a very flexible tool during the past 16 years. . . . In 1953, it was called upon to supply 564,000 men (59% of new entrants), while in 1961 draft requirements dropped to 60,000 (14% of new entrants)."[20] The Vietnam War ramped up reliance on the draft and once again severely tested that flexibility.

The Pentagon, however, did find shortcomings with the draft. It admitted that while efficient at meeting personnel requirements, there were "problems in the Selective Service process" that resulted in social and political flaws. The Pentagon classified major criticisms of the draft into four categories: First, "the present selection procedure calls the oldest men first—those who are most settled in their careers"; second, "past deferment rules have favored college men—those who may be the more fortunate economically"; third, "past deferment rules have favored married men without children—thus putting a premium on early marriages"; and fourth, "Department of Defense standards in recent years have disqualified men with lesser mental ability and educational attainment—those who may have been culturally deprived." The fact that a growing American population led to increased inequity in the draft drove many of these changes. Testifying before Congress, Morris explained how: "A principal problem affecting the operation of the draft system in the past has been the growing supply of draft-age men in relation to military requirements. A decade ago, only 1,150,000 men were reaching age 18. In 1965, the number of 18-year olds had increased by 50% to more than 1,700,000. This trend will continue into the coming decade; by 1974, the number of men reaching draft age will total more than 2,100,000—over 80% above the 1955 level." Population growth led to proportionally fewer Americans drafted into military service and increasingly more Americans receiving deferments. The Pentagon indicated, "As a consequence of this trend, a steadily decreasing percent of the Nation's manpower in the draft ages 19 through 25 has been called on to serve, and this trend may continue downward in the future": "One consequence of the growing imbalance in supply versus requirements in the past decade, was a trend towards more liberal deferment policies."[21]

The Pentagon study lasted roughly two years and reached its conclusions by 1966. It resolved that the all-volunteer force was prohibitively expensive and estimated that an AVF of approximately 2.65 million service members would cost at least $4 billion and potentially upwards of an additional $17 billion in defense spending. A large part of this estimate derived from the articulated requirement for significant pay increases in order to recruit the desired number of volunteers. For example, Department of Defense officials planned "that pay for first-term enlisted men would have to rise by 80 to 282 percent to attract a sufficient flow of true volunteers."[22] As a result, the Pentagon determined that the draft was necessary. Morris was adamant: "Clearly, there is no question about the success of the draft in meeting military manpower requirements, nor can there be any reasonable doubt as to the need for the draft in the present period." Pentagon officials also questioned the viability of any potential AVF. As Morris cautioned, "The findings clearly demonstrate that an all-volunteer force, under present policies, would fall far short of any force level which has been required since 1950." As a result, the Department of Defense defended the draft without qualification. Morris relayed that "we cannot look forward to discounting the draft in the next decade unless changing world conditions reduce force levels substantially below those needed since Korea."[23] Because the Vietnam War rapidly increased military personnel requirements at that time, this potential qualifier clearly did not resonate with military leaders during 1966.

There were two additional reasons why military leaders, especially those in the army, argued that the draft was essential. The first was the relationship between the draft and draft-induced volunteers. One of the unseen, but not accidental, purposes of the draft was to motivate individuals to enlist who otherwise might not in the absence of a draft. By enlisting, service members retained some control over duty assignment, location, and benefits, whereas if the draft later inducted them they lost such power. Estimates of draft-induced volunteers were both varied and indeterminate, but the issue was always a significant factor in debates. Worry about a potential all-volunteer force's impact on reserve forces spurred military leaders to analyze in great detail the prevalence of draft-motivated volunteers: "A Department of Defense survey of ready reserve personnel conducted in 1964 indicated that about 70 percent of non-prior-service reserve enlistees would not have enlisted in the absence of the draft; a comparable survey in 1968 indicated that the draft motivated group had risen to 80 percent."[24]

Draft-motivated volunteers continued to play a central role in debates regarding military personnel policies, especially when comparing the draft and the all-volunteer force. During later debates about the AVF, Army Chief of Staff William C. Westmoreland estimated the number as high as 60 percent of all volunteers. In a frank discussion with the Joint Chiefs of Staff and President Nixon, Westmoreland pleaded, "It is our estimate that over 60 percent of our volunteer enlistments are draft-motivated. . . . I can only conclude that for the next several years the Army will be heavily dependent upon the draft, and I believe that all of the other Services are also greatly dependent, either directly or indirectly. I am concerned that Congress and the public may have the impression that we have an alternative to the draft in the short-run."[25]

The second issue was the impact of the draft on reserve forces. This phenomenon was even more accentuated in the reserves, where draft-motivated volunteers represented upwards of 90 percent of all enlisted volunteers. In addition, the draft provided a general reserve of trained manpower known as the Individual Ready Reserve. Westmoreland feared that eliminating the draft fundamentally undermined the strength of reserve forces. As he warned, "I cannot conceive of any method of maintaining the Reserve Components at anything like their current authorized strength without a draft. Eighty-five percent of Reserve Component strength has been provided through the Reserve Enlisted Program, which is 90 percent draft motivated. Also, without the draft, the Individual Ready Reserve—a pool of one million trained men—will gradually dry up."[26]

Civilian policy makers increasingly focused their attention on the draft as well. President Johnson created the Marshall Commission in 1966 to study the Selective Service System. On 2 July 1966, while vacationing at his Texas ranch, President Johnson established the President's National Advisory Commission on the Selective Service by means of an executive order.[27] Executive Order 11289 outlined the commission's functions, explaining that "it is appropriate that the laws by which Government calls its citizens to serve should be reviewed by distinguished citizens from different walks of life, not only in the light of military needs but also with

President Lyndon B. Johnson (left) and Vice President Elect Hubert Humphrey during their trip to the LBJ Ranch near Stonewall, Texas. 2 November 1964. (Cecil W. Stoughton, courtesy Lyndon B. Johnson Library)

a view to other national, community and individual needs."[28] The twenty-member commission included vice president and general counsel of IBM Burke Marshall (chair), Yale University president Kingman Brewster Jr., former chief of the Women's Army Corps Oveta Culp Hobby, former assistant secretary of defense (manpower and personnel) Anna Rosenberg Hoffman, former secretary of defense Thomas S. Gates Jr., former White House press secretary George E. Reedy Jr., and Retail Clerks International Association president James A. Suffridge. The commission also had a sizeable staff, managed by executive director Bradley H. Patterson Jr., consultant for research John K. Folger, and reporter Harry J. Middleton. The staff included more than one dozen consultants, including Stuart H. Altman and Morris Janowitz.[29] The commission met intermittently throughout the last six months of 1966 and issued its final report to President Johnson in February 1967.

The fundamental task for the Marshall Commission was to determine "What are the present inequities of the Selective Service system and how can they be modified?"[30] It was notable that Burke Marshall chaired the commission. He previously served as assistant attorney general and led

Honorable Burke Marshall during a meeting in the White House Cabinet Room. 28 February 1967.
(Yoichi R. Okamoto, courtesy Lyndon B. Johnson Library)

the civil rights division within the Justice Department for both the Kennedy and Johnson administrations. President Johnson clearly meant his selection of Marshall as chair to counter charges that the Selective Service System unduly impacted African Americans. To achieve its task, the commission "sought to hear the nation's voice" and requested feedback from a wide swath of American society, including more than 120 private groups, "reflecting every sector of society." The Marshall Commission interviewed college presidents, numerous student leaders, roughly 250 student newspaper editors, more than 4,000 local draft boards, 97 appeal boards, every state governor and many city mayors, "every appropriate" federal department and agency, "representatives of the poor," and "many prominent private citizens." The commission also researched relevant congressional hearings and participated in three "national conferences on the draft." Marshall admitted that the group's lofty goals involved the difficult reality of ascertaining attitudes from coast to coast. He emphasized to President Johnson that "seeking to know the national mind was not, of course, enough. In the diversity of its interests, the nation does not think with one mind, or speak with one voice." In response, the committee determined "to find its own answers, based on its own comprehension of issues that involve both the national welfare and the rights of the individual."[31]

In February 1967, Marshall submitted to President Johnson the commission's report, entitled *In Pursuit of Equity: Who Serves When Not All Serve?* In his transmittal letter to the president, Marshall stressed that the report conveyed "the approval of all of the members of the Commission" and outlined their "final conclusions and recommendations." Marshall characterized the commission's task as "very difficult and intensely important" and relayed that they deliberated on the subject extensively, evidenced by "more than 3,500 pages of transcript." Marshall reiterated their central intention was "to find the means of securing the manpower needed for our national security in a manner as consistent as possible with human dignity, individual liberty, fairness to all citizens, and the other principles and traditions of a democratic and free society." In doing so, the commission analyzed an exhaustive list of topics, including "The Need for the Draft," "Profile of the Present System," "The Structure of the Proposed System," "The Individual in the System," "The Reserves," "Health Manpower and Aliens," "The Rejected," and "National Service." Marshall admitted that their work sought a delicate balance between national security and individual liberty. He underscored "the necessity to search for a method of manpower procurement which would assure the Armed Forces' ability to acquire the men they need, under any circumstances, to protect the nation's security and meet its commitments; and at the same time function as uniformly and equitably as possible with due regard for the problems and the rights of the individuals into whose lives it must intrude." The commission also considered all possibilities, "ranging from elimination of all compulsory service to compulsion for all." In doing so, it pointed out shortcomings of the Selective Service System, highlighting the high rejection rates of the Selective Service System as one of several "serious defects in our national life." It reported as evidence, "Of each group of men coming to draft age each year, from one-fourth to one-third of those examined are found ineligible for service because of educational or health deficiencies or both; almost 700,000 potential draftees were found unqualified to serve in the last fiscal year. A total of 5 million men between the ages of 18½ and 34 who have been examined for the draft are today considered ineligible to serve." Marshall warned that such high numbers of rejections "reveal weaknesses in our society."[32]

The Marshall Commission made thirteen specific recommendations,[33] including "continuation of a selective service system" that should be "consolidated . . . under more centralized administration." In order to market the Selective Service System, the commission recommended better public information to ensure that "both the registrant and the general public should be made fully acquainted with the workings of the improved system and the registrant's rights under it." The commission recommended, "The present 'oldest first' order of call should be reversed so that the youngest men, beginning at age 19, are taken first" in order to "reduce the uncertainty in personal lives that the draft creates." The commission also recommended changes to deferments "to insure fairness," implementation of "an order of call which has been impartially and randomly determined," and that "no further student or occupational deferments should be granted," with only minimal exceptions. By that time undergraduate student deferments were the most contentious critique of the draft, not the least because they explicitly highlighted social class divisions within American society. "To broaden the opportunities for those who wish to volunteer for military service," the commission suggested that "opportunities should be made available for more women to serve in the Armed Forces, thus reducing the numbers of men who must involuntarily be called to duty" and proposed creating "programs to achieve the objective, insofar as it proves practicable, of accepting volunteers who do not meet induction standards but who can be brought up to a level of usefulness as a soldier, even if this requires special educational and training programs to be conducted by the armed services." The Marshall Commission also "considered other propositions which it rejected." Chief among these was "elimination of the draft and reliance on an all-volunteer military force." It rejected this change primarily because "its inflexible nature, allowing no provision for the rapid procurement of larger numbers of men if they were needed in times of crisis." In addition to rejecting an all-volunteer force, the commission rejected universal military training, as well as both compulsory and voluntary national service.[34]

The Marshall Commission also singled-out race as a vital issue regarding U.S. military service. The members studied "the effect of the draft on and its fairness to the Negro" and reported, "His position in the military manpower situation is in many ways disproportionate, even though he does not serve in the Armed Forces out of proportion to his percentage of the population." The commission based its conclusion on several relevant findings that surfaced during its investigation and reported, "The number of men rejected for service reflects a much higher percentage (almost 50 percent) of Negro men found disqualified than of whites (25 percent). And yet, recent studies indicate that proportionately more (30 percent) Negroes of the group qualified for service are drafted than whites (18 percent)—primarily because fewer Negroes are admitted into Reserve or officer training programs." The commission observed, "Negro soldiers have a high record of volunteering for service in elite combat units" and determined, "This is reflected in, but could not be said to be the sole reason for, the Negro's overrepresentation in combat (in terms of his proportion of the population)." To emphasize this dynamic, the commission ascertained, "Although Negro troops account for only 11 percent of the total U.S. enlisted personnel in Vietnam, Negro soldiers comprise 14.5 percent of all Army units, and in Army combat units the proportion is, according to the Department of Defense, 'appreciably higher' than that." Marshall admitted that the cause was much broader than military service. As he reported, "Social and economic injustices in the society itself are at the root of inequities which exist. It is the Commission's hope that the recommendations contained in this report will have the effect of helping to correct those inequities."[35]

In August 1966, Secretary of Defense Robert S. McNamara initiated Project 100,000, which sought to promote military service among citizens previously disqualified due to poor test scores. The U.S. Air Force Recruiting Service documented, "During Phase I of Project 100,000, instituted in 1966, 15 percent of the total NPS accessions were to be taken from mental category IV." The recruiting service then revealed the purpose of doing so: "This project was an attempt to upgrade through military service and its attendant discipline and occupational training, men of lower mental caliber and/or educational achievement, as well as many suffering from easily remediable physical defects." The recruiting service finished by optimistically accepting the Pentagon's official stance on the program: "The Department of Defense directive establishing the program made it plain that Project 100,000 would not lower performance standards; rather, it would help young men meet the military's standards."[36] Project 100,000 sought to improve citizens through military service. It took previously rejected personnel (either because of low test scores or the lack of a high school diploma or both) and tried to use military service to better their condition. Project 100,000 purported to pursue the utopian ideal that military service advanced citizens through discipline and training. Of course, it also provided personnel at a time when military leaders desperately needed Americans in military service.[37] During its first year in operation, Project 100,000 introduced nearly 50,000 previously dis-

Secretary of Defense Robert S. McNamara during a national security meeting on Vietnam. 21 July 1965. (Yoichi R. Okamoto, courtesy Lyndon B. Johnson Library)

qualified Americans to military service, and most of them served in the army. From 1 October 1966 until 30 September 1967, Project 100,000 ran a pilot program and transitioned "some 49,000 formerly unaccept-able men—now referred to as New Standards men" into military service.[38]

In January 1968, William Leavitt reported, "The Army absorbed some 38,000, about 32,000 through the draft, the rest by enlistment. The Navy took about 3,600. The Marine Corps enlisted some 3,400. And the Air Force took about 3,400. All Navy, Air Force, and Marine Corps New Standards men are volunteers."[39] By far, the army participated in the project the most and did so primarily through compulsion. The other military branches exclusively used voluntary military service but also employed far fewer personnel in the project. Once again, the army proved the most concerned with meeting its larger personnel requirements, and therefore military personnel policy presented the biggest challenge for it. After op-erating the program for its first year, military leaders on 1 October 1967 expanded the program from Phase I to Phase II. The expansion of Project 100,000 presented two significant changes: "one, priorities one through six were now designated by three new categories, and two, the Air Force requirement of 15 percent was increased to 17 percent of NPS enlistees."[40]

As the project continued, the military modified and simplified it. Six categories, labeled "priorities," that evaluated Armed Forces Qualification Test (AFQT) scores and education level (i.e., whether the person was a high school graduate or not) merged into three.

Public reaction to Project 100,000 was mixed. William Leavitt characterized the program in social terms: "The armed forces, including the Air Force, are now accepting thousands of young men who until recently could not have met service entry requirements. The program has a frankly social purpose—the upgrading of youth through exposure to the educational opportunities and occupational training so widely available in the military—in order to help prepare them for useful reentry into the civilian world." Project 100,000 ostensibly presented military service as educational advancement and vocational training for disadvantaged youth and was therefore a program that purportedly blended both military and social purposes. Leavitt characterized Project 100,000 in sweeping terms: "Against a background of shooting war in Vietnam and civil strife at home, the armed forces, including the Air Force, are engaged in an historic experiment in manpower utilization and the salvage of disadvantaged youth. Its purpose is to bring into service as many as 100,000 young men a year who until recently could not have met the educational, mental, and in many cases, physical standards for enlistment or induction." The project was a social experiment that presumably used military service as a way to improve American youth, not dissimilar from earlier efforts such as the Universal Military Training Experimental Unit, located at Fort Knox, Kentucky, with its focus on morals and citizenship. Leavitt continued, "The program . . . is intended to upgrade, through military service and the discipline and occupational training that go with it, thousands of young men of lower mental caliber and/or underachievement in education—as well as many who are suffering from quickly remediable physical defects. The ultimate goal is to prepare them to reenter civilian life better equipped to live and work in a highly technical society."[41] Such a dynamic responded to high rejection rates under the Selective Service System and sought an offset to answer military personnel shortages.

Leavitt held high hopes for the program's future. Utilizing hyperbole, he considered initial participants to be "the vanguard of hundreds of thousands more to come. The Defense Department is, from all accounts, sufficiently heartened by the first year's results to be scheduling an influx of a full 100,000 during the second year of the project. Toward the second year's goal there is already a 'credit' of some 9,000 because all the services exceeded their combined first-year quota of 40,000 New Standards men." There was also a companion program named Project Transition that focused on smoothing the transition for enlisted personnel from military service to civilian life. Invoking a series of questions regarding the project and its implications for the relationship between military service and civilian life, Leavitt remarked, "Answers to these questions are just beginning to emerge from Project 100,000's 'first returns.' They tell a lot about our society, the untapped potential of people as a national resource that we dare not waste, and the enormous significance of the military as a producer of skilled citizenry for the civilian world."[42] The project bridged the gap between civilian and military life and also conveniently filled the ranks with much-needed personnel. Project 100,000 was one example where practical needs for additional personnel spurred military leaders to experiment with who served, in this case by including previously disqualified personnel.

Not all observers were positive. Even Leavitt conceded that there were "charges of those critics of Project 100,000 who have suggested that the program is nothing more than a plot to fill the infantry's ranks." Leavitt, however, countered, "Project 100,000 is different. It is in effect in all four services at the same time. The New Standards trainees are not segregated. They do not even know they are members of a separate group whose performance is being compared with men in higher mental categories as measured by scores in the Armed Forces Qualification and Aptitude Tests. Nor do their training instructors know the New Standards men as any different from the rest of their troops."[43] Conflicting views of the project abounded. Some characterized it as a ploy for additional personnel that targeted the most vulnerable American youth. Others considered it a legitimate mechanism to uplift citizens through military service. Such lively debates continued throughout the project's existence.[44]

As illustrated by the microcosm of Project 100,000, reliance on the draft intensified during the military mobilization for the Vietnam War. Draft calls swelled from 108,000 in 1964 to 233,000 the following year. They jumped to 365,000 in 1966, dropped temporarily to 219,000 the next year, and then vaulted to 299,000 in 1968. In addition to significantly amplified calls, the draft impacted volunteers. Draft-induced enlistments became ever more common, especially in the reserves and National Guard. Secretary of Defense Melvin R. Laird observed that during this time period "more than half of the young men in military service [volunteered] because of the draft, not because they were true volunteers. Thou-

President Lyndon B. Johnson (left) and Secretary of Defense Robert S. McNamara during a bipartisan congressional leadership meeting on Vietnam. 27 July 1965. (Yoichi R. Okamoto, courtesy Lyndon B. Johnson Library)

sands more enlisted in the Guard and Reserve because they perceived these organizations to be without a mission, undeployable, and a safe haven from the draft and the war in Vietnam."[45]

During the early and mid-1960s, contentious debates regarding military service simmered throughout society. At first, these debates centered on augmenting the expanded opportunities that the Fahy Committee had begun earlier. The Gilpatric memorandum and the Gesell Committee shifted emphasis from ensuring equality within the military to demanding equality for military service members in surrounding civilian communities. Military personnel policy made significant progress, but there were still many areas that demanded significant improvement—especially underrepresentation of minorities in officer ranks and far fewer opportunities for women compared to men. As military personnel requirements surged with the Vietnam War, so too did reliance on the draft to fill them. Draft calls multiplied, and critiques of the draft intensified along with them. Partly in response, first the army, then the Department of Defense, and finally President Johnson undertook extensive and highly publicized studies of the draft that all recommended its continuation.

Fear of the high cost of volunteers combined with concern over the loss of draft-motivated volunteers, especially in the reserves and National Guard, to prevent change. Pressed for personnel, the military services also experimented with alternative sources and instituted the experimental and controversial Project 100,000. Criticism of the draft mounted, however. On 6 March 1968, Richard M. Nixon busily prepared for the New Hampshire primary of the presidential campaign. On that day, he issued a campaign promise to end the draft and transition to an all-volunteer force. Nixon professed, "I believe we should have a volunteer armed services after the war is ended," so that young Americans would be "able to plan their lives rather than living as they are today with [the draft] hanging over them."[46] With that missive, Nixon launched an opening salvo at the draft that had far-reaching and even unintended consequences for U.S. military service.

CHAPTER SIX

CONSCRIPTION IS A TAX

President-elect Richard Nixon made just two explicit campaign promises. He promised to end the war in Vietnam. And he promised, after the war ended, to end the draft.[1]—*Newsweek*, 9 December 1968

The draft has been an accepted feature of American life for a generation, and its elimination will represent still another major change in a society much buffeted by change and alarmed by violent attacks on the established order. However necessary conscription may have been in World War II, it has revealed many disadvantages in the past generation. . . . The alternative is an all-volunteer force.[2] —Gates Commission, 20 February 1970

It ain't the old Army, buddy, and don't you ever forget it. These kids even have private rooms. Not really private, but only four to eight in one room. Back in '43, that was real basic training. Two hundred to a room. Double-decker bunks. Aren't even supposed to swear at these kids now. That makes it tough. They're called "gentlemen" now. Not even "trainees." "Gentlemen," or "soldiers." How're they going to know they're a long way from being soldiers yet unless we keep telling 'em? Those old words meant something. The Army's gone to hell.[3] —Ted Sell, *Los Angeles Times*, 19 July 1971

As the rafters crash down around him, let us pause to praise one of Mr. Nixon's finest achievements, the all-volunteer armed force. The evidence from fiscal year 1974, which ended June 30, is that the three major worries about the all-volunteer force—that there would not be enough volunteers, that they would not be of sufficiently high quality, that they would include "too

many" blacks—were unwarranted.[4] —George F. Will,
7 August 1974

As the Vietnam War raged, debates regarding military service took center stage once again. The inequities of the draft drew more and more criticism, and politicians noticed such public sentiments. Richard M. Nixon made concluding the war in Vietnam generally and ending the draft specifically major portions of his 1968 presidential campaign. Once in office, Nixon instituted significant reforms to the draft as a short-term remedy. He also created a presidential commission to propose changes that transitioned military personnel policy from dependence on the draft to an all-volunteer force. The Department of Defense established its own committee known as Project Volunteer to analyze the shift. By 1970, Nixon made the conversion official policy. Many observers doubted the feasibility or even desirability of the all-volunteer force. Such a move required monumental changes and occurred during a major war. Examples included the removal of irritants and increased advertising and recruiting, among others. The military services launched volunteer army (VOLAR) experiments to practice implementing such adjustments. The transition to the AVF met serious resistance from within the military and from many observers in American society. Recruiting shortfalls surfaced during and immediately after the transition, although by the mid-1970s many observers characterized the move as successful. One of the major results was a heightened focus by military leaders on demographics, minorities, and women, which in turn expanded opportunities for these groups within U.S. military service.

On 17 October 1968, Richard Nixon issued a stark challenge to an institution that had dominated American society since before World War II: he urged Americans that the time to end the draft was nigh. As Nixon avowed, "I say it's time we took a new look at the draft—at the question of permanent conscription in a free society. If we find we can reasonably meet our peacetime manpower needs by other means—then we should prepare for the day when the draft can be phased out of American life."[5] With those words, Nixon put in motion one of the major revolutions in modern U.S. military history—the conversion from the draft to the all-volunteer force. He also won a landslide presidential election in 1968 and claimed a mandate from the populace for his articulated goals.

President Richard M. Nixon. 6 January 1972. (Courtesy Richard M. Nixon Library)

Once in office, Nixon proceeded rapidly to move from the draft to the AVF. He initiated his efforts during the winter of 1969. On 29 January 1969 he informed Secretary of Defense Melvin R. Laird, "It is my firm conviction that we must establish an all-volunteer armed force after the expenditures for Vietnam are substantially reduced, and that we must begin now to move in that direction. . . . I request that you begin immediately to plan a special Commission to develop a detailed plan of action for ending the draft. This Commission should report to me by May 1, 1969, its findings and recommendations."[6] Nixon, therefore, charged the Gates Commission with determining the *best way* to end the draft, not to decide whether or not to end it. A little more than one week later, Nixon pressed Laird for progress and implored, "I am glad to learn that your department has already taken the initial steps for moving toward an all-volunteer armed force. . . . However, the very fact that some initial steps are already under way makes me feel all the more strongly that the time

President Nixon in the Oval Office during a meeting with General William C. Westmoreland, former U.S. Military Assistance Command, Vietnam (MACV) commander, and Secretary of Defense Melvin Laird. 17 August 1970. (Courtesy Richard M. Nixon Library)

has come to develop a detailed plan of action for ending the draft. . . . I, therefore, would like to have from you by the end of the week a list of suggested members for this Commission."[7] Spurred to action, the following day Laird provided Nixon a list of possible members, adding, "I would recommend Tom Gates as chairman and Jerome Holland as second choice."[8]

With that, Nixon formed a presidential body that analyzed various constructs of military service and ultimately recommended volunteer service as the one most effective for military strategy and most appropriate for a democracy. Such a task was a momentous decision regarding U.S. military service. On 27 March 1969, Nixon formed the Commission on the All-Volunteer Force and named as chair former secretary of defense Thomas S. Gates Jr. Nixon chartered the commission "to develop a comprehensive plan for eliminating conscription and moving toward an All-Volunteer Force."[9] The Gates Commission, as the group became known, immediately commenced to investigate the possibility and advisability of ending the draft.

The members were Thomas Gates (chair), former secretary of defense; Thomas Curtis, former U.S. representative from Missouri; Frederick Dent, president of Mayfair Mills; Milton Friedman, professor of economics at the University of Chicago; Crawford Greenewalt, chair of the finance committee at E. I. DuPont de Nemours; Alan Greenspan, chair of the board at Townsend-Greenspan; Alfred Gruenther, former supreme allied commander, Europe; Stephen Herbits, Georgetown University Law Center; Theodore Hesburgh, president of the University of Notre Dame; Jerome Holland, president of Hampton Institute; John Kemper, headmaster of Phillips Academy; Jeanne Noble, vice president of the National Council of Negro Women; Lauris Norstad, chair of the board of Owens-Corning Fiberglass corporation; W. Allen Wallis, president of the University of Rochester; and Roy Wilkins, executive director of the NAACP. Nixon urged the group to examine military service in its broadest context and to "study a broad range of possibilities for increasing the supply of volunteers for service, including increased pay, benefits, recruitment incentives and other practicable measures to make military careers more attractive to young men." In addition, he exhorted them to "consider possible changes in selection standards and in utilization policies which may assist in eliminating the need for inductions" and to "study the estimated costs and savings resulting from an all-volunteer force, as well as the broader social and economic implications of this program."[10]

The Gates Commission immediately commenced individual work and held its first formal meeting on 15 May 1969. Its members labored separately to analyze a multitude of official reports on the subject and met repeatedly as a group in Washington, D.C., often on weekends.[11] The commission considered its fundamental task as answering two distinct, yet related, questions related to military service: "Is an all-volunteer force feasible?" and "Regardless of whether an all-volunteer force is feasible, is it desirable?" In order to answer the second question the commission considered the intimate relationship between military service and democratic society: "Will voluntary recruitment weaken our democratic society and have harmful political and social effects?" The commission envisioned a military of between 2 million and 3 million service members and observed that "the United States has relied throughout its history on a voluntary armed force except during major wars and since 1948." During that latter time there was a projected need of 325,000 enlistments per year to maintain the force, but only about 250,000 true volunteers existed, significantly short of requirements. The commission argued that the difference between military personnel requirements and true volunteers necessitated a significant pay increase. It contended that the draft allowed "an entry pay that is roughly 60 percent of the amount that men of their age, education, and training could earn in civilian life" and maintained that "reasonable improvements in pay and benefits in the early years of service should increase the number of volunteers by these amounts." Therefore, the commission proposed enacting a basic pay increase on 1 July 1970 and asserted that doing so would allow an all-volunteer force by 1 July 1971. It estimated that the cost of the all-volunteer force would drop from initially $2.7 billion to eventually $2.1 billion per year due to lower personnel turnover and fewer training requirements, although critics vociferously disagreed with these estimates.[12]

In April 1969, Secretary Laird established the Project Volunteer Committee for "providing a working dialogue with the Gates Commission, and serving as the link point for its data." Roger T. Kelley, assistant secretary of defense (manpower and reserve affairs), chaired it. The committee understood its role "as the Department of Defense steering group responsible for directing overall plans for the All-Volunteer Force and for monitoring the effectiveness of action programs."[13]

Once the military began shifting from the draft to the all-volunteer force, several major requirements became evident. The first was improving military service members' quality of life. Often referred to as "irritants" by contemporary observers, it included things like kitchen police (KP) and janitorial duties. Without a draft, irritants deterred volunteers. Assistant Secretary of the Army William K. Brehm acknowledged that removal of irritants was a necessary precursor for the AVF. He admitted, "We cannot successfully advertise a product which retains some of the present deficiencies. Many of these deficiencies have become traditionalized and institutionalized as the result of long-term budgetary limitations." Brehm avowed that "to change the 'Beetle Bailey' image to a 'Steve Canyon' image will require more than advertising. It may require eliminating the repetitive rounds of KP, trash collecting, and latrine scrubbing that intrude on the soldiers' military training and development."[14]

Some of these quality-of-life changes were substantial. The *Chicago Daily News* reported, "The Army has gone a long way to make itself attractive to volunteers: no KP, five-day work weeks, two-man rooms instead of barracks dormitories, beer in the mess hall." The story considered the significant challenge that changing perceptions of military service presented to policy makers: "Still, an entrenched idea dies hard, and the Vietnam War played its part in giving the Army a bad image among the nation's youth."[15] The newspaper ended by commenting that a public relations campaign could overcome this challenge. Other issues were more surprising. John G. Kester reported to the assistant secretary of the army that haircuts were a significant morale issue in the early AVF. Kester observed, "During our recent trips to Fort Bragg and Fort Riley to gather information on race relations, our discussion with enlisted personnel time and again turned to a subject to which none of us had previously taken seriously: haircuts. . . . I am led to conclude that the current restrictions on hair styles of enlisted men are creating a significant morale problem deserving attention at the Department of the Army level." The reason was both simple and humorous: "Soldiers said that their short hair not only reduced their esthetic and biological appeal to the opposite sex, but also put a practical crimp in their style by marking them as soldiers even when off duty." Kester concluded that relaxing haircut standards to meet civilian expectations was a no-cost improvement in recruiting for the AVF. "We worry a good deal about making military service attractive at a time when the voluntary army looms," he remarked. "Some techniques to do so might not involve any monetary cost at all. For if there is ultimately any relation between a requirement of short hair and the best interest of the Army, it may turn out to be inverse."[16]

It quickly became apparent that one major requirement of an all-volunteer force was a substantial escalation in advertising and recruiting by the military. The draft allowed both of these aspects of military personnel policy to atrophy. This decay disproportionately had impacted the army. In contrast, the air force, navy, and marine corps had not relied as heavily on the draft; their advertising and recruiting efforts, therefore, had also not stagnated as much as the army's. If volunteers replaced draftees, then this had to change, especially for the army. Without successful advertising and recruiting efforts, the AVF would fail to attract sufficient numbers of volunteers. Alfred B. Fitt, who preceded Roger Kelley as assistant secretary of defense (manpower and reserve affairs), relayed to all his subordinates in the individual military branches that one critical goal was to "improve [the] overall image of military service." Fitt emphasized that accomplishing this mission required the military to "develop [a] comprehensive information program designed to enhance the overall public image of the Military Services; of the vital role they play in safeguarding our national security; of their related contributions to our society and of the many positive advantages of military service careers."[17]

In the absence of the draft, public relations and advertising proved crucial; they also transformed the U.S. military. Assistant Secretary of the Army William K. Brehm proposed more than a 1,000 percent jump in the army's recruiting advertising budget to accomplish the AVF. "The prerequisite to improvement in the enlistment and retention area is a sharp improvement in the image which the public has of the Armed Services. Service life, active and reserve, must not only be an accepted and honorable vocation, but a respected and attractive career," Brehm affirmed. For him, the solution was additional funding. As he relayed, "To this end, I am recommending a large increase in the Recruiting Command's advertising budget—now. We spend $8.5 billion annually on military pay and allowances, but only $3 million on recruiting advertising. I am proposing a better than tenfold increase in this advertising budget in order to let advertising do for the Army what it has done successfully for American business. A factual description of the positive benefits of Army careers must be conveyed to prospective recruits and their families."[18]

On 20 February 1970 the Gates Commission delivered its final report to President Nixon. As all members stressed, "We unanimously believe that the nation's interests will be better served by an all-volunteer force, supported by an effective standby draft, than by a mixed force of volunteers and conscripts; that steps should be taken promptly to move in this direction; and that the first indispensable step is to remove the present inequity in the pay of men serving in their first term in the armed forces."[19] In order to achieve the all-volunteer force, the commission recommended three specific steps. The first was to increase first-term basic pay (defined as the first two years of service) by approximately 75 percent, from $180 to $315 per month for enlisted personnel. The second was to "make comprehensive improvements in conditions of military service and in recruiting." The third was to create mechanisms for "a standby draft system" by 30 June 1971 that could "be activated by joint resolution of Congress upon request of the President."[20]

Once the Gates Commission determined that the all-volunteer force was feasible, it turned to the question of whether it was desirable. The group acknowledged "broader considerations which have prompted defenders of conscription to argue that an all-volunteer armed force will have a variety of undesirable political, social, and military effects. In our meetings we have discussed the opposing arguments extensively." The major arguments against the all-volunteer force included its "feasibility," its "undesirable political and social effects," and whether "it will gradually erode the military's effectiveness."[21] Critics questioned specific components of these broad categories, including such issues as cost, flexibility, impact on "patriotism by weakening the traditional belief that each citizen has a moral responsibility to serve his country," creation of "a separate military ethos," alterations to the racial and socioeconomic composition of the force, conditions that "stimulate foreign military adventures, foster an irresponsible foreign policy, and lessen civilian concern about the use of military forces," reductions in military effectiveness due to less qualified enlistees, and resulting cuts in other vital areas of military expenditures.

There were also more humorous critiques of the all-volunteer force. Banker E. Constantin Jr. of Dallas, Texas, warned Secretary of the Army Robert F. Froehlke that the AVF was too cushy and allowed soldiers to unionize. Railing that "Army recruits . . . have a number of privileges that other citizens do not enjoy, such as free lodging, food and other items that may be purchased at discount prices through the PX [post exchange]," Constantin concluded that "it is quite certain that the Army under those conditions will also be unionized. . . . I can hardly wait for the time to come when we are at war and an order is given by the commanding officer to march against the enemy and a steward representing the Union, if he did not agree with the order, would simply tell the officer that before his men can march or obey the order they would have to discuss the matter."[22]

The two major alternatives to either the draft or the AVF were mandatory national service and universal military training; the Gates Commission evaluated both. It determined that mandatory national service would require "service of all youth, though not necessarily in the military. Most would permit individuals to choose how they would serve from among a limited set of alternatives." It also concluded that mandatory national service for everyone entailed extremely high costs: "Assuming a very modest annual cost for each participant of $4,000 to $5,000, the cost of such a program would be a minimum of $16 billion, and perhaps as much as $40 billion—an amount equal to the entire current manpower budget of the Department of Defense." The commission determined that UMT occasioned many of the same problems, especially exorbitant costs and prohibitive numbers of trainees: "For one thing, it would impose on the military more untrained personnel than can be productively employed."[23]

The Gates Commission and Project Volunteer agreed on several key points regarding military service: "Both recommended substantial pay increases for junior enlisted personnel, selective pay incentives for specialists, additional ROTC scholarship support, and a greatly expanded recruiting program." There were, however, key differences between the two groups: "The main difference between Department of Defense conclusions and those of the Gates Commission was in timing the end of the draft." As Secretary Laird explained, "The Gates commission, assuming quick implementation of its legislative and other recommendations, recommended termination of induction authority on June 30, 1971, while [Project Volunteer] recommended extension of induction authority to July 1, 1973." After reviewing the conclusions and recommendations of both groups, Nixon applauded the Gates Commission but tempered his praise with the caution of Project Volunteer. Laird revealed, "President Nixon accepted the basic conclusions and recommendations of the Gates Commission, but cautioned that the draft could not be ended prematurely."[24]

Throughout 1970, Nixon took his plan to end the draft and transition to the all-volunteer force to the American public. On 23 April 1970 he addressed Congress and outlined actions that his administration would implement to end the draft and presented his administration's proposals to complete such a move. "The draft has been with us now for many years," Nixon lamented. "It was started as a temporary, emergency measure just before World War II. We have lived with the draft so long, and relied on it through such serious crises, that too many of us now accept it as a normal part of American life." Highlighting the recently released report of the Gates Commission, Nixon relayed, "After careful consideration of the factors involved, I support the basic conclusion of the Commission. I agree that we should move now toward ending the draft." Nixon buttressed his policy proposal with both economic and libertarian themes. "The starting pay of an enlisted man in our Armed Forces is—taking the latest raise into account—less than $1,500 a year," he reminded Congress. "This is less than half of the minimum wage in the private sector." In this way conscription was a tax. In addition to the economic argument of artificially low pay, Nixon added the libertarian argument that individual liberty must always temper national security. As he argued, "Ultimately, the preservation of a free society depends upon both the willingness of its beneficiaries to bear the burden of its defense—and the willingness of government to guarantee the freedom of the individual."[25]

In January 1971, Nixon pressed forward to achieve his policy to end the draft over a period of time. "While I am confident that our plan will achieve its objective of reducing draft calls to zero, even the most optimistic observers agree that we would not be able to end the draft in the next year or so without seriously weakening our military forces and impairing our ability to forestall threats to the peace," he warned members

President Nixon and Pat Nixon pose for an official state portrait by the stairway with General Lewis B. Hershey and Mrs. Hershey before attending a state dinner honoring General Hershey. 17 February 1970. (Courtesy Richard M. Nixon Library)

of Congress. Nixon instead sought to move cautiously and recommended that "Congress extend induction authority for two years, to July 1, 1973. We shall make every endeavor to reduce draft calls to zero by that time, carefully and continually reexamining our position as we proceed toward that goal."[26] After contentious hearings, Congress obliged and extended induction authority to 1 July 1973.[27]

The implications were momentous. Military service was no longer a universal obligation, but rather a voluntary choice by certain members of society. The biggest shift came in the form of pay: "The key element in this legislative program was a substantial and costly increase in pay and allowances for personnel in the lower enlisted grades—reflecting the fact that for 13 years, from 1952 through 1964, there were no pay increases for military first-term members." The pay increases took effect quickly and were hefty, in some cases doubling the pay of junior military service members: "The higher pay rates became effective November 14, 1971, and were followed by a cost-of-living increase in January 1972. A single man living on base, having just completed four months training, previously received $149 a month. His basic pay was more than doubled to $321. By correcting this inequity in pay, particularly as it affected junior enlisted personnel, the military services were enabled to compete for young people in the labor market."[28]

To implement the all-volunteer force, Army Chief of Staff William C. Westmoreland created the Modern Volunteer Army program in October 1970. His guidance to army leaders was clear: find ways to make military service more palatable. "Nothing is considered sacrosanct except where military order and discipline—the soul of the Army that insures [sic] success on the battlefield—are jeopardized," he ordered. "This we cannot and will not yield." Everything else was fair game. One major aspect of the program was VOLAR experiments, the first phase of which ran from 1 January to 30 June 1971. In January 1971 three U.S. Army installations stateside—Fort Carson, Colorado; Fort Benning, Georgia; and Fort Ord, California—as well as one in Europe tested changes anticipated in a volunteer force. A major emphasis during the VOLAR experiments was increased professionalism through the reduction of "irritants" in military service. In a comprehensive evaluation of the VOLAR experiment at Fort Benning, observers mentioned, "The most significant actions of the VOLAR test are those actions which enhance professionalism by reducing the number of details and the time spent by soldiers on relatively menial chores that are not a part of the soldiers' professional job, make no obvious contribution to the training of the individual or his unit and do not contribute to the accomplishment of the unit's mission."[29]

At Fort Ord, three infantry training brigades experimented with the transition to an all-volunteer force in one VOLAR experiment. Colonel Thomas Morgan commanded one of the brigades. Morgan had been a drill sergeant during World War II and confided, "The drill sergeants originally were against it. . . . The average drill sergeant felt his tool of discipline—that is, the threat of punishment—had been taken away from him." Morgan explained one main purpose of VOLAR experiments: "We're aiming at a reduction of the Mickey Mouse. . . . Mickey Mouse are those devices which produce an unnecessary pressure on a recruit." In addition to modified training methods, VOLAR experiments entailed logistical adjustments. Fort Ord reduced its weekly inductions from 1,150 to 850 personnel to "permit more individual attention" and also received $5 million "for modifications to barracks and such things as construction of new dining halls to provide the physical attractions for a more desirable army career." Morgan resolved, "Our mission hasn't changed. We're still assigned to produce soldiers who are physically fit, qualified on their weapons, and trained in the skills of soldiering."[30] What had evolved, however, was that the focus was now on potential volunteers rather than draftees. The second phase of VOLAR experiments lasted from 1 July 1971 until 30 June 1972. At that time the military expanded them to thirteen U.S. bases and three overseas installations.[31] Military leaders hailed the results as a success: "An overall analysis of the VOLAR experiment reveals that actions implemented pursuant to the experiment have caused massive positive changes in attitudes toward the Army, in expressed career intentions, in actual reenlistment performance, and in the Army's accession system."[32]

While building momentum toward eliminating the draft altogether, Nixon also reformed it early in his first term as a short-term solution. On 26 November 1969 he "signed into law a bill which reduced the period of draft vulnerability from seven years to one year, the latter being the calendar year following a young man's 19th birthday. The bill further provided that draft selections would be made by the drawing of sequence numbers at random, rather than by birth date." This was significant because it limited the impact of the draft to a shorter time period (one year) during a specific age (19–20 years old) and made the system random; in theory this made the draft more equitable. Nixon also reformed the draft system by limiting deferments. In April 1970, Nixon issued an executive order that phased out occupational and paternity deferments, "thereby further reducing the inequities of the draft system." In September 1971 he signed a draft reform bill that "contained key additional draft reforms. Principally, these reforms eliminated undergraduate student deferments for those entering college in the Fall of 1971 and thereafter, and established a uniform national call to insure that men throughout the country with the same sequence numbers would be equally liable to induction."[33] Doing so in late 1971, rather than earlier at the height of U.S. troop strength in Vietnam, had much less of an impact, however, primarily because overall U.S. force levels also were dropping precipitously at that time.

The early results of the transition to the all-volunteer force were less than favorable. As the final changeover date neared, serious doubt crept in among some military leaders whether the AVF was achievable. At the annual luncheon of the Association of the U.S. Army, Westmoreland acknowledged dedication to Nixon's policy but urged additional time and support to meet it. "I am announcing today that the Army is committed to an all-out effort in working toward a zero draft—a volunteer force. In accepting this challenge, we in the Army will bend every effort to achieve our goal," he signaled. "But we need support and understanding from the Administration, the Congress, and our citizenry." There were several reasons for hesitation among military leaders about whether 30 June 1971 was a realistic goal for the AVF. Most important, the Vietnam War still raged and hence required large numbers of personnel; the United States had approximately 300,000 service members in Vietnam at that time. High personnel requirements created misgiving as to whether the AVF would constrain strategic options by limiting the number of personnel available. As a result, Westmoreland urged postponement:

> If this Nation supports the President's chosen course in ending the Vietnam War, I believe the draft must be extended beyond its expiration date of June 30, 1971. Additionally, we must appreciate that movement toward a volunteer force will take time . . . and continuation of selective service will guarantee a transition period without jeopardizing this Nation's defenses. And finally, and most important, even though we reach a zero draft, selective service legislation should remain in force as national insurance. I am well aware of arguments both for and against selective service. Furthermore, I recognize that the Administration has committed itself to reducing the draft to zero. But I am also aware of the problems that confront the Army as we move toward a zero draft.[34]

As the transition toward the extended 1 July 1973 deadline neared, Westmoreland waivered once again. On 30 June 1972 he informed Nixon, "Despite intensive efforts, we have significant recruiting and strength shortfalls, and I can give you no assurance that we will achieve our goal of a volunteer force by 1 July 1973."[35]

In August 1972, Secretary of Defense Laird outlined to President Nixon and the chairs of the Armed Services Committees of the Senate and House of Representatives, John C. Stennis (D-MS) and F. Edward Hébert (D-LA), the military's progress on moving from the draft to the all-volunteer force. "During the three and one-half years of this Administration the draft system has been reformed and draft calls reduced from 300,000 to 50,000 a year, a quality force has been maintained with reduced draft pressure, and the proportion of true volunteers among those enlisting has increased from 40% to 75%," Laird boasted. "We are within reach of achieving an All-Volunteer Force composed of 2.3 million active duty and 1 million Selected Reserve members. Never before has a nation maintained a volunteer military force of that size." Laird confided that a significant issue was the draft's unpopularity due to its perceived inequities and revealed, "A variety of student and other deferments has undermined confidence in

President Nixon greeting and talking to U.S. Army soldiers of the First Infantry Division in Dian, South Vietnam. 30 July 1969. (Courtesy Richard M. Nixon Library)

the fairness of the draft system. For seven long years, from age 19 to 26, young men endured the uncertainty of an inequitable draft system which selected a few among the many who were subject to it. This prolonged term of uncertainty made it extremely difficult for them to plan for their education, career, and family."[36]

On 29 December 1972 the last draftee reported for duty with the army.[37] Shortly thereafter, upon taking over as secretary of the army in May 1973, Howard H. "Bo" Callaway embarked upon an ambitious tour of army units "in an effort to learn the problems of the new volunteer Army." In just his first five months, Callaway visited ten of the thirteen active army divisions. He found a discernable shift from racial concerns to a focus on living conditions and unrealistic expectations fostered by overly ambitious recruiters who often painted army life in rosy hues. Edward K. Delong of *Stars and Stripes* reported, "Racial problems no longer rank among the top concerns of America's fighting men, says Army Secretary Howard H. Callaway, but there are many other matters worrying the troops which must be dealt with before the all volunteer Army can succeed." Of course, Calloway understated the seriousness of racial problems in the army at that time. Although conditions in the continental United States had improved somewhat, racial tensions within the U.S. Army in Europe heightened during 1974–1975. Delong also relayed, "High among these present worries, the Georgia-bred Callaway has found, are poor housing conditions, promotion policies that seem unfair, failure to weed out misfits from among the volunteers, and disenchantment caused by recruiters who promise more than the Army can deliver."[38] Accordingly, military leaders sought to determine the success of their efforts. To do so, Callaway composed a report "as an indication of our progress during the first year in the volunteer experiment" entitled "The Volunteer Army—One Year Later." Callaway admitted, "While it outlines our successes to date, it also points to problem areas which we are confident can be overcome." After extensive review, Callaway proclaimed, "The volunteer Army is a reality. It is no longer just a concept. It is here now, on the ground, ready to fight if need be, stronger than when the draft ended. We intend to keep it moving in this direction."[39]

One of the major challenges of the transition to the all-volunteer force was resistance from the military services. Several events during 1973 demonstrated such opposition. The antagonism was palpable enough that Assistant Secretary of Defense Kelley convened a confidential meeting with Brigadier General Robert Montague and Deputy Secretary of

Defense William P. Clements Jr. to counteract it. Montague was deputy special assistant for the modern volunteer army, and Clements handled policy efforts for the Pentagon. Kelley confided, "Momentum, built up with great effort over past two years, is definitely slipping." He warned that the trouble was not natural but rather contrived by the military services to contest change; it was also not the first time that it had occurred. He remembered, "Services used quality issue to defeat the previous effort to end the draft in 1948. In effect, they priced themselves out of the market." Kelley argued that the military services had been successful in this earlier effort and now attempted the same tactic to foredoom the AVF. "Events are repeating themselves," he alerted. "*All* Services have raised quality criteria without adequate assessment of need or recruiting market conditions." Kelley provided examples to prove his point. He relayed that a "change in Army policy on February 1 to raise proportion of high school graduates to 70 percent was expected to result in recruiting shortfalls. But, 4,600 shortfall below 9,000 objective in April was far greater than anticipated. May shortfall may be nearly as large. Yet Army refuses to modify its policy." Kelley left no doubt as to the magnitude of the threat to the AVF from the military services. "I believe that the slippage in the AVF effort is serious. The Army appears to be drawing a hard line which will be fully exposed after your departure. The Marines are ready to ride out the storm until men are drafted again for the Army," he feared. "The numbers look so bad that I predict the Army will be seeking draft authority by next Christmas. Congress may demand drafting for the Reserves, or drafting for active forces to help Reserve recruitment, within a year. Yet, these measures are clearly not necessary. The AVF can work; we know how to make it work."[40]

The following week the Pentagon convened a task force on the all-volunteer force that included all the service secretaries and the Joint Chiefs of Staff; it met weekly. From the start, serious doubts surfaced among them regarding the viability of the AVF. Admiral Thomas H. Moorer, chair of the Joint Chiefs of Staff, discussed the nonextension of induction authority and cautioned, "I think it is a mistake to go out on a limb with optimistic statements. We should be cautious." Admiral Elmo R. Zumwalt, chief of naval operations, went further and questioned, "Is it too late to reconsider asking for standby [draft] authority? We will regret it by the end of the year if we don't." The army's chief of staff, General Creighton Abrams, supported the AVF and warned that any public doubts by senior leadership could have negative consequences. Abrams confided, "I do not question the validity of the All-Volunteer Force. But, how many people in the Army, officers and senior NCOs, think it is a bunch of crap. Our job is to make them exercise imagination to make the concept work. Thus, we've got to be careful about giving signals [that we are not sure about the concept]. Opponents would read something into our signals."[41]

During the summer of 1973, additional events intimated that the military services were pursuing their own agendas, often at the detriment of the all-volunteer force. At that time the air force increased its enlistment standards without consulting the secretary of defense and thereby triggered much alarm. "We investigated the rumor heard at the Knoxville AFEES [Air Force Enlisted Evaluation System] concerning a change in Air Force enlistment standards. It turns out that Air Force has already dispatched a message to its Recruiting Command which restricts starting June 1 enlistment of male non-high school graduates to individuals scoring in mental group I or II," Stephen Herbits relayed to Lieutenant General Taber and Brigadier General Montague. "Air Force previously did not accept non-high school graduates who scored in mental group IV. By eliminating mental group III non-high school graduates, the Air Force hopes to raise the percentage of high school graduate enlistments to better than 90% during the summer months." This increase in recruit quality clearly benefited the air force. The problem with such an uncoordinated change in policy was that it impacted other military services' recruiting and standards because all of them competed for the same available pool of personnel; it also provided grist for critics who argued that the AVF was not viable. Herbits complained, "This tightening of enlistment standards by one Service without consideration of overall supply of personnel for the DOD and without clearance from OSD [Office of the Secretary of Defense] again raises the question of OSD's role in managing the all-volunteer effort." Herbits demanded that civilian policy makers rein in such activity: "To the degree that we permit the Services to set standards which are unrealistic, we are encouraging criticism and contributing to the resurging belief that the AVF won't work. The issue is not just 'experimentation'; it is political. 'Standards' are a policy matter of the highest import and rightfully resides at the OSD level."[42]

One of the immediate results of the transition to the all-volunteer force was significant military service recruiting shortfalls, especially for the army. During the fall of 1973, recruiting deficits made headlines in major newspapers across the country. *Chicago Tribune* correspondent Nick Thimmesch reported that from January to September 1973, the army fell short of its military service recruiting goals by 24 percent and that during that entire time "the monthly recruitment goal hasn't been reached even once." Thimmesch recorded that while the army's experience was not representative of all military services, it was still highly significant due to the army's heavy reliance on personnel: "The Air Force, Navy and Marine Corps are doing far better than the Army in voluntary recruitment. But the Army accounts for half of the total U.S. military man [and woman] power, hence the concern in the Pentagon." To illustrate the "concern" in the Pentagon, Thimmesch relayed, "Defense Secretary James R. Schlesinger said on *Meet the Press* recently that while his people are working very hard to achieve success for the all-volunteer force, 'We cannot guarantee success.'" Thimmesch recounted that Schlesinger remarked, "We would be prepared to go back to the Congress and ask for renewal of draft authority," indicating a willingness to go back to the draft if necessary since, even though induction authority expired 30 June 1973, the Selective Service law remained. Thimmesch also highlighted a concern that the AVF was not representative of American society. "The Army faces a ticklish problem in that increasing numbers of its volunteers are black," he detected. "Where blacks make up 13.5 per cent of total U. S. population, some 21 per cent of Army volunteers since January are black, and in July, the figure soared to 35 per cent." Thimmesch concluded that many military leaders preferred the draft to the AVF for a variety of reasons and that alternatives to the AVF were equally problematic: "Meanwhile, it's no secret that some Pentagon thinkers are hoping the voluntary plan fails, so the draft can be reinstated. These folk also have an economic argument on their side. The all-volunteer Army is an expensive one." Thimmesch proposed an unlikely solution. "The long-range solution to this dilemma, it seems to me, is for Congress to pass a universal service bill. This long discussed program would conscript young men and women at 18, and give them the choice of public or military service," he suggested. "If the young person chose public, he or she might wind up working on environmental projects, with the poor, in a hospital, or serving in the Peace Corps. But I really doubt that Congress has the guts to pass universal service. The draft was unpopular enough."[43] Neither Congress nor the military at that time gave serious consideration to Thimmesch's recommended answer—a national service bill—and observers primarily outside government have often touted similar plans.[44]

On 22 September 1973 the *Chicago Daily News* characterized the all-volunteer force as a "new and different army" and highlighted the ominous fact that for the first seven consecutive months the army had missed its recruiting goals. "The all-volunteer Army program is encountering increasing trouble," the report discerned. "The Navy and Air Force are doing pretty well, but the Army, striving to maintain a strength of 815,000, has for seven consecutive times missed its monthly recruiting goals and is falling steadily further behind." Such shortfalls were despite advantages that should have made recruiting much easier under the AVF: "It is falling behind in spite of the fact that it has dropped its rule of requiring that 70 per cent of the recruits be high school graduates. The figure is now about half. The effort to have the Army reflect the national racial balance is failing, too. In July 35 per cent of the new volunteers were black." Because the $307 starting monthly pay for a recruit was "practically clear profit because housing, food, uniforms, medical and dental care are provided," higher pay should have alleviated problems for recruiting but failed to do so.

On 26 September 1973, *New York Times* correspondent C. L. Sulzberger asked a searing question: "Where Are Volunteers?" He explained, "United States reliance upon a volunteer military establishment does not seem to be working well, and if an improvement in the rate of enlistments doesn't materialize, the nation will either be forced to reduce overseas commitments more than its policy-makers desire or find a new defense budgeting approach." He listed specific reasons why: "Last month, recruiting for the four armed services fell 11 per cent short with 19 per cent of the lag in the Army. The more glamorous but smaller Navy and Air Force achieved their goals but the total of military recruits was under strength for the seventh consecutive time." Mentioning that estimates by U.S. allies, specifically the United Kingdom and Western European Union, and London's International Institute for Strategic Studies surmised the U.S. military would fall to 1.8 million personnel, Sulzberger scrutinized the incongruity between this force level and the one anticipated by U.S. policy makers: "Yet 1.8 million is nowhere near what Washington has so far counted on. The President's Commission on an All Volunteer Force reckoned in 1970 on 2.5 million." Sulzberger argued that such a contrast resulted from the disconnect of the AVF from American society. "Apart from the paramount requirement that a democracy must be able to defend itself and to reckon on doing so permanently, there is also (as the French recognize) a philosophical aspect," he commented. "Should not each youngster feel a duty to serve his state one year?" Such views resonated with some high-level military leaders. As Sulzberger recalled, "I discussed this four years ago with Gen. Earle G. Wheeler, then chairman of the Joint Chiefs of Staff. He said succinctly: 'The draft gives a cross-section of young American society. You would lose this with a professional [volunteer enlistment] army.'"[45]

On 29 October 1973 the *Atlanta Journal* highlighted initial problems with the transition to the all-volunteer force. "Since the Army dropped reliance on the draft last January—a full six months before legislation would require such a step—the reports concerning the Army have been anything but encouraging," it reported. The journal witnessed, "Bonuses have been offered to spur enlistment within the combat arms branches. Recruitment fell below the goals set. The bonuses were increased. The goals were still not met. These were the reports and it began to appear that we had two choices—either return to the draft or watch the Army sink below acceptable strength levels."[46]

On 11 February 1974, Bo Callaway reported to President Ford on the transition to the all-volunteer force. Callaway proudly presented Ford with a recap of the successes and challenges of the conversion.[47] One of the major points of contention regarding the AVF was whether it was representative of American society. As a result, the Department of Defense amassed a plethora of statistics on demographics. On 17 December 1974, William Brehm provided them to the chair of the Senate Armed Services Committee, John C. Stennis (D-MS). Among the major findings, the AVF was fairly representative of American society, except that it had higher numbers of African Americans, service members from the South and West, and rural service members than their respective proportions in American society. Brehm relayed, "In FY 1974, the representation of new enlistees and the active force as a whole was close to that of the general population with the exception of minority representation. Black personnel constituted about 21 percent of new enlistees compared to 13 percent in the general population." In addition, Brehm detected that "geographically, the number of new enlistees from each State tended to be proportional to the youth population in that State. Regionally, there was a slightly greater representation from the South and the West than from the North and, more particularly, the Northeast." Finally, Brehm relayed, "The 57 largest metropolitan areas provided a slightly lower share of new enlistees than their proportion of the population (46 percent vs 50 percent)."[48]

On 30 June 1974 the army reached its authorized strength under the AVF construct. Callaway reported the news to Major General John A. Wickham Jr., military assistant to the secretary of defense. As Callaway crowed, "It is with a great deal of pride that I report to you that on 30 June 1974 your Army ended the fiscal year at its authorized manpower strength of 781,600 persons. This noteworthy achievement is clear evidence that the volunteer Army is a success."[49] Callaway also provided Wickham a comprehensive report entitled "FY 74 Volunteer Army Highlights," dated 1 July 1974, that celebrated the AVF's first year: "30 June 1974 marked the completion of the first full year without a draft authority and therefore is a good point at which to assess the results of efforts to make the Volunteer Army a success." Callaway mentioned one recurrent concern regarding the representativeness of the AVF: "At year end, the minority content of the Active Army was about 21 percent[,] of whom 19 percent are Black. This represents an increase of about 4 percent in minority content since end FY 73. This increase is due primarily to enlistments which ran about 27 percent Black for FY 74, indicating that group's positive perception of the opportunities available in the Army."[50]

Although some cautious optimism existed that the all-volunteer force would improve discipline, motivation, and personnel stability, resistance from various military leaders, especially within the army, lasted for quite some time. Such antagonism often centered on concerns among senior military leaders about the size of the force and principled adherence to the citizen-soldier ideal. In 1975 former secretary of the army Robert F. Froehlke appeared before the Defense Manpower Commission's hearing on "Future Needs and Methods of Providing Manpower for the Defense of the United States of America." Froehlke criticized the move to the AVF as political and left open the possibility of a return to the draft. "A political decision was made a number of years ago to rely on volunteers for our military manpower. It is important that we recognize that it was a political—not a military[—]decision," Froehlke railed. "Thus, should the political climate ever change, this nation could again consider reverting to the draft for its manpower." Froehlke urged committee members and the audience to consider why such a shift had occurred. He asked, "What caused the political climate to dictate volunteerism over the draft?" After pausing for effect, Froehlke provided his answer: "Obviously there were a number of factors. However, two factors predominate." They were "a very unpopular war" and "a very unfair draft." Froehlke warned of the dangers of a military that was not representative of the society that it defended: "It is important to bear in mind that in a democracy, at least, the military must be made up of a cross-section of its citizens. An all white or black, rich or poor, educated or uneducated military would tend to be dangerous to the well being of the democracy." In closing, Froehlke urged expansion of military service and situated its value directly to citizenship. He recommended that "if we can again adopt the service concept for all our people," then three specific benefits would accrue. First, "Our nation will truly be of, by and for the people." Second, "We will learn, in the process of serving, that different people are just different—not better or worse." Third, "Our nation's defense will be on a sounder foundation."[51] At that time, few observers predicted that the AVF would result in a dramatic rise in recruit quality beginning in the early 1980s.

The late 1960s witnessed significant debates regarding military service. Richard Nixon made the draft a significant issue during the 1968 presidential election. Once in office, he created the Gates Commission to spearhead the shift to the all-volunteer force. Project Volunteer provided military input and recommended extending the deadline by two years. The Gates Commission report emphasized pay increases to ensure the feasibility of the AVF, while some observers also contested its desirability. Alternative options ranged from continuing or reforming the draft to instituting universal military service or national service. The removal of "irritants" transformed U.S. military service, and advertising and recruiting took on newfound urgency. The army conducted VOLAR experiments and tested modifications necessary for the AVF. Ending the draft did not come without challenges, however, as the military services resisted in various ways. As the last draftee reported for service in the army, military service underwent seismic shifts. Recruiting shortfalls persisted and caused angst in some quarters of American society that a return to the draft was necessary. The AVF also emphasized ensuring fairness with previously underrepresented groups, including minorities and women. As a result, policy makers placed much more emphasis on increasing the number of women in military service, partly to offset the loss of draftees. All the military services began dramatically expanding the number of women and the available opportunities for them more than ever before.

CHAPTER SEVEN

MORE THAN EVER BEFORE

Increased recruitment and utilization of uniformed women provides an additional method of reducing requirements for recruitment of men for service. Women have and can be utilized in a very wide range of occupational duties and functions, other than those involving direct combat operations. In an all-volunteer force, the use of military women should be extended insofar as recruiting capability and rotation requirements for enlisted men make it practical to use them.[1]—Project Volunteer, 14 August 1970

Some 80 female plebes who entered the United States Naval Academy yesterday are part of the 345 young women who are entering the nation's military academies for the first time, thanks to legislation passed by Congress last year. With the taste of that victory still fresh, some egalitarians—including several members of Congress—have started massing for an offensive on their next military target: the legal and institutional barriers now preventing women from being assigned to so-called combat jobs.[2] —Martin Binkin, 7 July 1976

More than ever before, women are increasingly present in the United States Armed Forces. When the United States military went to war in Southeast Asia, women accounted for fewer than two percent of all uniformed personnel. By the start of the Persian Gulf War in 1991, women accounted for nearly 11 percent of all active-duty personnel.[3] —Presidential Commission on the Assignment of Women in the Armed Forces, August 1992

Women have a long history of service within the U.S. military. Military personnel policy, however, has often constrained that role, especially prior to the advent of the all-volunteer force. Women first served in a uniformed capacity during 1917–1918. Their role in the military became permanent with the passage of the Women's Armed Services Integration Act of 1948. The law, nonetheless, placed ceilings on both the number of female enlisted and officer personnel, as well as on the rank that women could hold. In 1951, Secretary of Defense George C. Marshall further formalized women's roles in U.S. military service when he established the Defense Advisory Committee on Women in the Services (DACOWITS). Such gender limits cast a long shadow on the opportunity for women's participation in military service throughout much of the 1950s and 1960s. Beginning in 1969, Project Volunteer explored ways to accomplish the conversion from the draft to the AVF. Both military and political leaders increasingly saw women as one potential personnel offset for the loss of male draftees. Therefore, momentum for increasing the number of women serving in the military and expanding opportunities available to them gained traction. Such discussions led to tangible results, as the number of women in military service increased steadily throughout the 1970s. U.S. Air Force Major General Jeanne M. Holm epitomized the shifting terrain for women in military service, both within military circles and to audiences beyond. By 1975 additional barriers to women's participation in military service had fallen. Congress mandated that the military service academies admit females and that ROTC programs increase the availability of scholarships for them. Later that year, the U.S. Air Force opened pilot training to women, although the prohibition against combat roles in all the military services remained. Operation Desert Shield/Storm placed the issue of women in military service front and center for the American public, resulting in the President's Commission on the Assignment of Women in the Armed Forces, the largest examination of the issue ever.

On 12 June 1948, Congress made women's roles in military service permanent with the passage of the Women's Armed Services Integration Act of 1948. The law restricted women to only 2 percent of enlisted service members and no more than 10 percent of officers.[4] According to Michelle Sandhoff and Mady Wechsler Segal, the law "created a permanent place for women in the U.S. military, though women's roles were tightly constrained."[5] It also enacted a specific gender ceiling by forbidding women to hold military rank higher than O-5, a level equivalent to lieutenant colonel (army, air force, marines) or commander (navy).[6] In addition, the law prevented women from assignments likely to lead to either air or naval combat, although oddly not specifically from ground combat.[7]

Within a month, women transferred from the reserves to the active forces of the U.S. military. On 7 July 1948, Rear Admiral George L. Russell (judge advocate general), Captain Joy B. Hancock (WAVES), and Secretary of the Navy John L. Sullivan officiated a ceremony "swearing the first six enlisted women into the regular Navy under the provisions of the Women's Armed Services Integration Act." The group consisted of Wilma J. Marchal of Tell City, Indiana; Edna E. Young of Springfield, Massachusetts; Ruth Flora of Bowling Green, Kentucky; Kay L. Langdon of Burton, Washington; Frances T. Devaney of Baltimore, Maryland; and Doris R. Robertson of Ord, Nebraska. Sullivan characterized the event as "a milestone in the history of this department." The following day at the Pentagon, Army Chief of Staff Omar N. Bradley swore in Vietta M. Bates as "the first member of the Women's Army Corps to enter the Regular Army." Until that fall, women in the reserves had the chance to transfer to the permanent military. After that point, the military increased recruiting efforts specifically targeted at women. The *New York Times* reported, "Officers of the Women's Services said today that from now until mid-September opportunity would be given to those now on duty to transfer to the regular service. Then recruiting will start simultaneously in all services to build up to authorized strength."[8]

One minute past midnight on 8 July 1948, the role of women in U.S. military service shifted. The bill that President Truman had signed into law the previous week took effect. Military personnel at Third Army headquarters, located at Fort McPherson, Georgia, commemorated the occasion with a formal ceremony attended by General Alvan C. Gillem Jr., commander of the Third Army. Major Mary M. Pugh, the Third Army's WAC staff director, inducted twelve women into the regular army. "We think our girls are the first in the country to become regular members of the armed forces," she exclaimed. "That's why we held our induction ceremony at such an unorthodox hour!" Pugh pondered the significance of the change that the law produced. "Until today, women in the Wac and Waves have been reservists on temporary active duty," she pronounced. "Now they'll serve their hitches and be eligible for pensions just like the menfolk." General Gillem mingled with attendees and congratulated inductees. He remarked to Sergeant Cornelia P. Atterbury of Atlanta, "Women proved themselves during the war; we're proud to have them in the Regular Army."[9]

One of the first post–World War II efforts to evaluate personnel policy related to women in military service was the establishment of the Defense Advisory Committee on Women in the Services. Secretary Marshall created it in 1951 to offer "civilian support and advisement on the expanding scope of Service women" and to "contribute valuable assistance to the Department of Defense and the Services on various manpower matters pertaining to women in the Armed Forces." The role and mission of DACOWITS expanded throughout the 1950s. In 1956 the committee put forward initiatives "to permit payment of a quarters allowance to married Military women." In 1960 it sought "to remove grade restrictions on female officers so that they could be promoted to a rank above lieutenant colonel." Throughout its existence, DACOWITS forced consideration of expanded opportunity for women in military service. Although the progress was often far too slow, Congress enacted many of its recommendations, and the Pentagon changed military personnel policy as a result. By 1975 the committee comprised "30 women from throughout the Nation who have achieved outstanding reputations in business, professions, public service and civic leadership. Each member is invited by the Secretary of Defense to participate for three years, and each member serves as an individual, not as a representative of any organization. Meeting semiannually, the committee concentrates on areas which affect the retention rate, housing, pay and allowances, job opportunities, and promotion policies for Military women, as well as existent inequities in policies."[10] The committee's work gained momentum in the 1960s.

During the last half of 1967, air force recruiting objectives for women remained low, primarily because enlisted ceilings constrained them: "Women in the Air Force (WAF) enlistment objective for the reporting period, prior and non-prior service, was 1,365. Production was 1,367, or 100.1 percent. The WAF enlisted program continued as a ceiling program, with input restricted to a specified number of enlistees in a weekly training class." The number of women in military service generally was also relatively low, mainly because of this same ceiling. There was, however, some interest in expanding the role of women throughout the air force, as demonstrated by an emphasis on advertising projects specifically targeted at them. When discussing advertising and publicity, the U.S. Air Force Recruiting Service admitted, "Highest priority in advertising projects was given to all women's programs, followed by OTS [officer training school] and prior service. Fewer quantities of NPS projects were produced, with these funds transferred to nurse and WAF materials." The

U.S. Air Force stressed women's programs in its advertising even though the number of women in military service was relatively small. This was one early indicator of interest by policy makers of expanding the role of women in military service. At the same time that prominence of advertising and publicity on women's programs amplified, it did so in unique ways, including ads in *Mademoiselle* magazine. For example, "The WAF officer campaign was to accent femininity, and the nurse campaign was to stress both aerospace nursing and the humanitarian role of the Air Force nurse." In contrast to women's programs, male programs highlighted far different themes: "The prior service campaign was to use an 'About Face' theme, in the hopes of inviting the prospect to return to military service. The OTS campaign concentrated on two programs: science and engineering and pilot."[11] Such obvious disparities demonstrated complicated and gendered dimensions of military service at that time: the air force was interested in advertising specifically to women, but it employed chauvinistic language regarding them and initially maintained limited conceptions of possible women's roles in the military.

The restrictions on women in military service remained in force until Congress eliminated them in 1967.[12] Even with the removal of previous restrictions, however, actual numbers of women in military service failed to reach even those paltry earlier limits. In 1964 under the limitations, there were 19,186 enlisted women serving in the U.S. military. This total represented 0.8 percent of the U.S. military. By 1969, two years after Congress had formally lifted restrictions, 26,323 women served in the U.S. military. This represented 0.9 percent, a very nominal increase. It was not until 1973 and the advent of the all-volunteer force that the number of women serving in the U.S. military topped 2 percent: 42,627 women served during 1973, representing 2.2 percent of the U.S. military.[13] One estimate counted women's participation in military service as hovering consistently around 1 percent of the total force from 1948 until the AVF's introduction in 1973.[14]

Noticeable changes regarding women in military service occurred with the move from the draft to the all-volunteer force. As political leaders spurred the move and military leaders formulated plans to implement it, the likelihood of recruiting shortfalls among men became evident. Increased emphasis on recruiting women became one way to offset them. Over time, the results were expanded participation and opportunities for women in military service. "The percentage of women in the armed forces steadily increased from less than 2% at the end of FY1972 to 13.9%

at the end of September 1997,"[15] one government report documented. Such massive shifts began as small ripples.

On 10 April 1969, Project Volunteer, "whose membership includes the Assistant Secretary of Defense (M&RA), the Assistant Secretaries of the Military Departments (M&RA), and the Deputy Chiefs of Staff for Personnel of each Military Service," deliberated on ways to accomplish the all-volunteer force.[16] By 13 April 1970, Secretary of Defense Melvin R. Laird addressed the members of DACOWITS at their semi-annual meeting. In his remarks, he made clear that the Pentagon planned to expand opportunities for women in military service. "Throughout the years, women in the Military Services have provided a true source of *volunteer* manpower," Laird indicated. "We recognize this and I believe that in the future, women will play an even greater and more active part in our National Defense, particularly in view of our plans to reduce the draft."[17] There was a growing recognition among many policy makers that women represented one important counterbalance for the impending loss of male draftees. Policy makers on all sides of debates were fairly certain that without the draft, the number of male military personnel would drop precipitously; therefore, how the military compensated for this loss in personnel became a vital question. As a result, there were pragmatic as well as ideological considerations that led to the expanded role of women in U.S. military service.

As was noted in Chapter 6, Project Volunteer outlined major challenges to the all-volunteer force along with recommendations to address them. On 14 August 1970 the group admitted, "There are several issues which remain to be resolved before a fully volunteer force is achieved." They endorsed extending induction authority beyond 30 June 1971, the date when the Military Selective Service Act of 1967 was set to expire, to "at least" 30 June 1973. The formal recommendations of Project Volunteer covered a plethora of issues, including public understanding of the armed forces, military pay and benefits, educational and training benefits, housing, military personnel utilization and management, recruitment programs, physicians and dentists, and reserve and National Guard forces. The main areas of Project Volunteer proposals each had numerous sub-points. For example, under "Military Personnel Utilization and Management," Project Volunteer affirmed, "Increased recruitment and utilization of uniformed women provides an additional method of reducing requirements for recruitment of men for service."[18]

The group envisioned an expansion of women in military service in both numbers and specialties: "Women have and can be utilized in a very wide range of occupational duties and functions, other than those involving direct combat operations. In an all-volunteer force, the use of military women should be extended insofar as recruiting capability and rotation requirements for enlisted men make it practical to use them." Women, therefore, represented a planned offset. The focus, however, was on non-combat roles to lessen the need for recruiting men in the absence of the draft. Over time, this emphasis sparked a significant expansion of the number of women in military service and the opportunities available to them. Such a shift had already begun:

> In recognition of the desirability of expanding this source of manpower, the Air Force has under way a program to increase the number of WAF on active duty. The Army recommends a similar program for expanding WAC strength subject to funding of necessary modifications of base housing accommodations. The Navy and Marine Corps plans to continue their present strength levels of approximately 6,000 in Navy and 2,800 in Marine Corps. The Navy believes that sea-shore rotation considerations limit significant additional use of military women; the Marine Corps considers 1% of total strength an optimum strength for women Marines. It is recommended that the proposed Service programs be supported. An all-out recruiting campaign will be needed. The Defense Advisory Commission on Women in Services (DACOWITS) has indicated its availability to assist in this effort.[19]

Project Volunteer represented civilian oversight of military personnel policy from the Pentagon and strongly accentuated the value of women in military service as compensation for the loss of male draftees. The air force and army agreed and had already launched major augmentations of women in their respective services. The reason varied by service. The army suffered the most from losing the draft, so it needed any and all offsets available. The air force reasoning was less clear, although similar to its leading role in military desegregation: it was the most progressive branch regarding social reforms. The navy and marine corps were the most resistant to change on this issue. The navy had the unique and legitimate issue of shipboard service, whereas the corps' resistance was largely due to tradition, including its combat-centric ethos inculcated in recruits with the often-voiced phrase "every Marine a rifleman."

As discussed in the previous chapter, Project Volunteer determined that "Major improvements in military pay are an essential first step in any program for moving to an all-volunteer force." In addition, however, Project Volunteer considered the "utilization of uniformed women" and how it related to the switch from the draft. The Program Evaluation Group on the All-Volunteer Force observed that the air force sought "to increase the number of WAFs on active duty by more than 100% from pre-Vietnam levels to 15,000 by 1974. The Army recommends a similar program for expanding WAC strength by 12,000 or 100%."[20] These initial changes became models for further enlargement later.

In a lengthy interview in May 1971, Army Chief of Staff William Westmoreland examined the evolution of the all-volunteer force. One specific topic he analyzed was the impact of the changeover on women in military service. In a venue labeled "straight talk from the chief," the interviewer asked Westmoreland, "There is considerable evidence to show that more women are interested in military careers than can be accepted under current policies. What are the prospects of expanding the range of duties performed by women, even to such combat jobs as air-defense artillery radar operators?" Westmoreland answered, "Project Volunteer recommended that a study be made to determine the feasibility of expanding the strength of the Women's Army Corps by 80 percent. The Deputy Chief of Staff for Personnel is currently pursuing this study." As Westmoreland explained, "The duties performed by women in the Army are constantly under review, and military occupational specialties are added or deleted from time to time. By law, women are classified as noncombatants; therefore, there is no possibility that women will be used in combat or combat-related jobs." Instead, Westmoreland conceded, "It is much more likely that the range of jobs for WACs will be expanded for service support roles in areas like communications, medical care and treatment, automatic data processing, administration, and finance. Under current strength authorizations, all qualified women applicants applying for enlistment at current rates in the armed forces can be accepted in one of the women's services."[21]

At that time, policy makers recognized that expanding the opportunities for women in the military compensated for the heightened number of male volunteers required in the absence of the draft. Secretary of the Army Howard "Bo" Callaway explicitly admitted this. Regarding the possibilities inherent in expanding the Women's Army Corps, Callaway affirmed, "The great potential of 'woman power' to offset the requirement for men was early recognized by the Army. In 1972 we undertook a study to determine those jobs which can be filled by either men or women. This

General William C. Westmoreland during a meeting in the White House Cabinet Room. 14 October 1968. (Yoichi R. Okamoto, courtesy Lyndon B. Johnson Library)

study resulted in the identification of 434 of the Army's 484 occupational specialties being opened to female enlistees. Skills excluded are those either in or directly related to the combat arms."[22]

Viewing greater employment of women as a potential recompense for the increased number of male volunteers required was not unique to the army. Secretary of Defense Melvin Laird reported to President Ford and the chairs of the armed services committees of the Senate and the House of Representatives, "We are determined that the All-Volunteer Force shall have broad appeal to young men and women of all racial, ethnic, and economic backgrounds. This objective was reinforced by the Human Goals program initiated by the Department of Defense in 1969, which emphasizes equality of opportunity for all uniformed members."[23] The AVF shifted focus of the military toward equality of opportunity, especially as it pertained to women in military service. There was an action-and-reaction cycle. Critics contended that the AVF would be either all African American, all poor, all female, or all of the above. In response, the Department of Defense paid greater attention than had traditionally been the case on ensuring that the military was representative of American society. Within such a context, including both minorities and women in military service progressively became a priority, as illustrated by Laird's comments.

Secretary Laird also outlined "remaining problems" with the transition to the all-volunteer force and delineated "how to solve them." He revealed how fears of military recruiting shortfalls spurred action within the Department of Defense: "Current trends indicate that a series of vigorous actions must be taken to avoid enlisted shortages in the Active Forces that could be about 40,000 in the Army and 15,000 in the Navy in FY 1974 after the draft ends." He interpreted such deficits as necessitating forceful exploits to mitigate, including both improved retention and expanding the role of women in military service. As Laird explained, "These actions include a continued intensification of efforts to attract more recruits to both Army and Navy. But considerably more must be done to limit the need for recruits overall, both by retaining more trained and qualified personnel through reenlistment and by selectively replacing military men in jobs that can be performed as well and as economically by civilians and military women."[24] Laird's attention to recruiting shortfalls and his recommended solution to solve them demonstrated that prior to the enactment of the AVF, civilian leaders within the Department of Defense pointed toward women as one way to equalize the lack of draftees. Laird envisioned that improved retention provided one counterweight, and expanding the role of women in military service provided another. His views and resulting policies were an important start toward expanding opportunity for women in military service.

The first potential counterweight to ending the draft that Laird highlighted was retention through improved marketing of military service as a career. "The attractiveness of military service, and the capacity to retain qualified career people, is strongly affected by public attitudes toward military service," he relayed. "It is essential that the vital role of the Armed Forces in national security and the many challenges of military life be projected in ways that will enhance public understanding and respect for military people, their profession, and the uniform they wear."[25] The first offset, therefore, was retention; it demonstrated a shift toward promoting military service as a career where people remained long-term instead of only several years as under the draft. That goal required an alteration in attitude among the public and also necessitated the military to sell service as a career.

The second offset that Laird stressed was increased use of civilians and women in military service. Laird indicated, "Many support-type jobs now filled by military men can be performed effectively and economically by civilians and military women. The expanded use of these alternate sources of manpower can reduce the requirement for male recruits."[26] In addition to an action-and-reaction cycle, there were unintended consequences of such an emphasis. To end the draft, policy makers needed to compensate for lower numbers of male volunteers. One way to do that was to open up more jobs for women. Once they did that, however, the result created pressure to unlock even more specialties, even ones that policy makers had not envisioned ever opening (e.g., combat roles). As a result, debates regarding military service forced significant changes: first in military personnel policy and second in American society. In this instance, the practical pressure for more people in military service during times of change compelled a search for additional personnel, including civilians and women in military service. Over time, these openings spurred expanded opportunity and future change.

Such a change in emphasis had tangible results. Laird revealed that the Department of Defense considerably increased both the number of civilians in support roles and the number of women in military service. "Under this Administration the proportion of civilians to total employment in the Department of Defense has increased from 30 percent in January 1969 to 33 percent in June 1972," he recounted. "The Services are developing plans for using an even higher proportion of civilians in the work force." The department planned an even greater comparative increase in the role of women in military service. As Laird disclosed, "The Services are preparing plans which would nearly double the number of enlisted women in the Services from 31,000 to 59,000 by June 1977, with the addition of another 3,000 female officers. These plans will be implemented to the extent they are effective and feasible."[27] Increased numbers of civilians in support roles and women in military service were two offsets that benefited the AVF in the absence of the draft. Heightened numbers of women in military service also resulted in a notable shift toward expanded opportunity, probably far more than Laird or anyone else envisioned at that time. They started the process, however, and it gained momentum later.

The following month, Assistant Secretary of Defense (Manpower and Reserve Affairs) Roger Kelley distributed guidance from Laird throughout the Department of Defense and highlighted the opportunity represented by the "recruitment of women." Kelley argued, "The supply of qualified women who can effectively perform military jobs now held by men is greater than the number currently being recruited. Both the Army and Navy, who will have the greatest difficulties recruiting sufficient men in

FY 1973, have initiated actions to expand greatly the number of women enlisted. . . . The Air Force and Marine Corps, whose recruiting problems are far less severe, are studying the use of more military women." The total number of female recruits for the four services was approximately 14,000 in 1972. The Department of Defense increased its 1973 goal to 20,500 and again boosted its 1974 target to 26,000, almost double the total of women from just two years before. Pentagon planning figures underscored that even this significant rise "may be revised upward" once the air force and marine corps completed their ongoing studies on increasing the recruitment of women.[28]

It was not only civilian leaders within the army and the Pentagon that encouraged greater employment of women within the all-volunteer force. John C. Stennis (D-MS), chair of the Senate Armed Services Committee, urged enhanced recruiting of women and greater opportunities for them within the AVF. "I think young girls who are willing to go into the Service should be encouraged," he asserted. "It seems to me that they should be given more and more places and used more and more by the Services—especially the Air Force and the Army—but not for combat. They are an abundant source of talent[,] and more extensive experiments of their use should be made."[29]

Interest in expanding opportunities for women in military service was not just discussed. There was also a determined effort to augment the number of women serving in the military, largely to counter difficulties that the services experienced recruiting sufficient numbers of men during the early switch to the all-volunteer force. On 28 November 1973, Brigadier General Robert Montague Jr., deputy special assistant on the modern volunteer army, reported to Stephen Herbits what Montague characterized as an "emphasis by command group" on the Women's Army Corps: "You might be interested in this summary on enlisting women in the Army. We will easily meet the 12,000 objective and beat the goal of 14,400 also. We have momentum and confidence."[30] Montague provided Herbits details compiled by Colonel Forest G. Crittenden, the director of recruiting operations. Crittenden revealed that on 9 October 1973, "the Army Chief of Staff approved a plan to expand the Women's Army Corps over the next six years." Crittenden also outlined the planned significant expansion of the WAC in specific terms and disclosed that the official objective was 12,000 women for fiscal year 1974, 17,000 women in FY 1975 and 1976, 18,000 women in FY 1977, and 19,000 women in FY 1978 and 1979. Such an upward trajectory represented an increase of almost 60 percent within a five-year span. Crittenden revealed that military planners did not consider such an increase an anomaly, but rather the beginning of further growth. "In support of this planned expansion, a General Officer Steering Committee on Women in the Army was activated," he relayed. "The primary purpose of this Committee has been to determine the feasibility of greatly expanding utilization of women."[31]

On 11 February 1974, Secretary Callaway disseminated "ideas to enhance recruiting for the volunteer army" to every general officer on active duty. One of the key ideas was to "expand WAC recruiting." Each letter included a copy of a detailed memorandum on the subject. Under that same heading, Callaway remarked that in October 1973, "a plan was approved for implementation that will increase the WAC to a level of approximately 50,000 by FY 79." As Callaway further explained, "All but 48 MOS [military occupational specialties] have been opened to women," and "numerous enlistment options previously closed to women have been revised to include qualified women applicants." As he concluded, he reiterated that these changes would begin immediately: "FY 74 procurement objectives for women have been increased from 12,000 at the beginning of the fiscal year to 14,400."[32]

Other events provided publicity and momentum. Around the world, contemporaries heralded 1975 as International Women's Year. On 19 April 1975 the popular magazine *Ladies Home Journal* sponsored a ninety-minute national television broadcast of its annual Women of the Year awards ceremony in New York City to commemorate the occasion. During the show, sponsors honored female leaders from around the world in eight categories. The journal named U.S. Air Force Major General Jeanne M. Holm "woman of the year" in the category of government and diplomacy for her longtime and committed role in "expanding opportunities for women in the Armed Forces." Observers acknowledged, "General Holm is the first military woman to be honored by the *Journal*'s Women of the Year awards program." Holm was the only female major general in the armed forces at that time. Although she retired soon after, she continued her advocacy for expanded opportunities for women in military service. Holm's award demonstrated that the issue of women in military service also received increased attention in American society after the transition to the AVF.

Holm was a long-standing presence in the air force and personally impacted military personnel policy. She was director of women in the air force from November 1965 to February 1973, "and during that time,

President Nixon standing in the Oval Office with female brigadier generals (left to right) Jeanne M. Holm, Elizabeth Hoisington, Mildred Bailey, Lillian Dunlap, and Anna Hays, along with Assistant Secretary of Defense (Manpower and Personnel) Roger T. Kelley. 6 December 1971. (Courtesy Richard M. Nixon Library)

policies affecting women were updated, the number of Air Force women more than doubled, job assignment opportunities greatly expanded, and uniforms were modernized." Throughout her career, Holm led many efforts to expand opportunities for women in military service. While much of her military career predated the all-volunteer force, it nonetheless foreshadowed many subsequent transformations. For example, during her tenure in the air force the number of women doubled, a significant sign of change. Holm argued that expanded opportunities for women in military service were undeniable: "Confident that women will be making far greater contributions to national defense than ever before," the journal reported that "she also predicts that Military women in the future will attend the Service academies, fly Air Force planes, serve aboard Navy ships of the line, and have many combat arms fields open to them."[33] Holms's prophecies were quite prescient, with most of them coming to fruition shortly after she retired, although allowing women in combat remained debated and contested for years to come.

Soon after the transition to the all-volunteer force, expanded opportunities appeared for women in U.S. military service. Although Congress capped the number of women in the military at 2 percent prior to the AVF, by 31 December 1975 "there were 32,356 Air Force women on active duty. This total included 1,633 women line officers, 3,406 women medical officers, and 27,317 enlisted women. At this time women represented 5.4% of the total active duty strength."[34] Without formal limits and with many military and civilian leaders anxiously looking for ways to compensate for the loss of draftees, the percentage of women quickly increased within the AVF. Whereas beforehand the percentage of women in military service remained at roughly 2 percent, by 1975 it had already jumped to more than 5 percent, and it continued to climb thereafter.

In addition to raising the number of women in military service, other significant shifts regarding women were occurring in the 1970s. One was admission of women to military service academies. On Friday, 26 September 1975, Congress broke the gender barrier at the historically all-male institutions through the Department of Defense Appropriations Authorization Act for 1976: "The significance of that event to this Committee is that one section of that Act contains an earthshaking new provision—it requires the three Service academies to open their doors to women as of next summer."[35] Although Congress, and not the military, seized the initiative and resolved the issue at that time, the increased number of enlisted women serving in a broader range of specialties focused greater attention on limitations placed on female officers. Remarkably, this major shift rapidly transitioned from President Ford's signature to implementation in less than one year.

On 7 October 1975, Ford signed Public Law 94-106 and therefore made admission of women to service academies a reality: "The law provides that women will be eligible for appointment and admission to the service academies and that standards required for appointment, admission, training, graduation, and commissioning of women will be the same as those for men except that adjustments required for physiological differences be made."[36] As a result, service academies opened to women in the summer of 1976 and removed a major barrier to female success in military service, as many senior officers were service academy graduates.

On 11 July 1975, Assistant Secretary of Defense (Manpower and Reserve Affairs) William Brehm "directed a major new policy change in

the number of Senior Reserve Officer Training Corps (or ROTC) Scholarships open to women." As he explained, "Prior to this policy change,
ROTC Scholarships were being awarded to women only in very limited
numbers. For example, in Fiscal Year 1975, the Army had 120 women
in the ROTC Scholarship Program, the Navy 70, and the Air Force 45."
Brehm compared these numbers to their male counterparts. "By contrast,
in Fiscal Year 1975, the Army had 6,380 men in their ROTC Scholarship
Program, the Navy 5,412, and the Air Force 5,851," he found. "The reason
for such small numbers of female participants is that women have not
been allowed to compete on an equal basis with men for those scholarships." Brehm's increase of ROTC scholarships was another example of
expanded opportunity for women in military service during the 1970s.
He granted more women scholarships; this in turn better prepared them
for military careers. Brehm went further, though. On the same day, he
"issued a memorandum to the Secretaries of the military departments
directing them to adopt a new policy with regard to the numbers of ROTC
Scholarships available to women. In that memorandum, Mr. Brehm directed that women be allowed to compete fully for that number of scholarships which equals the maximum number of female officer graduates
needed from ROTC for that fiscal year. This figure, in turn, is based on the
total number of female officer billets available in that service."[37] Therefore, Brehm not only increased the number of ROTC scholarships for
women but also directed that the competition for them be fair.

Another major shift was the admission of women to pilot training
within the air force. On 20 November 1975, U.S. Air Force Chief of Staff
General David C. Jones "approved a proposed program for the training of
women pilots. The Air Staff Working Group which convened to develop
program parameters addressed selection, training, and initial aircraft
assignment limitation for the test group. The following personnel concepts were assumed: a. Women pilots should be considered no differently
(consistent with combat exclusion) in their opportunities for retraining,
promotion, and career Air Force status, and b. Women entries into pilot
training subsequent to the test group will come from normal sources."[38]
As a result, the air force opened up previously off-limits areas to women
in military service. As before, personnel needs drove experimentation
with alternate sources of personnel that in turn further illuminated inequities in military service opportunities between men and women. Such
exposure then broadened opportunities for women. It was a slow process,
but one that moved toward egalitarian ideals.

While there were some early signs that the advent of the all-volunteer force enlarged prospects for women in military service, some significant areas of military service remained closed. Most contentious among them was opening combat roles to women. In a legislative briefing to DACOW-ITS during their fall 1975 meeting, Carole Frings of the office of the assistant secretary of defense general counsel relayed that DACOWITS's previous recommendation "to remove the total prohibition that women in the Navy may not be assigned to vessels of the Navy or to aircraft engaged in combat missions" had made some recent progress. As she conveyed to the group, "A bill to accomplish this result has been introduced in Congress—H.R. 58, 94th Congress. The Department of Defense was asked by the Congress to present the views on this bill. The report on the bill, which was prepared by the Army and concurred in by the Navy and Air Force, takes a very strong position opposing the bill." Frings conveyed the Department of Defense's public position of steadfast opposition to women in combat: "It is recognized that the issue of women in combat is an active political question which has provoked sharp differences of opinion in the Congress and among the American people. It appears that the weight of public opinion, as expressed by the Congress in past legislative practice, favors the continued exclusion of women from combat. Examples of this policy are found in sections 6015 and 8549 of Title 10, *United States Code*, which restrict combat assignments for certain women of the Navy and Air Force. For practical, as well as policy reasons, the Department of Defense supports this view."[39] As a result, opportunities for women in military service expanded in the 1970s, but combat roles remained closed. This resulted partly from resistance by segments of American society and somewhat from the military's desire and ability to assign combat roles in a linear fashion. As long as combat was predominately linear, policy exclusions differentiating combat from noncombat roles were controllable, even when unjust. Such power would lessen severely with the emergence of asymmetric conflict and nonlinear combat lines, beginning in the Vietnam War and proliferating ever more in the post-9/11 wars of Iraq and Afghanistan.

Frings, however, contrasted the military's resistance to extending combat roles to women at that time with the military's willingness to multiply openings in other areas of military service: "To optimize the use of women, the services have rapidly increased the opportunities for female enlistment with 86 percent of all career field specialties within the Department of Defense open to them. The Department of Defense will continue to change regulations and policies as appropriate in order to eliminate disadvantages to women." Even such an advocate for women's participation in military service as Frings admitted that during the 1970s the issue of women in combat was as unlikely as it was contentious. "Such an evolutionary approach is most likely to lead to results that are satisfactory both to the armed services and to society at large." She cautioned, "Legislation which would propel women into combat roles would cause severe personnel disruptions and assignment problems and would require significant additional costs—all at a time of severely constrained budgets and without a mandate that such legislation reflects the considered judgment of the American people."[40] Frings's assessment illustrated the dichotomy between the need to increase the number of women in military service and expand opportunities for them and the stiff resistance against opening combat roles to them. Personnel requirements propelled opportunities that then presented complicated and often unpopular related issues such as combat roles for women.

By the early 1980s, these changes illuminated the shifting terrain of women in U.S. military service. On 25 October 1983, Operation Urgent Fury commenced and sought the evacuation of American citizens from Grenada in the Caribbean. The initial deployment of U.S. personnel included four female service members assigned to military police duty after the invasion; however, 82nd Airborne Division Commanding General Edward Trobaugh ordered the women back to their home base at Fort Bragg, North Carolina. Much debate ensured. Eventually, XVIII Airborne Corps Commanding General Jack Mackmull intervened, and the women participated in the operation beginning on 2 November 1983.[41] Six years later, during the U.S. invasion of Panama known as Operation Just Cause, no one endeavored to keep women out of the operation even while debates regarding their roles still surfaced.

In January 1988 the Department of Defense Task Force on Women in the Military highlighted the difficulty of defining a "combat mission" for the purposes of assignment policy. At that time, force structure changes had made military units far more self-sufficient than in the past; those changes also resulted in much greater integration between combat and support personnel in the same unit. The task force urged the Pentagon to clarify its definition of "combat mission" for the purposes of assignment policy, especially as it related to women.[42] As a result, the Pentagon issued the "risk rule" that restricted women to only those noncombat support units where the risk of "direct combat, hostile fire, or capture" was less than the risk in the combat units that they supported. The risk rule also forbade the colocation of women with combat units.[43]

The massive military mobilization, buildup, and deployment from 2 August 1990 until January 1991 for Operation Desert Shield drove momentum toward reexamining the role of women in military service. The National Defense Authorization Act for Fiscal Years 1992 and 1993 dealt specifically with "Assignment of Women in the Armed Forces." The law repealed statutory limitations on assignment of women in the armed forces to combat aircraft and established a commission, "to be known as the Commission on the Assignment of Women in the Armed Forces." As a result, Operation Desert Shield both accentuated and influenced military personnel policy. Restrictions whereby women could not serve on combat aircraft drew harsh criticism. The timing of this reconsideration was no coincidence. In fact, as demonstrated in previous chapters, major military personnel policy changes often coincided with war, as practical concerns such as personnel shortages and political and social concerns such as the heightened visibility of military service during wartime influenced policy. The general duties of the commission were to "assess the laws and policies restricting the assignment of female service members" and to "make findings on such matters." The group evaluated assignment policies, emphasizing the magnified presence of women in military service and considering the implications. It looked at a plethora of issues, including "combat readiness of the Armed Forces"; "public attitudes in the United States on the use of women in the military"; "legal and policy implications," including both voluntary and involuntary assignment of female service members to combat positions; registration of women for the Military Selective Service Act; "the extent of the need to modify facilities and vessels" if women were assigned to combat roles; the costs of such modifications; and "the implications of restrictions on the assignment of women on the recruitment, retention, use, and promotion of qualified personnel in the Armed Forces."[44] The law required the commission to submit its final report to the president no later than 15 November 1992, and the president to then transmit it to Congress by 15 December of the same year.

Retired U.S. Air Force General Robert T. Herres served as chair. Herres graduated from the U.S. Naval Academy but served in the U.S. Air Force. During his thirty-six years of military service, he held a number of significant roles, including commander of 8th Air Force, commander-in-chief of U.S. Space Command, and vice chair of the Joint Chiefs of Staff at the time of his retirement. Fifteen members served with Herres on the commission, including retired U.S. Army Major General Mary Elizabeth Clarke. During her more than thirty-six years in military service, Clarke had been commandant of the military police corps and chemical corps; had commanded Fort McClellan, Alabama; and had served as the director of the Women's Army Corps. Former draftee Charles Moskos, professor of sociology at Northwestern University and chair of the Inter-University Seminar on Armed Forces and Society, also served as a member.[45]

On 13 January 1994, Secretary of Defense Les Aspin removed the "risk rule" that had been in place since 1988. This elimination paved the way for further removal of restrictions on women serving in combat.[46] In the early 1990s, Congress rescinded other barriers that prevented women from performing air and naval combat roles in the military.[47] In 1994, however, the Department of Defense issued a policy that effectively banned women from serving in "units, below the brigade level, whose primary mission is to engage in direct combat on the ground."[48] Such a policy prevented women from serving in combat arms military occupational specialties: infantry, artillery, armor, special operations, and combat engineers.

By the end of the twentieth century it became readily apparent to informed observers that the most significant remaining constraint on women's full participation in military service was the restriction placed on women serving in ground combat. "As long as combat jobs are closed to women, there is likely to be a lower proportion of women in the senior officer grades, as these tend to be filled by officers whose careers have been involved in the central mission of the armed forces, which is combat,"[49] one government report professed in 1998.

The long-standing participation of women in U.S. military service underwent massive changes in the aftermath of the all-volunteer force. The Women's Armed Services Integration Act of 1948 first made women's roles in the military permanent, but it constrained both the number of women allowed in military service and the ranks that they could achieve. George C. Marshall's creation of DACOWITS in 1951 signaled a strengthened emphasis on women in military service, although significant changes awaited the transition to the AVF. The air force led the way by specifically targeting recruiting of women and increasing their numbers. When Congress lifted formal restrictions on women in military service in 1967, the climate for change was ripe. As military and civilian leaders grappled with the monumental task of ending the draft and creating the AVF, women became an important offset for the loss of male draftees and initial recruiting shortfalls among male volunteers. Military services sought to double the number of women in uniform, although the extent varied by service. As more women donned military uniforms, policy makers opened additional jobs to them, albeit with staunch resistance against unlocking combat roles. U.S. Air Force Major General Jeanne Holm personified many of these developments as the senior female officer in the military. As the number of women in military service rose, long-standing barriers such as admission to service academies, increased ROTC scholarships, and pilot training fell in rapid succession. Resistance to women in combat, however, remained fierce, as demonstrated by Operation Urgent Fury and institution of the risk rule in January 1988. Operation Desert Shield/Storm provoked the most intensive reexamination of women in U.S. military service in history. At the beginning of the 1990s policy makers proudly and correctly claimed that women served in the military more than ever before. Debates regarding military service shifted from the issue of gender to sexual orientation when candidate William J. Clinton made open military service by homosexuals a campaign promise during the 1992 presidential campaign.

CHAPTER EIGHT

TO SERVE IN SILENCE

You have no idea what it is like to serve in silence.[1]
—Anonymous service member responding to survey
regarding repeal of "Don't Ask, Don't Tell" policy, 2010

I don't think it's going to be such a big, huge, horrible
thing that DoD is telling everyone it's going to be. If it is
repealed, everyone will look around their spaces to see
if anyone speaks up. They'll hear crickets for a while. A
few flamboyant guys and tough girls will join to rock the
boat and make a scene. Their actions and bad choices
will probably get them kicked out. After a little time has
gone by, then a few of us will speak up. And instead of
a deluge of panic and violence . . . there'll be a ripple
on the water's surface that dissipates quicker than you
can watch.[2]—Anonymous service member responding
to survey regarding repeal of "Don't Ask, Don't Tell"
policy, 2010

No longer will our country be denied the service of
thousands of patriotic Americans who were forced to
leave the military—regardless of their skills, no matter
their bravery or their zeal, no matter their years of
exemplary performance—because they happen to be
gay. No longer will tens of thousands of Americans in
uniform be asked to live a lie or look over their shoulder
in order to serve the country that they love.[3]—President
Barack H. Obama, 22 December 2010

[Repeal of DADT] didn't change anything. . . . We've got
a guy in the unit who is gay. We've been working together
for years and everyone knew, but no one ever cared. For
us it's all about whether or not you're good at your job
. . . it's all about quiet professionalism, not about your
sexual orientation.[4]—U.S. Army Ranger, 9 April 2012

As the U.S. military proved victorious in Operation Desert Shield/Storm in Iraq, policy makers assessed the war and its implications for military service. Initial focus highlighted the war as vindicating the all-volunteer force, although concerns remained. Some of these were not new. Apprehensions regarding the representativeness of the AVF resurfaced in the aftermath of the war, while the war also highlighted major increases of women in military service. Most important, however, the early 1990s witnessed a shift in debates regarding U.S. military service. Governor of Arkansas and presidential candidate William J. Clinton made a campaign pledge to lift restrictions on homosexuals openly serving in the U.S. military. After his election as president, Clinton sought to make good on his promise. He immediately encountered fierce resistance from military leaders, including the chair of the Joint Chiefs of Staff, Colin L. Powell, who so adamantly opposed Clinton's proposal that he threatened to resign. Partly due to the broad and diverse support that Powell attracted, Clinton tempered his goal. A compromise policy emerged, colloquially referred to as "Don't Ask, Don't Tell" (DADT), that was a slightly modified ban on homosexuals in military service. Enacted on 30 November 1993, the policy suffered from both exclusion and ambiguity. Complicated cases proliferated, and by 1998 they spurred an extensive Pentagon review of the policy. When President Obama took office, he quickly urged Congress to repeal the law. Many generals and admirals protested, and the Pentagon again analyzed the issue in great detail, including one of the largest efforts to survey the American military since Samuel Stouffer's G.I. survey during World War II and Leo Bogart's Project Clear surveys during the Korean War. Ultimately, the Pentagon recommended repealing DADT and allowing open military service. In 2010 first the U.S. House of Representatives and then the U.S. Senate voted to repeal DADT. Three days before Christmas 2010, President Obama signed the law, and open military service became a possibility. The military branches still had to certify that the policy change did not undermine military effectiveness, and certification occurred the following summer. The military personnel policy requiring American service members to serve in silence had become an echo of the past.

After the conclusion of the Persian Gulf War, U.S. policy makers considered many issues related to the conflict, including such personnel issues as mobilization, force quality, and military effectiveness. Representative Les Aspin (D-WI), chair of the House Armed Services Committee, released on 26 April 1991 a report that analyzed the all-volunteer force in much detail.[5] Aspin focused generally on the representativeness of the force and specifically on its potential reliance on African Americans in probable scenarios for war. As he revealed, the group "examined three scenarios for armed conflict, and estimated the proportion of black service members at risk." Aspin further explained, "In conflicts involving chiefly air power, or air power and Navy ships, blacks were underrepresented compared to their proportion of the population as a whole. In a ground war, blacks were somewhat overrepresented."[6]

The following year, Representative William L. Dickinson (R-AL) joined Aspin to again scrutinize the war and military personnel issues. They characterized the Persian Gulf War as the first serious test of the all-volunteer force since its creation roughly two decades before: "The Gulf war tested for the first time whether the All Volunteer Force would be effective in war. By all accounts, the AVF passed with honors." Indeed, the Persian Gulf War validated the AVF to many observers. The AVF proved exceptionally well-suited to the war and achieved complete victory. Harkening back to the early difficulties that the force encountered throughout the 1970s, Aspin and Dickinson concluded, "The performance of the AVF in the Gulf war may have surprised those who remembered the problems of the 1970s. In 1973 the United States had established an all-volunteer force based on marketplace incentives—good pay and benefits for all who volunteered. By the late 1970s, the effect of lower enlistment standards for recruits and higher discipline problems raised serious concerns about force quality and effectiveness."[7]

The lessons of Operation Desert Shield/Storm were not entirely positive, though. Aspin and Dickinson warned, "The war also raised anew the questions of representativeness of minorities and the poor in the AVF—whether, in fact, it was fair. Black Americans of recruitment age comprise about 14 percent of the population as a whole, but 26 percent of new Army recruits and about 18 percent of new Marine Corps recruits. Overall, blacks comprise 31 percent of enlisted Army soldiers and 21 percent of enlisted Marines, compared to 12 percent of the general population aged 18 to 24. It is this disproportionate representation which gave rise to concerns of disproportionate risk for blacks." Of course, worries about the representativeness of the AVF existed prior to the war. They were palpable enough during the Persian Gulf War, however, that the Congressional Budget Office initiated an extensive review of the issue. "Where many commentators said the All Volunteer Force was chiefly dependent on the lower economic classes," the Congressional Budget Office "found the socio-economic characteristics of the AVF to be generally reflective of the larger society."[8] As a result, Aspin and Dickinson concluded that the AVF performed well in the Persian Gulf War and was also fairly representative at that time.

The Persian Gulf War also reinforced previous trends in two specific personnel areas related to U.S. military service. First, the conflict continued to enlarge the role of women in military service, continuing a trend detailed in the previous chapter: "Women served in greater numbers and performed a wider variety of military occupations in Operation Desert Storm than in any other conflict. More than 35,000 servicewomen were deployed to Southwest Asia as logisticians, air traffic controllers, engineers, equipment mechanics, drivers, reconnaissance aircraft pilots, and scores of other positions. Two women were taken as prisoners of war. Fifteen were killed in the conflict, five by enemy fire." During the Persian Gulf War, women served in the military in greater numbers and in a wider array of roles than ever before. That growth continued throughout the 1990s. While there were, of course, debates about such an expansion, American society generally noted the shift in positive terms. "During Operation Desert Storm, American society continued to display its willingness to accept the enhanced role for military women that had first revealed itself in Operation Just Cause," Aspin and Dickinson explained. "While there were some undercurrents of disapproval, discussions more often focused on women's competence and willingness to serve. As a result of the Operation Desert Storm experience, Congress last year repealed the law prohibiting women aviators from flying combat missions."[9] The Persian Gulf War solidified the fact that broadening women's opportunities in the military worked and did not limit military effectiveness. Instead, it stimulated useful debates regarding military service that resulted in the repeal of the air combat mission exclusion. As in earlier examples, military service prodded alterations to military personnel policy; it highlighted areas of discrimination and limited opportunity that became more difficult to maintain whenever someone from that previously excluded group—in this case women—willingly served in the military.

Second, the Persian Gulf War established a heightened use of reserve and National Guard personnel: "The U.S. response to the crisis in the Gulf involved the largest mobilization of reserve components since the Korean War of 1950, and the first major mobilization since the Berlin Crisis of 1961–1962," Aspin and Dickinson observed. "The U.S. response also provided the first test of the Total Force Policy. In 1973, following the end of the Vietnam War, the Department of Defense implemented the Total Force Policy, integrating the active and the reserve components into a combined fighting force," the duo continued. "How this mobilization was carried out, how the reserve components performed and what lessons might be learned for the future are the subjects of this portion of the inquiry."[10] Such an approach to using reserve forces contrasted sharply with the manner in which U.S. policy makers would utilize reserve and National Guard units during Operations Iraqi Freedom and Enduring Freedom in Afghanistan, which subsequent chapters will cover. The Gulf War involved a huge mobilization including reserves and National Guard personnel, whereas Operations Iraqi Freedom and Enduring Freedom used reserves far more actively than previous conflicts but without a general mobilization, partly to downplay the necessary force levels required. In the prior instance, this newfound reliance on reserves and National Guard personnel through general mobilization also rallied public support. Such an approach contrasted sharply with the latter case, where during Operations Iraqi Freedom and Enduring Freedom reserves and National Guard personnel became an offset in the absence of sufficient active duty personnel, with far more negative consequences.

Shortly after the Persian Gulf War, debates regarding American military service shifted toward the issue of sexual orientation. During the 1992 presidential campaign, governor of Arkansas and Democrat presidential candidate William Clinton made a campaign pledge to issue an executive order to remove the ban on homosexuals openly serving in the military. This prohibition had existed since the Articles of War of 1916, but enforcement of the exclusionary military personnel policy was uneven, especially during times of war when personnel shortages intensified.[11] In 1949, military leaders solidified the policy and enacted a complete ban on homosexuals openly serving.[12]

There was an immediate firestorm of backlash from military leaders, including the nation's most senior military officer, Joint Chiefs of Staff chair General Colin Powell. On 18 November 1992, Powell proclaimed resistance among many in the military against open service by homosexuals. As he protested, "It is a very big problem for us, and it is not just the generals and the admirals who are saying it." Powell argued that the existing policy banning open service was in fact quite useful. "We continue . . . to believe that the policy we have been following is a sound one," he stated, "that there are issues of enormous legal and administrative difficulty associated with a change in that policy, and there are significant issues of privacy associated with it." In a brutally honest moment, though, Powell revealed that the choice was not his to make. He relented, "At the end of the day . . . it's a judgment that will have to be made . . . by our civilian political leaders." In the end, Powell admitted, "The armed forces will do what we are told to do."[13]

On 29 January 1993, President Clinton directed the Pentagon to study the issue and expressed his intent to eliminate sexual orientation as a disqualifying factor in military service. This action ended a hectic week that began with Clinton announcing his intention; Senator Sam Nunn (D-GA), chair of the Senate Armed Services Committee, publicly opposing him; and intense deliberations over the next several days. The move was anything but smooth. President Clinton's policy rested on four pillars: "One, service men and women will be judged based on their conduct, not their sexual orientation. Two, therefore the practice . . . of not asking about sexual orientation in the enlistment procedure will continue. Three, an open statement by a service member that he or she is a homosexual will create a rebuttable presumption that he or she intends to engage in prohibited conduct, but the service member will be given an opportunity to refute that presumption. . . . And four, all provisions of the Uniform Code of Military Justice will be enforced in an even-handed manner as regards both heterosexuals and homosexuals." Clinton concluded by stressing the compromise that he expected from military leaders: "And thanks to the policy provisions agreed to by the Joint Chiefs, there will be a decent regard to the legitimate privacy and associational rights of all service members." At the same time, Clinton halted the questioning of new service members regarding sexual orientation.[14]

Combative congressional hearings in both the Senate and House Armed Services Committees commenced and continued throughout the spring and summer of 1993. Although hearings lasted from 29 March to 22 July 1993, Senator Nunn announced in May a compromise that he characterized "as a 'don't ask, don't tell' approach." DADT explicitly forbade homosexuals from openly serving in the U.S. military. The proposal maintained, "Presence in the armed forces of persons who demonstrate a propensity or intent to engage in homosexual acts would create an unacceptable risk to the high standards of morale, good order and discipline, and unit cohesion which are the essence of military capability."[15] Under this policy, military officials refrained from asking questions concerning the sexual orientation of prospective and current members of the military while requiring individuals to keep their homosexual orientation to themselves. If they refused, then they were discharged from military service or denied the opportunity for enlistment or appointment.[16] Historian Beth Bailey has shown how "policy discussions about gays in the military centered on questions of military efficacy rather than on the morally charged issue of sexual behavior," even when at their core debates were always about moral beliefs.[17]

On 19 July 1993, President Clinton, surrounded by the Joint Chiefs of Staff, announced his endorsement of a compromise policy on homosexuals serving in the military. Labeled "Don't Ask, Don't Tell," it limited the military's ability to investigate the sexual orientation of a service member (Don't Ask), but also restrained the service member's ability openly to disclose it (Don't Tell). Although Clinton maintained, "Under this policy, a person can say, 'I am a homosexual, but I am going to strictly adhere to the Code of Conduct,'" he did not clarify exactly how this would be done. Homosexual acts, even those off base, warranted discharge from the military under the compromise policy. Clinton faced fierce resistance on the issue, even from members of his own political party. Senator Nunn argued that open service damaged military effectiveness; he parried Clinton's attempt to loosen restrictions on it as a result.[18] Although President Clinton originally sought a "Don't Pursue" addition to the policy that limited the military's ability to investigate service members for homosexual conduct, he did not include it in his public announcement on 19 July 1993.[19] Initial reactions to DADT drew attention to its complexity and ambiguity, including outright confusion in congressional testimony by Secretary of Defense Les Aspin as to whether a statement of homosexuality by a military service member was indeed grounds for discharge.[20]

On 30 November 1993, President Clinton signed into law the Fiscal Year 1994 National Defense Authorization Act; it made DADT law.[21] The law provided grounds for discharge for any service member who "has engaged in, attempted to engage in, or solicited another to engage in a homosexual act or acts; . . . states that he or she is a homosexual or bisexual; or . . . has married or attempted to marry someone of the same sex."[22] The DADT policy determined that "service by those who have a propensity to engage in homosexual conduct creates an unacceptable risk to morale, good order and discipline, and unit cohesion, and that the long-standing prohibition of homosexual conduct therefore continues to be necessary in the unique circumstances of military service."[23] The policy, however, attempted to separate sexual orientation from conduct. For example, Department of Defense Directive 1332.30, which implemented the policy, characterized sexual orientation as a "personal and private matter" that "is not a bar to current military service . . . unless manifested by homosexual conduct."[24] Such a development was significant. Because Clinton enacted the compromise through a congressional act (instead of an executive order), it converted the military personnel policy of DADT into law. Therefore, only a new law was capable of undoing it.

As the name implied, the new policy also eliminated questions about sexual orientation from the enlistment process: "Questions concerning homosexuality are no longer permissible and are no longer included on enlistment forms."[25] The ambiguity and vagueness of DADT quickly became apparent as service members attempted to navigate its waters. In 1994, U.S. Navy Lieutenant Maria Zoe Dunning found herself before a military tribunal for proclaiming, "I am a lesbian!" at a public rally the previous January. Her case highlighted definitional opacities within the DADT policy because the navy argued that her statement constituted sexual conduct, whereas her lawyers successfully countered that it simply declared her sexual orientation. Partly in response to such uncertainties, in August 1995 the Department of Defense Office of the General Counsel shifted the emphasis in the policy away from sexual orientation toward conduct by removing mention of the former and reinforcing that statements belonged to the latter.[26]

As the number of high-publicity cases involving DADT proliferated, civilian leaders pressured the Pentagon to reevaluate its policy. In April 1997, Secretary of Defense William S. Cohen ordered a review of "the effectiveness of the application and enforcement" of the DADT policy. The extensive assessment was partly in response to a recent scathing critique by the Service Members' Legal Defense Network. As part of the appraisal, the Defense Manpower Data Center detailed statistics for "discharges based on homosexual conduct for Fiscal Years 1980 through 1997." In April 1998 the Pentagon published its findings on the implementation of the "Department's Policy on Homosexual Conduct in the Military." In an understatement, the military concluded, "The balance that the policy strikes between the prohibition of homosexual conduct in the military and the privacy rights of our service members has posed a challenge to the Services." The examination found that discharges under the DADT policy had "in fact risen since the new policy became effective in 1994." Admitting that such a development was "cause for some concern," Under Secretary of Defense (Personnel and Readiness) Rudy de Leon concluded, "The large majority of the discharges for homosexual conduct are based on the statements of service members who identify themselves as homosexuals, as opposed to cases involving homosexual acts." Although DADT distinguished sexual orientation from conduct, such a task was exceedingly difficult because the policy also characterized statements as conduct. De Leon recognized the conundrum: "The consistent upward trend from 1994 to 1997 raises questions about how our policy is working in practice." The review also found that in limited instances, "primarily the Coast Guard on the East Coast," older enlistment forms that included questions on sexual orientation still were used, ostensibly "as a cost savings measure." In August 1997 the Pentagon mandated new enlistment forms across the military. Despite such problems, de Leon resolved that the DADT policy had, "for the most part, been properly applied and enforced."[27]

In a clear parallel to Clinton, Barack H. Obama advocated repeal of DADT in his presidential campaign. As President Clinton's efforts had before, Obama's pronouncement engendered much resistance from military leaders. More than 1,000 retired generals and admirals protested in March 2009; they claimed that DADT repeal "would undermine recruiting and retention, impact leadership at all levels, have adverse effects on the willingness of parents who lend their sons and daughters to military service, and eventually break the All-Volunteer Force."[28] Unfazed, President Obama specifically advocated repeal of DADT in his first State of the Union address: "This year, I will work with Congress and our military to finally repeal the law that denies gay Americans the right to serve the country they love because of who they are. It is the right thing to do."[29]

On 2 March 2010, Secretary of Defense Robert M. Gates named the Honorable Jeh C. Johnson and U.S. Army General Carter F. Ham to cochair a committee to consider consequences of repealing the DADT policy within the U.S. military. In one of the largest surveys of attitudes among service members since Samuel Stouffer's G.I. survey during World War II and Leo Bogart's Project Clear surveys during the Korean War, the committee surveyed almost 400,000 service members and received over 115,000 responses as a result; the group also surveyed more than 150,000 service member spouses and received nearly 45,000 responses as a result. Approximately 100,000 additional service members voiced their opinions as a result of numerous "information exchange forums," focus groups, and a special "online inbox for Service members and their families to offer their views." Johnson and Ham also solicited assessments from senior military leaders, members of Congress, and foreign allies, as well as both veterans and civilian groups. The committee combed through previous personnel policies and service member surveys for an intense nine months. Its resulting report claimed with satisfaction, "To our knowledge, our nine-month review and engagement of the force was the largest and most comprehensive in the history of the U.S. military, on any personnel-related matter." The committee's conclusion was simple and straightforward: "Based on all we saw and heard, our assessment is that, when coupled with the prompt implementation of the recommendations we offer below, the risk of repeal of Don't Ask, Don't Tell to overall military effectiveness is low." While the report admitted that there was risk of "limited and isolated disruption to unit cohesion and retention," the committee decided that long-term benefits more than made up for it. Johnson and Ham explained: "Longer term, with a continued and sustained commitment to core values of leadership, professionalism, and respect for all, we are convinced that the U.S. military can adjust and accommodate this change, just as it has others in history."[30] The Department of Defense also released a support plan for implementation that accompanied its comprehensive review; the support plan proved instrumental in the transition to open service.[31]

Johnson and Ham based their conclusions on the results of their extensive survey of military service members and spouses: "The results of the Service member survey reveal a widespread attitude among a solid majority of Service members that repeal of Don't Ask, Don't Tell will not have a negative impact on their ability to conduct their military mission." The survey of service members disclosed that the largest group of respondents asserted that repeal only marginally impacted them or the overall military; there were also minorities on either side who deemed that it produced either positive or negative effects. "Consistently, the survey results revealed a large group of around 50–55% of Service members who thought that repeal of Don't Ask, Don't Tell would have mixed or no effect." Johnson and Ham disclosed "another 15–20% who said repeal would have a positive effect; and about 30% who said it would have a negative effect." The results of the survey of military spouses evidenced an even greater majority that anticipated no significant impact from repeal: "74% said repeal would have no effect, while only 12% said 'I would want my spouse to leave [the military] earlier.'" Of course, not all survey responses were positive. Nearly one-third of military service member respondents maintained that repeal would negatively impact the U.S. military. The working group reported to Secretary Gates that "around 30% overall (and 40–60% in the Marine Corps and in various combat arms specialties) . . . predicted in some form and to some degree negative views or concerns about the impact of a repeal." Johnson and Ham contended that this result demanded "caution" but still insisted that "the risk of repeal to overall military effectiveness is low."[32]

Johnson and Ham related the repeal of DADT to other historical transitions within the U.S. military that previous chapters of this book have detailed, such as racial desegregation during the 1940s and 1950s and the expansion of opportunities for women after the advent of the all-volunteer force. They concluded that in context, "The general lesson we take from these transformational experiences in history is that in matters of personnel change within the military, predictions and surveys tend to overestimate negative consequences, and underestimate the U.S. military's ability to adapt and incorporate within its ranks the diversity that is reflective of American society at large." As Johnson and Ham insisted, "Repeal would work best if it is accompanied by a message and policies that promote fair and equal treatment of all Service members, minimize differences among Service members based on sexual orientation, and disabuse Service members of any notion that, with repeal, gay and lesbian Service members will be afforded some type of special treatment."[33]

Among many debates, two specific areas of concern arose regarding the potential repeal of "Don't Ask, Don't Tell." The first involved standards of conduct. Johnson and Ham determined, "Many of these concerns were about conduct that is already regulated in the military environment, regardless of the sexual orientation of the persons involved, or whether it involves persons of the same sex or the opposite sex." The working group recommended an egalitarian approach that emphasized equality as the best policy. As the committee contended, "Concerns for standards in the event of repeal can be adequately addressed through training and education about how already existing standards of conduct continue to apply to *all* Service members, regardless of sexual orientation, in a post-repeal environment." The second area of concern involved moral and religious trepidations. Johnson and Ham reported, "In the course of our review, we heard a large number of Service members raise religious and moral objections to homosexuality or to serving alongside someone who is gay. Some feared repeal of Don't Ask, Don't Tell might limit their individual freedom of expression and free exercise of religion, or require them to change their personal beliefs about the morality of homosexuality. The views expressed to us in these terms cannot be downplayed or dismissed." Johnson and Ham, however, concluded, "The reality is that in today's U.S. military, people of sharply different moral values and religious convictions . . . and those who have no religious convictions at all, already co-exist, work, live, and fight together on a daily basis." Therefore, as their report stated, "Service members will not be required to change their personal views and religious beliefs; they must, however, continue to respect and serve with others who hold different views and beliefs." Johnson and Ham conveyed, "We are both convinced that our military can do this, even during this time of war. We do not underestimate the challenges in implementing a change in the law, but neither should we underestimate the ability of our extraordinarily dedicated Service men and women to adapt to such change and continue to provide our Nation with the military capability to accomplish any mission."[34]

On 27 May 2010 the U.S. House of Representatives voted on H.R. 5136, the National Defense Authorization Act for Fiscal Year 2011 as amended to repeal DADT. After contentious debate, 230 representatives voted for repeal, 195 voted against it, and 8 representatives did not vote. The measure then proceeded to the U.S. Senate. On 18 December 2010 the U.S. Senate voted; 63 senators voted in favor of repeal, easily carrying the measure forward.[35] Much had changed, both in the U.S. military and in American society, in the nearly two decades since DADT had emerged as the pivotal debate of its era regarding military service. Most important, public opinion had shifted decidedly toward open service. As Beth Bailey has shown, "While only 44 percent of Americans had believed that gay men and lesbians should be able to serve openly in the U.S. military in 1993, 77 percent did so in 2010."[36]

At 9:10 a.m. on the morning of 22 December 2010, President Obama addressed an expectant crowd gathered at the Department of the Interior building in Washington, D.C. He was there to sign Public Law No. 111-321, which repealed the previous military personnel policy of "Don't Ask, Don't Tell." Before signing the law, the president remarked on the moment's significance. He told the poignant story of two friends, Lloyd Corwin and Andy Lee, who served together with the 80th Division of Patton's Third Army during the Battle of the Bulge in World War II. Taking enemy gunfire and at great risk to his own life, Lee saved Corwin after the young army private fell down a ravine where enemy fire pinned him in place. As President Obama relayed, "For the rest of his years, Lloyd credited this soldier, this friend, named Andy Lee, with saving his life, knowing he would never have made it out alone." Obama continued, "It was a full four decades after the war, when the two friends reunited in their golden years, that Lloyd learned that the man who saved his life, his friend Andy, was gay. He had no idea, and he didn't much care. Lloyd knew what mattered. He knew what had kept him alive; what made it possible for him to come home and start a family and live the rest of his life. It was his friend." Throughout his remarks, President Obama connected the repeal of "Don't Ask, Don't Tell" to previous changes in military personnel policy. He confirmed, "Because of these efforts, in the coming days we will begin the process laid out by this law. Now, the old policy remains in effect until Secretary Gates, Admiral Mullen, and I certify the military's readiness to implement the repeal. And it's especially important for servicemembers to remember that. But I have spoken to every one of the service chiefs, and they are all committed to implementing this change swiftly and efficiently. We are not going to be dragging our feet to get this done." President Obama concluded his remarks by affirming, "We are a nation that welcomes the service of every patriot. We are a nation that believes that all men and women are created equal. Those are the ideals that generations have fought for. Those are the ideals that we uphold today."[37] With that, he signed the law that repealed "Don't Ask, Don't Tell."

As Obama noted in his remarks on 22 December 2010, repeal required that military leaders certify that the new policy did not imperil national security or military efficiency. As legal analyst for the Congressional Research Service Jody Feder recorded, "Under the Don't Ask, Don't Tell Repeal Act of 2010, DADT repeal became effective 60 days after the President, the Secretary of Defense, and the Chairman of the Joint Chiefs of Staff certified that they considered the recommendations contained in a Department of Defense (DOD) report on the effect of repeal; that DOD prepared the necessary policies and regulations to implement the new law; and that the implementation of such policies and regulations 'is consistent with the standards of military readiness, military effectiveness, unit cohesion, and recruiting and retention of the Armed Forces.'" When Congress voted and President Obama signed the repeal of DADT, they initiated a review; ultimately, military leaders had to certify that the repeal did not conflict with national security and military readiness. On 22 July 2011, President Obama, Secretary of Defense Leon Panetta, and Joint Chiefs of Staff chair Admiral Michael Mullen certified that repeal of the DADT policy "is consistent with the standards of military readiness, military effectiveness, unit cohesion, and recruiting and retention of the Armed Forces."[38] As a result, repeal officially took effect on 20 September 2011, and open service became a reality.

Many observers characterized the transition from silent service to open service as a success. The Congressional Research Service concluded, "In general, DADT repeal appears to have proceeded smoothly."[39] Others agreed. Beginning six months after repeal, a diverse group of eminent scholars conducted a rigorous half-year investigation into "the impact of DADT repeal on military readiness." They performed extensive research utilizing interviews, survey analysis, fieldwork, pretests, posttests, and media analysis. Most important, the group "made a particularly vigorous effort to solicit the views of opponents of DADT repeal by seeking input from 553 anti-repeal retired generals and admirals and 22 well-known activist and expert opponents of repeal, as well as senior staff members from 9 anti-repeal and veterans service organizations." In the end, "based on all of the evidence available to us," the group determined "that DADT repeal has had no overall negative impact on military readiness or its component dimensions, including cohesion, recruitment, retention, assaults, harassment, or morale." The group went further, however, and declared, "If anything, DADT repeal appears to have enhanced the military's ability to pursue its mission."[40]

The 1990s witnessed many debates regarding U.S. military service. The Persian Gulf War reintroduced concerns regarding the representativeness of the all-volunteer force, although detailed investigations concluded that it was a success. Concerns regarding race resurfaced, and the expanded role of women in military service appeared in heightened terms. After the war, debates regarding military service shifted to the issue of sexual orientation when presidential candidate William Clinton pronounced his intent to lift the long-standing ban on open service. Amid fierce criticism from military leaders, President Clinton compromised and endorsed DADT. Congressional hearings highlighted the issue for the American public but also brought into sharp relief the ambiguity of the new policy. After DADT's introduction in 1993, high-publicity cases of homosexual service members multiplied and led to an extensive Pentagon review of the policy in 1998. A decade later, President Obama reignited the issue, countered critics, and spurred Congress to action. In 2010 Congress voted to repeal DADT. By the end of that year, Obama signed the repeal into law. Certification followed and made silent service open. In the shadows, though, a new and troubling development lurked. The wars in Iraq and Afghanistan dramatically increased military personnel requirements.

With a smaller and completely voluntary military, the demand for additional service members created an uneasy relationship that replaced sole reliance on American service members with the convenient, but highly problematic, dependence on private security contractors, often third-party nationals, to augment U.S. military service.

CHAPTER NINE

AN UNEASY RELATIONSHIP

Iraqis do not know them as Blackwater or other PSCs
but only as Americans.[1]—Iraqi Interior Ministry official,
20 September 2007

There were 18,971 private security contractor personnel
in Afghanistan. This represents the highest recorded
number of private security contractor personnel used
by DOD in any conflict in the history of the United
States.[2]—Congressional Research Service, 13 May 2011

At the same time that debates regarding American
military service focused on repeal of "Don't Ask, Don't Tell," a new incar-
nation of an old phenomenon emerged from the shadows. Reliance on
private military contractors significantly increased, while the utilization
of private security contractors presented novel dilemmas. The terrorist
attacks of 11 September 2001 provoked U.S. involvement in Operations
Iraqi Freedom and Enduring Freedom in Afghanistan, and U.S. policy
makers embroiled the nation in two simultaneous foreign wars. Secretary
of Defense Donald Rumsfeld's vision of defense transformation emphasized technology and eschewed large numbers of personnel. As a result,
he sought to minimize the number of American service members mobilized for both wars. Over time, this initial context resulted in a greatly
enhanced reliance on military contractors generally and private security
contractors specifically to offset the lack of sufficient numbers of American service members. More than half of all personnel involved in the
two wars were contractors, and private security contractors consistently
numbered in the tens of thousands in each country. It is important to put
the extraordinary presence of private security contractors in perspective.
At their peak during June 2012 in Afghanistan, there were 28,686 private
security contractors. This total equated to the personnel of approximately
six additional brigade combat teams and was roughly 50 percent more
personnel than U.S. military leaders added to force totals during the surge

in Iraq. As a result, contractors suffered significant casualties and pre-sented exorbitant costs. The private security contractor company Blackwa-ter epitomized this metamorphosis, both with its pivotal role in sparking the heated battle for Fallujah in Iraq and for its notorious involvement three years later in a deadly mass shooting in Bagdad's Nisour Square that left seventeen Iraqis dead, the vast majority of whom an FBI investi-gation later determined were innocent civilians. Though Operations Iraqi Freedom and Enduring Freedom in Afghanistan evidenced unique differ-ences regarding military contractors, they both demonstrated the palpable and problematic drift toward acceptance of private security contractors as one counterweight for the dearth of American service members relative to U.S. commitments. Problems with this uneasy relationship abound. It lessens public debates regarding waging war because it masks the overall costs of doing so in lives and money. In addition, it often works against American strategic interests, because the U.S. government has far less control than is the case with service members. Finally, the recent trend in the industry away from American employees toward international ones as a cost-saving measure only exacerbates these dilemmas. In the end, the uneasy relationship between military service and private security contrac-tors has become the major contemporary challenge to military personnel policy and contributes a unique critique of the all-volunteer force to the many other prescient ones that have been raised.

One of the more troubling recent developments of the AVF has been the increasing use of private military contractors to fill roles traditionally reserved for military service members.[3] Of course, the military has used private contractors throughout American history. As counterinsurgency scholar Thomas X. Hammes demonstrated, "The presence of contractors on the battlefield is obviously not a new phenomenon but has dramatically increased from the ratio of 1 contractor to 55 military personnel in Vietnam to 1:1 in Iraq and 1.43:1 in Afghanistan."[4] Other observers agree. At the nadir of the Iraq War in 2004, *Atlantic* writer Matthew Quirk observed that private military contractors in Operation Iraqi Freedom represented a force that was "ten times as many per military soldier as served in the 1991 Gulf War."[5] In addition to an order of magnitude increase in the number of private military contractors relative to service members, the roles con-tractors filled became more varied. The recent drift is unique, however, in how private security contractors participated in Operations Iraqi Freedom and Enduring Freedom in Afghanistan. In these recent conflicts, private security contractors regularly filled combat roles—a departure from previous practices. Moshe Schwartz of the Congressional Research Service reported, "The United States is relying heavily, apparently for the first time during combat or stability operations, on private firms to supply a wide variety of security services," and therefore these two conflicts presaged "new challenges" regarding private security contractors.[6]

As both the deployment of and involvement by private security contractors enlarged, ominous incidents resulted that sparked debates regarding a plethora of military, ethical, and legal implications of such a phenomenon. On 31 March 2004, Iraqi insurgents killed four private security contractors working for Blackwater Security Consulting in a brutal ambush, and a local mob subsequently displayed their charred bodies on a bridge overlooking the Euphrates River. This gruesome event sparked the heated First Battle of Fallujah, also known as Operation Vigilant Resolve, led by Marines from 4 April to 1 May 2004.[7] As a result, it clearly foreshadowed the increasingly intimate linkages between private security contractors and U.S. military service. *New York Times* correspondent Jeffrey Gettleman echoed the outrage felt by many Americans when he characterized the attack as "one of the most brutal outbursts of anti-American rage since the war in Iraq began." Most commentators, nevertheless, initially made few distinctions between these private security contractors and American military service members.[8] In fact, reports directly compared the grisly incident in Fallujah to the irreverent display of the body of an American service member in Mogadishu, Somalia, more than a decade earlier.[9] As time went on, though, observers grew ever more critical of the deployment of private security contractors to augment force levels and raised numerous questions regarding their expanded usage. On 16 September 2007, Blackwater personnel unleashed a torrent of firepower in Baghdad's Nisour Square and killed seventeen Iraqis. The deadly event spurred intense investigations in both Baghdad and Washington.[10] As a result, the issue of private security contractors garnered significant attention in Congress, with multiple hearings dedicated specifically to it.[11]

It is important to distinguish between private military contractors and ones tasked with security. The former are far more common and fill support roles for American service members. Examples included logistics, information technology, linguistics, and maintenance, among many others. Private military contractors have a more established historical context and do not routinely employ deadly force; therefore, they are far less problematic. Private security contractors, in comparison, are a relatively new manifestation related to U.S. military service.[12] In Iraq and Afghanistan they progressively filled such roles as armed convoy security, armed installation security, and training of local security forces, which American service members had traditionally accomplished in previous conflicts.[13] Even though the broader category of private military contractors is not new, the prevalence of them in both Iraq and Afghanistan was staggering. Deborah Avant and Renée de Nevers estimated, "More than one-half of the personnel the United States has deployed in Iraq and Afghanistan since 2003 have been contractors," representing approximately 50 percent of U.S. forces in Iraq by 2008 and as much as 62 percent of U.S. forces in Afghanistan by 2009.[14] Hammes added, "At the height of the surge in April 2008, DOD stated it had 163,900 contractors supporting 160,000 troops in Iraq," and roughly two years later the ratio was 207,000 contractors to 175,000 American service members, equating to approximately 50 percent of total U.S. personnel in Iraq and 59 percent in Afghanistan.[15]

Because contractors outnumbered U.S. military service members in both war zones, it was not surprising that they also suffered significant casualties. Hammes documented, "By the end of 2009, contractors reported almost 1,800 dead and 40,000 wounded in Iraq and Afghanistan."[16] In addition to suffering large numbers of casualties, military contractors were very expensive. Between fiscal year 2007 and 2013, the total cost of contractors in Iraq and Afghanistan hovered above $25 billion per year; it peaked at $32,684,200,570 in fiscal year 2008.[17]

The historic increase in the overall use of private military contractors in war zones demonstrates one important development, but the enlarged deployment of private security contractors is far more challenging. Although the first noticeable occurrences of this trend occurred during the Balkans, the usage of private security contractors rose significantly during Operation Iraqi Freedom. The Department of Defense did not report the number of private security contractors in Central Command prior to December 2007; therefore, estimates before that time remain hazy at best. Even so, from December 2007 to December 2011 the number of private security contractors eclipsed 10,000 every month and peaked at 15,279 in June 2009.[18] In Iraq the vast majority of these private security contractors were third-country nationals. In March 2011 there were 9,207 private security personnel in Iraq. Of these, 7,727 (84 percent) were third-country nationals, 917 (10 percent) were Americans, and 563 (6 percent) were Iraqis. Therefore, vast numbers of third-country nationals represented U.S. strategic interests in Iraq in lieu of American service members. Understandably, local Iraqis held the United States responsible for everything that these private security contractors did or failed to do. In addition, private security contractors there suffered casualties in higher proportion than American service members. "Adjusting for the difference in the number of PSC personnel compared to troops, a PSC employee working for DOD in Iraq was 1.2 times more likely to be killed in action than uniformed personnel," reported the Congressional Research Service.[19]

In Afghanistan, the same general trend of employment of private security contractors to augment force levels revealed subtle differences. "From December 2008 to March 2011, the number of U.S. troops and DOD contractor personnel in Afghanistan increased," revealed one government report. "However, the number of security contractors increased at a much faster rate (414%) than total contractors (26%) or troop levels (207%). As of March 2011, security contractor personnel made up 21% of all DOD contractors and was equal to 19% of the size of total U.S. troop presence in Afghanistan." As more and more private security contractors deployed to Afghanistan, they established a new apex for the number of private security contractors used in American history: "According to DOD, as of March 2011, there were 18,971 private security contractor personnel in Afghanistan. This represents the highest recorded number of private security contractor personnel used by DOD in any conflict in the history of the United States." Even more troubling, "Local nationals made up 95% of all security personnel."[20] As the Obama administration sought to limit the number of American service members deployed to Afghanistan, the number of private security contractors there skyrocketed, peaking at 28,686 in June 2012.[21] As of March 2013 there were still approximately 18,000 private security contractors in Afghanistan.[22] As in Iraq, they suffered significant numbers of casualties. The Congressional Research Service testified, "According to DOD, from June 2009 to November 2010, 319 private security contractor personnel working for DOD have been killed in action in Afghanistan, compared to 626 U.S. troops killed in action over the same period. Adjusting for the difference in the number of PSC [private security contractor] personnel compared to troops, a PSC employee working for DOD in Afghanistan is 2.75 times more likely to be killed in action than uniformed personnel,"[23] more than double the comparable rate in Iraq.

The historic increase in the number of private military contractors involved in Operations Iraqi Freedom and Enduring Freedom in Afghanistan—especially the striking rise in the deployment of private security contractors to both war zones—highlighted significant problems relative to military personnel policy. As Hammes observed, "Contractors reduce the political capital necessary to commit U.S. forces to war, impact the legitimacy of a counterinsurgency effort, and reduce its perceived morality. These factors attack our nation's critical vulnerability in an irregular war—the political will of the American people."[24] There are also military implications. Ryan Kelty conducted a detailed study of the relationship between contractors and National Guard personnel, especially its influence on unit cohesion and retention. His results were stunning. "The findings in this study indicate that both social comparisons with contractors and general attitudes toward contractors have negative impacts on retention attitudes. The data also show that the relative deprivation motivated by comparisons with contractors has detrimental effects on perceptions of unit cohesion," Kelty observed. "Taken together, this is powerful evidence that military and civilian leaders need to seek a better understanding of the unintended consequences of the current trend towards integrating civilian contractors with military units."[25]

One deadly example demonstrated the dangers of employing large numbers of private security contractors to lessen reliance on American service members. On 16 September 2007 private security contractors working for Blackwater responded to the detonation of a bomb in Baghdad's Nisour Square. A firefight, chaos, and death ensued; the private security contractors fired machine guns and grenade launchers from armored vehicles and helicopters into surrounding cars, many of them stuck in snarled traffic with no means of escape. When the gunfire ceased and the smoke cleared, seventeen Iraqis lie dead in the street and twenty-four others suffered serious wounds.[26] Other infamous incidents of misconduct occurred in Afghanistan, most notably in the Maiwand district from 2006 to 2009. Not surprisingly, such events engendered significant criticism from local populations and damaged U.S. strategic interests throughout the region.[27]

These incidents and others like them spurred increased concern among civilian leaders regarding the heightened reliance on private security contractors during the past two conflicts. The Fiscal Year 2008 National Defense Authorization Act "required the Secretary of Defense, in coordination with the Secretary of State, to prescribe regulations and guidance relating to screening, equipping, and managing private security personnel in areas of combat operations." The following year, the Fiscal Year 2009 National Defense Authorization Act included a "provision that private security contractors should not perform inherently government functions, such as security protection of resources in high-threat oper-ational environments."[28] In January 2009, Secretary of Defense Robert M. Gates revealed that the increased use of private security contractors was neither a well-conceived nor a purposeful military personnel policy, but rather an improvised process that occurred without sufficient civilian oversight: "We have not thought holistically or coherently about our use of contractors, particularly when it comes to combat environments or com-bat training."[29]

As a result of heightened angst and intensified scrutiny from civilian policy makers, the Pentagon increased oversight and issued policy guid-ance regarding private security contractors. In July 2009, Under Secretary of Defense Ashton B. Carter clarified policy on private security contractors through guidance entitled *Private Security Contractors (PSCs) Operating in Contingency Operations*. In it, Carter grappled with complicated issues surrounding private security contractors and reinforced Department of Defense oversight of them.[30] To ensure effective control, Congress estab-lished the Commission on Wartime Contracting in Iraq and Afghanistan, an independent and bipartisan effort to consider the many problems asso-ciated with recent occurrences in this arena.[31] The commission issued its final report to Congress in August 2011. The report distilled several years of intense research into wartime contracting and made numerous rec-ommendations regarding private security contractors. "The use of private security companies can present especially sensitive risks, because their armed employees can become involved in incidents that injure or endan-ger innocent civilians," the report noted. The commission also observed that other significant problems existed. In Afghanistan the use of private security contractors for convoy security "invites pay-for-protection extor-tion that diverts taxpayers' funds to local warlords and insurgents." As a result, the commission recommended that the U.S. government "phase out use of private security contractors for certain functions."[32] Increased concern in Congress over the enlarged role of private security contractors prompted additional investigations. On 17 May 2013, the Congressional Research Service reported on the "Department of Defense's Use of Con-tractors to Support Military Operations" and documented a significant tendency. It concluded: "Over the last decade in Iraq and Afghanistan, and before that, in the Balkans, contractors accounted for 50% or more of the total military force." It also cautioned, "DOD's extensive use of con-tractors poses several potential policy and oversight issues for Congress and has been the focus of numerous hearings."[33]

In part, the increased use of private security contractors derives from a shortage of military personnel relative to U.S. commitments. Ryan Kelty observed: "However, as the number of missions and the frequency of deployments have continued to rise in the wake of the Cold War's end, increasing numbers of civilian contractors have been hired to compensate for the reduction in military personnel," something Kelty characterized as mostly "a reactive and ad hoc process."[34] After thoroughly discussing many problems resulting from increased use of private security contractors, Hammes observed that in Afghanistan "the shortage of ISAF [International Security Assistance Force] troops and sheer difficulty of maintaining security . . . mean that there is currently no feasible alternative" to private security contractors.[35] U.S. Army Colonel Scott L. Efflandt detected, "In Iraq and Afghanistan, the numbers of such personnel did not count against 'force caps' or troop strength limitations, and thus minimized the public exposure as to the level of U.S. involvement."[36] David Isenberg at the International Peace Research Institute in Oslo, Norway, maintained, "Private contractors fill the gap between geopolitical goals and public means. The low visibility and presumed low cost of private contractors appeals to those who favor a global U.S. military presence, but fear that such a strategy cannot command public support."[37] Such problematic developments know no political boundaries. The Clinton administration experimented with private security contractors in the Balkans, the Bush administration greatly expanded their use in Iraq, and the Obama administration continued using contractors unabated in Afghanistan. After Blackwater president Erik Prince sold his company in 2010, the company changed its name to Academi. The Obama administration subsequently awarded the group approximately $220 million in private security contracts.[38]

While the most prominent private security contractor firm has receded in influence, other companies providing private security contractors have proliferated, including DynCorp International and Triple Canopy. Their nature continues to evolve as well. In 2013, *The Economist* observed that an increasing number of these companies were foreign-owned and more often utilized local personnel.[39] On 22 October 2014 a federal jury convicted the four Blackwater employees involved in the Nisour Square shooting. The move concluded an eleven-week trial that illuminated in sharp relief many of the problems with heightened use of private security contractors.[40] The following year, on 14 April 2015, a federal judge in Washington, D.C., handed down sentences; three received 30 years in prison and one received life in prison. Of the seventeen Iraqis killed that September day in 2007, fourteen of the deaths "were unjustified and violated deadly-force rules for contractors," according to a lengthy FBI investigation. The *New York Times* emphasized the significance of the shooting: "It also high-lighted the heavy reliance of the United States government on security contractors, whom many Iraqis had come to loathe as cowboys operating outside the bounds of the law."[41] Private security contractor companies took notice: "Industry officials say that one of the consequences of the 2007 shooting has been to impose more rigorous controls on contrac-tors handling diplomatic security for the State Department, as Blackwater was doing when its security guards fired into Baghdad's crowded Nisour Square, killing unarmed Iraqis, enraging the country."[42]

Human rights groups also took notice. Amnesty International issued a dire warning regarding the use of private military contractors: "As the United States engages in the 'war on terror,' it is outsourcing key secu-rity and military support functions, particularly in Iraq and Afghanistan, to private companies to carry out the work. The number of contractors now exceeds the number of military personnel." The human rights group further explained, "The work that is contracted out to companies ranges from logistical support to security for U.S. government personnel and reconstruction projects, to training military and security personnel, to operating and maintaining weapons systems. But the contracted compa-nies have also served in more sensitive roles, such as interrogation and translating during questioning of alleged terrorist suspects."[43] Amnesty International pleaded for U.S. policy makers to reassert control over what appeared to be a chaotic and potentially explosive arena.

If anything, the trend is expanding. Former officer and paratrooper in the U.S. Army's 82nd Airborne Division and DynCorp International private security contractor Sean McFate perceived, "America turned to the private sector for personnel that its all-volunteer military could not mus-ter. In Iraq half of the personnel in war zones were contracted, and in Afghanistan it was closer to 70 percent. America may fight future wars mainly with contractors." In addition to having a large presence to aug-ment U.S. military personnel, private security contractors have prolifer-ated worldwide. McFate continued, "Now others are following America's lead. Nigeria hired hundreds of mercenaries to fight Boko Haram. Russia is allegedly using them in Ukraine. And oil companies and humanitarian organizations are turning to private military companies to protect their workers and property in dangerous places, and there is an argument that the United Nations should use this industry to augment thinning peace-keeping missions."[44] As a result, the negative implications of this uneasy relationship have multiplied.

Scott L. Efflandt has argued that "private security companies are contesting the U.S. military's preeminence" because as they "become alternative agents to apply lethal force for the state[,] a competitive situation emerges." Previously, competition existed between U.S. military services, between U.S. government agencies, or between U.S. military forces and other nations' military forces. Now, however, "a fourth competitive relationship emerged where private companies began to compete with the military for jurisdiction over its core task—the employment of lethal force."[45]

Overall, private security contractors have essentially reversed the dynamic that we have seen in previous debates regarding U.S. military service. Before, offsets for the lack of necessary personnel spurred civilian policy makers to bring previously excluded groups into military service. Now, a lack of civilian oversight has turned the dynamic on its head. Private security contractors have themselves become a counterweight for the dearth of necessary service members relative to the nation's ambitious strategic designs, often quietly used when and where convenient. As a result, private security contractors have served to sever the vital connection between citizenship and military service. Civilian policy makers now have the expedient ability to avoid either clearly articulating the justification for additional service members or paring down international commitments to correlate to existing force levels. In addition, military leaders have become far too comfortable with the use of private security contractors, similar to the way that they became at ease with its antonym from an earlier era, the draft. The difference, of course, is the clear disconnect between military service and citizenship that the usage of private military contractors encourages. The draft had flaws all its own, but it nonetheless drew citizenship and military service closer together in a tighter bond, whereas offloading military service to private security contractors works in the opposite direction. Military leaders often euphemistically characterize private military contractors as nothing more than a surge capability. Even so, private security contractors provide a significant addition of military personnel without forcing policy makers publicly to justify their usage to the American people in the way that using increased numbers of American service members always requires. Therein lies the rub.

CHAPTER TEN

THE NATION'S CONSCIENCE

The performance of the Nation's military is tied to
the individual's belief that he or she will be treated
fairly regardless of his or her background.[1]—Military
Leadership Diversity Commission, March 2011

The U.S. military is a learning organization capable
of adapting to change and the needs of the Nation,
provided that the Nation's highest leaders are willing
both to change and to provide a clear vision of success
that is followed by the sustained oversight needed
to succeed. The Armed Forces have led the Nation
in the struggle to achieve equality. To maintain this
leadership, they must evolve once again, renewing their
commitment to providing equal opportunity for all.
The time has come to embrace the broader concept
of diversity needed to achieve military goals and to
move the Nation closer to embodying its democratic
ideals.[2]—Military Leadership Diversity Commission,
March 2011

As a result of the terrorist attacks of 9/11, the United
States engaged in Operations Iraqi Freedom and Enduring Freedom in
Afghanistan. Over the course of the first decade of the twenty-first century,
these two conflicts demonstrated that warfare has changed significantly.
As with wars before them, they also kindled debates regarding U.S. military service. The uneasy relationship that first lurked in the shadows and
then came into full view after 9/11 has fueled questions about the role of
military service in American society. As discussed in previous chapters,
warfare demands large numbers of personnel; this in turn stokes debates
regarding the very nature of military service. The wars in Iraq and Afghanistan involved approximately 200,000 troops at their height, primarily
from 2003 to 2009.[3] Of course, that number would have been drastically

higher without the use of private security contractors as an offset for the minimal numbers of American service members available. Therefore, both the massive scope of personnel involved in long-term military operations and the deployment of far more private security contractors in the first decade of the twenty-first century have placed military service back in the spotlight with the official conclusion of Operation Enduring Freedom in December 2014.[4]

In addition to the heightened involvement of private security contractors, from September 2001 to 28 February 2013 nearly 300,000 women deployed in support of Operations Iraqi Freedom and Enduring Freedom in Afghanistan. Approximately 800 of them sustained wounds, and more than 130 died.[5] When combined with Operation New Dawn, these three campaigns resulted in 161 female service members killed and 1,015 wounded as of April 2015, representing 2 percent of total casualties incurred during the three operations. To recognize the changed context, the military awarded more than 9,000 women Army Combat Action badges.[6] Both conflicts also demonstrated a shift wherein American military service members engaged primarily in counterinsurgency.[7] As a result, distinctions between combat and noncombat units became far less rigid, as improvised explosive devices, snipers, and ambushes often targeted noncombat units and personnel as well.

Partly as a result of increased numbers of women exposed to combat, Congress created the Military Leadership Diversity Commission through the Fiscal Year 2009 National Defense Authorization Act. The commission's task was straightforward: "Conduct a comprehensive evaluation and assessment of policies and practices that shape diversity among military leaders."[8] The dilemma was that the U.S. military, though largely successful in expanding opportunities for participation, still fell far short in terms of multiplying leadership positions for minorities and women. Upon beginning its work, the commission found, "Since [1948], the U.S. military force has endeavored to become an inclusive organization dedicated to the equality of all its members, regardless of their background. Its dedication to equal opportunity has resulted in increased representation of racial/ethnic minorities and women among the top military leaders in recent decades." The committee's chair, Lester L. Lyles, cautioned, "Despite undeniable successes, however, the Armed Forces have not yet succeeded in developing a continuing stream of leaders who are as diverse as the Nation they serve." Lyles warned that if left unchecked, this shortcoming would only escalate in coming years: "Marked changes in the demographic makeup of the United States will throw existing disparities into sharp relief, creating a recruiting pool that looks very different from the pool of 30–40 years ago, from which today's leaders were drawn." The commission held nationwide hearings with public citizens, service members, veterans, military leaders, and business executives. Its charter required that the group submit a final report to the president and Congress within one year of its initial meeting.[9] On 7 March 2011 the commission made available online its final report, *From Representation to Inclusion: Diversity Leadership for the 21st-Century Military*.[10] It was presented to President Obama and members of Congress the following week. Overall, Lyles concluded that there was still room for improvement in expanding opportunities in the military, especially regarding leadership: "While we find the promotion policies and practices of the Department of Defense and the Services to be fair, we find also that there are some barriers to improving demographic representation among military leaders." Lyles characterized the commission's role as "to support the U.S. military's continuing journey of becoming a preeminently inclusive institution."[11]

The commission recommended that the Department of Defense standardize its definition of diversity among the services to "inspire a common vision and elicit the needed changes." It also recommended a definition: "Diversity is all the different characteristics and attributes of individuals that are consistent with Department of Defense core values, integral to overall readiness and mission accomplishment, and reflective of the Nation we serve." Lyles found that one of the most problematic trends in U.S. military service was a less than representative senior leadership pool. He contended "that top military leaders are representative neither of the population they serve nor of the forces they lead. The extent to which racial/ethnic minorities and women are underrepresented varies across the Services, but the Commission found, on average, low racial/ethnic minority and female representation among senior military officers." The commission discovered a low proportion of racial and ethnic minorities, as well as an even lower proportion of women, in senior leadership positions throughout the military. Lyles reported that "in each Service, at least one racial/ethnic minority group was underrepresented. The review also revealed that women were underrepresented across all the Services."[12]

The commission also found evidence of "institutional barriers" that limited prospects for advancement among women. Lyles insisted, "DoD and the Services must remove institutional barriers in order to open traditionally closed doors, especially those relating to assignments—both the initial career field assignment and subsequent assignments to key positions. An important step in this direction is that DoD and the Services eliminate combat exclusion policies for women, including removing barriers and inconsistencies, to create a level playing field for all service members who meet the qualifications."[13] The commission first connected the ideal of military service to democracy and then related it directly to military personnel policy: "Among its recommendations, the commission stated that DOD should take deliberate steps to open additional career fields and units involved in direct ground combat to women. The commission's recommendations prompted Congress to direct DOD, in the Ike Skelton National Defense Act for Fiscal Year 2011 (P.L. 111-383), to conduct a review to 'ensure that female members have equitable opportunities to compete and excel in the Armed Forces.'"[14]

Sweeping changes occurred quickly. Debates revolved around contested notions of two important concepts: full participation in military service, and military readiness. *Congressional Research Service* analyst David F. Burrelli summarized the various positions for members of Congress: "Many women's right [sic] supporters contend that the former exclusionary policy, or standards that, de facto, act in an exclusionary manner, prevents women from gaining leadership positions and view expanding the roles of women as a matter of civil rights. Critics view such changes as potentially damaging to military readiness." Unconvinced by the latter argument, Secretary of Defense Robert M. Gates announced on 23 February 2010 that the navy had eliminated its restrictions on women serving aboard submarines. Within a couple years, more than two dozen women had served on submarines, all as officers. On 24 January 2013, Secretary of Defense Leon Panetta removed the prohibition against women serving in combat units that had existed since 1994, known formally as the Direct Ground Combat Definition and Assignment Rule.[15] Critics contended that such restraints were increasingly anachronistic because nearly 300,000 women were deployed to Iraq and Afghanistan, and women represented approximately 2 percent of casualties in those two war zones.[16] In June 2015 the national military strategy specifically highlighted gender integration, contending that "critical to building the best military possible are our efforts to further integrate women across the force by providing them greater opportunities for service."[17] That same month, the navy extended the submarine program to enlisted service members and chose four female chief petty officers and thirty-four female petty officers to attend Basic Enlisted Submarine School in Groton, Connecticut. Upon completion of their training they would serve aboard the USS *Michigan* (SSGN-727), an Ohio-class ballistic missile submarine.[18]

Major changes occurred in the army as well. On 18 August 2015, First Lieutenant Shaye L. Haver and Captain Kristen M. Griest successfully completed U.S. Army Ranger School, "becoming the first females to complete the grueling combat training program and earn the right to wear Ranger tabs on their uniforms." Both West Point graduates, the two female soldiers joined ninety-four male classmates who endured the intense eight-week course at Fort Benning, Georgia. Their graduation speaker, Major General Scott Miller, emphasized to the class that standards remained the same as when he had graduated from the school thirty years before: "A 5-mile run is still a 5-mile run. Standards do not change. A 12-mile march is still a 12-mile march."[19] To reinforce Miller's assessment, Army Secretary John McHugh remarked, "Each Ranger School graduate has shown the physical and mental toughness to successfully lead organizations at any level. This course has proven that every soldier, regardless of gender, can achieve his or her full potential." Echoing much of the commission's findings, McHugh also argued, "We owe soldiers the opportunity to serve successfully in any position where they are qualified and capable."[20] Shortly thereafter, Major Lisa Jaster became the first U.S. Army Reserve female to graduate from the school.[21]

In late 2015 such reverberations cracked formal barriers to women's participation in military service that had existed throughout the nation's history. On 3 December 2015, Secretary of Defense Ashton B. Carter announced that all military occupational specialties within the military would be open to women beginning in January 2016. Carter contended, "This means that as long as they qualify and meet standards, women will now be able to contribute to our mission in ways they could not before. They'll be allowed to drive tanks, fire mortars, and lead infantry soldiers in combat. They'll be able to serve as Army Rangers and Green Berets, Navy SEALS, Marine Corps infantry, Air Force parajumpers and everything else that was previously open only to men." Such a seismic shift was not without opposition. Whereas all three secretaries of the military services, commander of U.S. Special Operations Command, army chief of staff, air force chief of staff, and chief of naval operations agreed with Carter's policy, Marine Corps Commandant Joseph F. Dunford dissented and requested an exception for his service. He argued that the corps objected to Carter's proposal in certain combat specialties and protested that a wholly gender-integrated military negatively would impact combat effectiveness.

Carter countered, "While the Marine Corps asked for a partial exemption ... we're a joint force and I have decided to make a decision which applies to the entire force."[22]

Partly as a result of more than a decade of war and partly in response to the many changes in military service discussed throughout this book, many contemporary observers rightly have critiqued the all-volunteer force on a number of important grounds; eminent scholars have criticized it more and more over the past several years. They have questioned the AVF on a host of significant grounds. Andrew J. Bacevich demonstrated, "With a pronounced aversion to collective service and sacrifice (an inclination indulged by leaders of both political parties), Americans resist any definition of civic duty that threatens to crimp lifestyles." Bacevich cogently argued that the AVF has fostered military adventurism by detaching the military from American society. He concluded, "The all-volunteer force is not a blessing. It has become a blight."[23] Karl W. Eikenberry reinforced this relationship between the AVF and military adventurism. As he recorded, "Nineteen overseas military deployments occurred in the twenty-seven-year draft period versus more than 144 during the thirty-nine-year course, to date, of the AVF. This translates into an AVF-deployments-per-annum ratio five times higher than that of the draft force."[24] Other distinguished voices have joined in with criticisms all their own. David R. Segal and Lawrence J. Korb illustrated, "The replacement of the high personnel turnover of the conscription era with a smaller force of personnel who serve longer has raised questions about whether there is now a culture gap between the American military and the society it serves." In addition, the authors explored the high cost of the AVF and its impact on the sustainability of the force. At its founding, proponents argued that one main advantage of it was cost savings compared to a force comprised of large numbers of draftees. Many observers at that time questioned this proposition; contemporary defense budgets reveal that the AVF might not be the cost-saving device it was once touted as. Segal and Korb demonstrated quite the reverse: "In fiscal 2013, the government is due to spend more than $100 billion on military retirement. If corrections are not made, these costs will grow to $217 billion by 2034." The authors also illuminated the impact of the AVF on the reserves and National Guard, especially in Iraq and Afghanistan: "The American military began to rely on the reserve forces to a degree not seen since World War II, but in this case without the support of conscription."[25] Major General (retired) Dennis Laich took this critique further and showed how U.S. military leaders shifted the application of the reserves and National Guard from a strategic reserve to an operational one:

> The reserve components became a viable and ready source of manpower to meet the needs of combatant commanders in Iraq and Afghanistan. Prior to 2001, the reserve was seen as a strategic reserve that would have time to be alerted, trained, and deployed in an emergency. It was further assumed that a reservist might deploy once in an emergency. . . . The concept of the reserve components in the AVF changed as soon as the AVF itself was at risk. This new operationalization of the reserve components had profound effects on individual service members. In the decade following 9/11, approximately 240,000 members of the National Guard and 170,000 reservists have been deployed at least once.[26]

Such changes have powerful implications for military personnel policy, especially recruiting and retention. Michael Runey and Charles Allen revealed that potentially 96 percent of American youth are either unwilling to serve in the military, unqualified to do so, or both.[27] Other modern experts questioned the AVF on civil-military grounds. David M. Kennedy remarked, "The advent of the AVF also severed the link between citizenship and service. No American today is obligated to serve in the military."[28] Robert L. Goldich took this shortcoming one step further: "In the midst of a civilian society that is increasingly pacifistic, easygoing, and well adjusted, the Army (career and non-career soldiers alike) remains flinty, harshly results-oriented, and emotionally extreme. The inevitable and necessary civil-military gap has become a chasm."[29] James Wright applies these dynamics to the treatment of veterans. He argues that Americans "pay lip service to our 'sons and daughters' at war, even if the children of some 99 percent of us are safely at home." He also admits, "These current wars and American views of military service remain works in progress."[30] Indeed.

There is other evidence of growing fissures in the viability of the all-volunteer force. In fiscal year 2008 moral waivers eclipsed more than 25 percent of total enlistments, over twice the percentage from only four years earlier. The vast majority of these recruits entered the army. Such a development indicated that the military repeatedly abandoned its own established enlistment standards due to significant shortages of personnel. The military issued approximately 80,000 moral waivers from 2005 to 2008, exposing severe personnel pressures.[31] On 31 March 2015, President Obama announced that Congress had enacted sweeping changes to the military retirement system in the Fiscal Year 2016 National Defense Authorization Act, largely in response to concerns about its fiscal sustainability. Referring to a January 2015 report by the Military Compensation and Retirement Modernization Commission, he declared, "I believe the recommendations are an important step forward in protecting the long-term viability of the All-Volunteer Force."[32]

Such cogent questions raise important issues; one is whether the AVF is effective. Since the terrorist attacks of 9/11, policy makers repeatedly and extensively have utilized the U.S. military. One estimate calculated that in just the first five years after 9/11, "over 1 million active-duty personnel and 400,000 reserve personnel had been deployed." In addition, the use of reserves and the National Guard dramatically rose. After conducting wide-ranging research regarding the effectiveness of the AVF, the Congressional Budget Office determined, "Before the first Gulf War in the early 1990s, reservists spent an average of one day per year on active duty in support of exercises and operations. In the years before the terrorist attacks of September 11, 2001, that measure rose to about 14 days; since 2003, it has grown to more than 70 days per year, on average." Amid intensifying debates regarding the viability of the AVF, government officials sought to determine its effectiveness.[33]

In July 2007 the Congressional Budget Office published a comprehensive report on the subject. Such "deployments and recruiting problems" elevated "concerns among decision makers, military analysts, and other observers" about the all-volunteer force. They specifically considered three of these concerns: "That the armed forces will not have enough troops available to accomplish their missions, that military personnel and their families are experiencing significant hardships that the rest of the U.S. population is not sharing, or that less-affluent people are more likely than other groups to serve in those operations." The Congressional Budget Office also perceived that debates had strengthened enough that "some observers have called for reinstituting a military draft as a way to alleviate those strains and to spread the demands of war more evenly throughout society." The office determined that the all-volunteer force had been effective in terms of education, test scores, and experience. It reported, "The AVF has attracted a greater proportion of recruits with high school diplomas or with AFQT scores at or above the median than in the youth population as a whole or than the services obtained through the draft during the Vietnam War." The report also remarked, "Experience levels in the military have also risen during the years of the AVF, as initial enlistment periods have grown longer, on average, and retention rates have increased." The same study found that the AVF has also proven more expensive. Although cost comparisons between the draft and the AVF are difficult due to the hidden costs of the draft, such as depressed wages for both draftees and draft-motivated volunteers, research clearly showed that the AVF was far more expensive than proponents had predicted it would be: "There is evidence that budgetary costs have been higher under the AVF than under the Vietnam-era draft system." The AVF is also fairly representative of American society. Even though it drastically amplified the number of women in military service, women remain significantly underrepresented within it in terms of both overall numbers and senior leadership positions. The Congressional Budget Office declared, "The current all-volunteer force is representative of society along many dimensions—although, partly because of the unique demands of military service, it is younger than the population as a whole and has a smaller proportion of women." Demographically, women represent approximately 14 percent of the AVF but roughly 50 percent of the civilian population. African Americans represent approximately 19 percent of the AVF but only 14 percent of the civilian population. Hispanic Americans represent approximately 11 percent of the AVF and 14 percent of the civilian population.[34]

The issues discussed in the preceding chapters suggest a unique way to evaluate the all-volunteer force. That approach is to consider the many trends of U.S. military service that have led to it and to ponder the challenges that now exist within it. Some of these changes have been positive, such as greatly expanded opportunities for minorities and women. Others, such as the recent drift toward private security contractors as one offset for the lack of sufficient American service members relative to U.S. commitments, portend troubling consequences if continued or expanded. This uneasy relationship is an accelerant that fuels many of the problems identified in aforementioned critiques of the AVF. It serves to disconnect further the military from American society, to lessen further political accountability for the use of military force, and to heighten further military adventurism. Ultimately, the ideal of military service, as it has in the many previous debates considered throughout this book, can reflect the dangers of this drift so that civilian leaders will redefine military service as a bond between citizens and their nation, just as they redefined military service countless other times whenever it strayed from the values of a democracy.

Though a generation of Americans has reached adulthood with the understandable perception that military service is a fixed and static ideal, it most certainly is not. American military service has always been a shifting and mutable concept. Such questions as who served in the military and how they served have permeated recent American history. The only thing constant about these debates is that they have changed repeatedly over time. From the selective service idea to such a sound and democratic principle as universal military training, how Americans served in the military has been highly contested. In addition, who served forced consideration of race as a segregated military slowly gave way to an integrated one in which the freedom to serve was eventually accorded to all races. A growing population, the Vietnam War, and increasing inequity in the draft sparked debates concerning who serves when not all serve. First candidate and then President Nixon argued that conscription is a tax, abolished the draft, and instituted the AVF, largely for political reasons. Such a move ensured that women served in the military in numbers greater than ever before. First candidate and then President Clinton forced debates concerning military service toward sexual orientation, arguing that certain Americans should not have to serve in silence. More recently, debates regarding military service revealed an uneasy relationship, wherein policy makers outsourced military service to private security contractors with problematic implications.

The many manifestations of U.S. military service from World War II to the Iraq and Afghanistan wars demonstrate its disputed nature. Throughout those years military service served as a contested arena within which individuals, groups, and society grappled with the values of a democracy. They critiqued, pushed, pulled, reshaped, reformed, and ultimately redefined military service in ways that expanded opportunities and promoted broader inclusion. Such occurrences highlight the valuable role that military service serves within a democracy. It is, and always has been, a mirror reflecting the nation's conscience. Throughout this study, military service exposed the best and worst in American society. Such issues as compulsion, liberty, universality, race, inequity, volunteerism, gender, sexual orientation, and privatization of force all brought American values into sharp relief. Oftentimes, this reflection fell far short of the best American values. As a result of the struggle, however, military service also revealed one of the true strengths of American society: civilian control of the military. Throughout these various debates, civilian leaders prodded the military to change personnel policies that did not accurately reflect American values. In doing so, they demonstrated a profound irony. Whereas the military as a social organization is often justifiably cast as rigid, hierarchical, conservative, hidebound, and resistant to change, civilian leaders often forced it to change for the better. This is because the military as a social organization does not exist within a vacuum, beholden only to itself. Instead, the system of American civil-military relations dictates civilian control of the military. As a result, civilian leaders have time and again forced change upon the military that would not have occurred otherwise. Civilian leaders effected drastic changes to military personnel policy that the military initially protested vehemently; once implemented, these changes left little more than ripples in their wake. That was true in 1948, and it is still true today with such issues as the repeal of DADT and the inclusion of women in combat. Therefore, military service displays two enduring roles in American society: reflection of American values for better or for worse, and malleability when that persona warrants correction. When civilian leaders determine that they do not like the image that they see, they can provide a clear vision of needed reform. With perseverance and persistent oversight they can then transform it into reality.

If Americans visit any post office across the nation, chances are they will likely find tucked away in a dusty corner a Selective Service System brochure. In ominous language it warns, "Do the Right Thing: It's Quick, It's Easy, It's the Law." Many Americans probably pass by without even noticing it. Some may even use it to jot down a few notes or a grocery list on the back. Many Americans, however, would be surprised to learn that the last draftee retired in the fall of 2014 or that the Selective Service System is scheduled for consideration once again in 2016. This deliberation will likely include contentious debates regarding registration for women, especially as civilian policy makers have now lifted ground combat restrictions for females. All this brings us back to Camp Red Cloud, Korea. When Chief Warrant Officer 5 Ralph Rigby retired on 28 October 2014 as the last continuously serving draftee in U.S. military service, his distinguished career served as a timely and cogent reminder of the mutable constructs of military service since World War II and the many lively and heated debates that have surrounded them.

The reality is that many Americans today view military service as a fixed construct. They laud the military's servicemen and -women, as they should, but military service is not, and has never been, a constant. Through the past seven and one-half decades, U.S. military service can be characterized as a duality. How Americans serve in the military has been linked primarily to fundamental and perennial debates in democracy over the appropriate balance between compulsion and liberty. Selective service reigned supreme from 1940 to 1947 and again from 1948 to 1973. Its ascendancy was supported by the idea that national security often demanded compulsion. The all-volunteer force reigned supreme from 1973 onward.

In addition to illuminating *how* Americans served in the military, this book has explored the various military personnel policies that have defined *who* served in the military. In this regard, military service often served as a litmus test for American values. The constant debate and continual redefinitions of who served at times attempted either to restrict participation or expand it, depending on the historical context. Civilian leaders from outside the military or practical concerns such as personnel shortages within the military often forced changes to military personnel policy that eventually broadened inclusion. Ultimately, this dynamic resulted in expanded opportunities for Americans in military service.

The past seventy-five years of debate regarding U.S. military service also illuminate a fundamental strength of democracy regarding civil-military relations. The military is vitally a social organization. It is defined by organizational hierarchy and deference to authority. Civilian leaders often leveraged these characteristics to produce malleability and drive much-needed alterations in personnel policy. Whereas military leaders often resisted, delayed, and undercut such efforts, persistent civilian leaders ultimately forced progress. This dynamic illustrates that civilian leaders can foster change in the military, at times more directly and more quickly than in civil society.

The U.S. military has often been described as traditional, conservative, and slow to change; by itself it is this and much more. What is less obvious, however, is that the nature of American civil-military relations creates a unique dynamic regarding the military as a social organization. The very characteristics that make it seem reactionary—adherence to orders, rigid vertical hierarchy, strict regimentation, and practical concerns with military efficiency and readiness—also make it highly malleable under the control of civilian leaders. Civilian leaders have demonstrated this dynamic over time by how they influenced military personnel policy, often in advance of and contributing to broader change throughout American society. As a result, these civilian leaders have often used military service as a conduit for breaking down barriers to participation, expanding opportunities, and ensuring equality, both in the U.S. military and beyond. In this sense, military service has served its own purpose far from its obvious application on the battlefield. Perennial debates, negotiations, and redefinitions regarding who served in the military and how they served all illustrated another valuable role that military service served from World War II to the Iraq and Afghanistan wars. The U.S. military has not only defended democracy in wars abroad but also stood in defense of democracy at home, ensuring that every American willing and able to serve can.

INDIVIDUALS OF NOTE

Civil Rights Leaders

A. Philip Randolph, international president, Brotherhood of Sleeping
    Car Porters
Channing H. Tobias, director, Phelps-Stokes Foundation
Lester B. Granger, Urban League
Mary McLeod Bethune, president, National Council of Negro Women
Roy Wilkins, executive director, NAACP
Walter White, executive secretary, NAACP

Congress

Andrew J. May (D-KY), chair, House Military Affairs Committee
Chan Gurney (R-SD), chair, Senate Armed Services Committee
Clifton A. Woodrum (D-VA), House Select Committee on Postwar
    Military Policy
Dewey J. Short (R-MO), member, House Military Affairs Committee
Edwin C. Johnson (D-CO), member, Senate Military Affairs Committee
Harry L. Towe (R-NJ), sponsor of the Towe Bill
James W. Wadsworth (R-NY), House Select Committee on Postwar
    Military Policy
Leo E. Allen (R-IL), chair, House Rules Committee
Robert A. Taft (R-OH), chair, Senate Republican Policy Committee

War Manpower Commission (18 April 1942–19 September 1945)

Arthur J. Altmeyer, executive director
Paul V. McNutt, chair
William Haber, director, planning division

Selective Service Directors

14 October 1940–30 July 1941: Clarence B. Dykstra
31 July 1941–15 February 1970: Lewis B. Hershey
6 April 1970–1 May 1972: Curtis W. Tarr
2 April 1973–31 July 1977: Byron V. Pepitone

President's Advisory Commission on Universal Training (19 December 1946–29 May 1947)

Anna M. Rosenberg, War Manpower Commission
Charles E. Wilson, chief executive officer of General Electric
Daniel A. Poling, president and editor of *Christian Herald*
Edmund A. Walsh, founder of Georgetown School of Foreign Service
Harold W. Dodds, president of Princeton University
Joseph E. Davies, former ambassador to the Soviet Union
Karl T. Compton, chair; president of Massachusetts Institute of
 Technology
Samuel I. Rosenman, presidential speechwriter
Truman K. Gibson, civilian aide to the Secretary of War

President's Committee on Equality of Treatment and Opportunity in the Armed Services (26 July 1948–22 May 1950)

Alphonsus J. Donahue, president of A. J. Donahue Corporation
Charles H. Fahy, chair; former U.S. Solicitor General
Charles Luckman, president of Lever Brothers
Dwight R. G. Palmer, president of General Cable Corporation
John H. Sengstacke, publisher of *Chicago Defender*
Lester B. Granger, executive secretary of the National Urban League
William E. Stevenson, president of Oberlin College

President's Commission on an All-Volunteer Armed Force (27 March 1969–20 February 1970)

Crawford Greenewalt, Finance Committee chair of E. I. duPont de
 Nemours
Frederick Dent, president of Mayfair Mills
Milton Friedman, University of Chicago professor of economics
Stephen Herbits, Georgetown University Law Center
Thomas B. Curtis, former U.S. representative (R-MO)
Thomas S. Gates, chair; former secretary of defense

War Department

Dwight D. Eisenhower, Army Chief of Staff, 1945–1948
George C. Marshall, Army Chief of Staff, 1939–1945
Henry L. Stimson, secretary of war, 1940–1945
Howard C. Petersen, assistant secretary of war, 1945–1947

John J. McCloy, assistant secretary of war, 1941–1945
John M. Palmer, special advisor to Army Chief of Staff
Omar N. Bradley, Army Chief of Staff, 1948–1949
Robert P. Patterson, secretary of war, 1945–1947
Truman K. Gibson, civilian aide to the secretary of war, 1943–1945
Walter L. Weible, director of military training
William H. Hastie, civilian aide to the secretary of war, 1940–1943

Department of Defense (Created 1947)

James V. Forrestal, secretary of defense, 1947–1949
J. Thomas Schneider, chair, Personnel Policy Board
Stephen E. Herbits, special assistant to the assistant secretary of defense
(manpower and reserve affairs) for All-Volunteer Force Action
William K. Brehm, assistant secretary of defense (legislative affairs),
1976–1977; assistant secretary of defense (manpower and reserve
affairs), 1973–1976; assistant secretary of the army (manpower and
reserve affairs), 1968–1970

Department of the Army

Frank Pace Jr., secretary of the army, 12 April 1950–20 January 1953
Howard H. Callaway, secretary of the army, 15 May 1973–3 July 1975
Jacob L. Devers, commanding general, Army Ground Forces
John M. Devine, commanding general, UMT Experimental Unit
Kenneth C. Royall, secretary of the army, 18 September 1947–27 April
1949
Robert F. Froehlke, secretary of the army, 1 July 1971–14 May 1973
Stanley R. Resor, secretary of the army, 5 July 1965–30 June 1971

Gillem Board (4 October 1945–4 March 1946)

Aln D. Warnock, U.S. Army brigadier general
Alvan C. Gillem Jr., chair; U.S. Army lieutenant general
Lewis A. Pick, U.S. Army major general
Winslow C. Morse, U.S. Army brigadier general

CHRONOLOGY

20 June 1940	Burke-Wadsworth bill introduced in Senate by Edward R. Burke (D-NE)
21 June 1940	Burke-Wadsworth bill introduced in House by James W. Wadsworth Jr. (R-NY)
28 August 1940	Burke-Wadsworth bill passed in Senate
7 September 1940	Burke-Wadsworth bill passed in House
14 September 1940	Burke-Wadsworth bill sent to President Roosevelt
16 September 1940	President Roosevelt signed Selective Training and Service Act of 1940
16 September 1940	President Roosevelt called for the first peacetime registration for Selective Service System
14 October 1940	President Roosevelt appointed Clarence B. Dykstra director of the Selective Service System
16 October 1940	First peacetime registration for Selective Service System held
19 December 1940	President Roosevelt appointed Lewis B. Hershey deputy of the Selective Service System
21 March 1941	Clarence B. Dykstra resigned as director of the Selective Service System
1 April 1941	Dykstra's resignation became effective
26 May 1941	President Roosevelt called for the second peacetime registration for the Selective Service System
1 July 1941	Second peacetime registration for the Selective Service System held
31 July 1941	President Roosevelt appointed Lewis B. Hershey director of the Selective Service System
8 December 1941	United States declared war with Japan
11 December 1941	United States declared war with Germany and Italy
18 April 1942	Executive Order 9139 created War Manpower Commission
14 May 1942	Congress created the Women's Army Auxiliary Corps (WAAC)
30 July 1942	Congress rescinded restrictions on women serving in the Naval Reserve, and the U.S. Navy activated Women Accepted for Voluntary Emergency Service (WAVES)

5 December 1942	Executive Order 9279 terminated voluntary enlistment in the armed forces
1 July 1943	Congress authorized the Marine Corps Women's Reserve and converted the WAAC to the Women's Army Corps (WAC)
8 May 1945	Victory in Europe Day
9 May 1945	President Truman signed bill to extend the Selective Training and Service Act to 15 May 1946
15 August 1945	Victory in Japan Day
29 August 1945	Executive Order 9605 restored voluntary enlistments in the armed forces for registrants in the age group acceptable for induction
6 October 1945	President Truman signed Public Law 190, 79th Congress, to stimulate voluntary enlistment in the army and navy through immediate and deferred monetary and other benefits
27 April 1946	War Department issued Circular 124, "Utilization of Negro Manpower in the Postwar Army Policy"
31 March 1947	Selective Service Act expired
26 July 1947	President Truman signed the National Security Act of 1947
26 April 1948	James V. Forrestal held National Defense Conference on Negro Affairs
12 June 1948	President Truman signed the Women's Armed Services Integration Act
24 June 1948	Selective service resumed
26 July 1948	President Truman issued Executive Order 9981 "Establishing the President's Committee on Equality of Treatment and Opportunity in the Armed Services"
29 July 1948	President Truman clarified in press conference that his intent with Executive Order 9981 was to end segregation in the armed forces
18 September 1948	President Truman designated members of the Fahy Committee
12 January 1949	President Truman held first meeting with four service secretaries and Fahy Committee
6 April 1949	Secretary of Defense Louis A. Johnson issued antidiscrimination directive

1 May 1949	Secretary Johnson ordered military services to submit their programs for implementation of Executive Order 9981 to the Personnel Policy Board, Office of Secretary of Defense
11 May 1949	Secretary Johnson approved air force program for implementation of Executive Order 9981
7 June 1949	Secretary Johnson approved navy program for implementation of Executive Order 9981
30 September 1949	Secretary Johnson approved army program for implementation of Executive Order 9981
16 January 1950	Army issued policy statement on Special Regulations Number 600-629-1, "Utilization of Negro Manpower in the Army"
22 May 1950	The President's Committee on Equality of Treatment and Opportunity in the Armed Services presented its final report, *Freedom to Serve*, to President Truman
25 June 1950	North Korean forces invaded South Korea, triggering the Korean War
19 June 1951	President Truman signed the Universal Military Training and Service bill
1955	Congress renewed the draft
1959	Congress renewed the draft
1963	Congress renewed the draft
1 July 1967	Congress changed the Universal Military Training and Service Act to the Military Selective Service Act of 1967
8 November 1967	Congress repealed restrictions on the percentage of women in American military service
17 October 1968	Richard M. Nixon's radio address announced his intention to end the draft and transition the military to an all-volunteer force
27 March 1969	The White House issued a press release on the Gates Commission
10 April 1969	Secretary of Defense Melvin R. Laird established Project Volunteer
15 May 1969	Gates Commission held its first meeting
7 October 1975	President Gerald R. Ford signed Public Law 94-106 allowing the admission of women to the military service academies

25 October 1983	Operation Urgent Fury commenced and included the deployment of four female service members assigned to military police duty after the invasion
2 November 1983	XVIII Airborne Corps Commanding General Jack Mackmull intervened and ensured that women participated in the operation
29 January 1993	President Clinton announced an interim compromise to remove questions regarding sexual orientation from enlistment forms
29 March– 22 July 1993	Congress held hearings on "Don't Ask, Don't Tell" (DADT) policy
19 July 1993	President Clinton announced DADT policy
30 November 1993	Congress made DADT law by means of the Fiscal Year 1994 National Defense Authorization Act
11 September 2001	Terrorist attacks of 9/11
31 March 2004	Iraqi insurgents killed four private security contractors working for Blackwater Security Consulting
16 September 2007	Blackwater private security contractors engaged in firefight in Baghdad's Nisour Square
23 February 2010	Secretary of Defense Robert M. Gates announced that the navy had eliminated restrictions on women serving aboard submarines
22 July 2011	President Obama, Secretary of Defense Leon Panetta, and chair of the Joint Chiefs of Staff Admiral Michael Mullen certified the repeal of DADT
20 September 2011	DADT repeal became effective
24 January 2013	Secretary of Defense Leon Panetta removed restrictions on women serving in combat
June 2015	Navy extended the submarine program to allow enlisted female sailors to participate
21 August 2015	First Lieutenant Shaye L. Haver and Captain Kristen M. Griest became the first female soldiers to graduate from U.S. Army Ranger School
16 October 2015	Major Lisa Jaster became the first U.S. Army Reserve female to graduate from the school
3 December 2015	Secretary of Defense Ashton B. Carter opened all military occupational specialties to women

The National Archives and Records Administration, located in College Park, Maryland, houses the majority of military records from the twentieth century. Record Group 147 provided exhaustive details into the operation of the Selective Service System. Especially useful were the Selective Service System Director annual reports, which contained meticulous particulars regarding World War II and military personnel policy. Within Record Group 147, Protest File, 1940–1942 and "Fan Mail," May 1943–December 1944 were remarkably informative. The Protest File includes letters and telegrams debating age limits of the draft and the "work or fight" order issued on 9 June 1941. "Fan Mail" contains letters illuminating perceived inequities of the draft during World War II and elaborating on individual Americans' views on how to eliminate them. Taken together, they offered insights into reactions to and public debates about the draft during World War II. Record Group 211 outlined the workings of the War Manpower Commission and highlighted the close relationship between military personnel policy and civilian efforts to resolve personnel challenges of both war and non-war industry. Record Group 330 revealed disputes over military personnel policy at the level of the office of the Secretary of Defense, including understandings into DACOWITS, the Universal Military Training and Service Act of 1951, the National Security Training Committee, and Anna M. Rosenberg's role as assistant secretary of defense (manpower and personnel). Record Group 220, Records of Temporary Committees, Commissions, and Boards, Presidential Commission on the Assignment of Women in the Armed Forces, lent comprehension of heated debates over military personnel policies regarding women during the 1990s, including the impact of the Tailhook scandal, the repeal of the combat exclusion for warships, and the continuation of the direct combat exclusion for combat aircraft and ground combat.

The Dwight D. Eisenhower Library, located in Abilene, Kansas, houses the records of the Eisenhower administration as well as other pertinent collections. The Dwight E. Eisenhower papers proved expressly valuable. The Pre-Presidential papers illuminated the nuanced differences between George C. Marshall's preference for universal military training and Eisenhower's penchant for universal military service. The J. Lawton Collins papers explained early efforts at military desegregation, especially how the Korean War influenced military personnel policy. The Courtney H. Hodges papers articulated the rationale for UMT, as well as the broad support that the plan held among such policy makers as Henry L. Stimson, James V. Forrestal, George C. Marshall, and John M. Palmer, among many others.

The U.S. Army Military History Institute, located in Carlisle, Pennsylvania, houses the records of the U.S. Army, veteran surveys, and the original War Department Library. The All Volunteer Army Collection clarified the trials of and responses to the army's transition to the AVF in the late 1960s and early 1970s. The Alvan C. Gillem Jr. papers revealed Gillem's vital role in the desegregation of the army, both with the board that bore his name and its resultant work, which would become the foundation for the later Fahy Committee created by President Truman's Executive Order 9981.

The U.S. Air Force Historical Research Agency houses the records of the U.S. Air Force. Principally beneficial for this book were U.S. Air Force oral history interviews, including those with James C. Evans that revealed his important role in the campaign for expanded opportunity for African Americans in military service and the impact of Project Clear on military desegregation. U.S. Air Force Recruiting Service records shed much light on Project 100,000 and its purported connections between military service and civil society. Also useful were records of the Directorate, Women in the Air Force (WAF), which contextualized women's military service in the air force both before and after the advent of the AVF, including the significant increase in women's opportunities and participation. Examples included efforts to make pilot training, service academy admission, and an increased number of ROTC scholarships available to women. Records pertaining to Representative Les Aspin (D-WI), especially *Defense for a New Era: Lessons of the Persian Gulf War*, illustrated military personnel policy challenges during that war. Records there also demonstrated the vital roles that Jeanne M. Holm and DACOWITS played in broadening prospects for women in military service, especially in the air force.

The Gerald R. Ford Library houses the records of the Ford administration. Especially helpful were sources explaining many of the debates and policies accompanying the conversion to the all-volunteer force. Most important for this book were the Melvin R. Laird papers. This collection contributed ample material on the AVF, including surveys, policy documents, memoranda, and speeches. It also contains a chronological listing of documents related to the AVF that proved particularly informative. The

Arthur F. Burns papers comprised detailed minutes of the Gates Commission meetings and many of President Nixon's policies to reform the draft. The Gerald R. Ford Vice Presidential papers offered useful material on national defense and the military draft in general. The Patricia Lindh and Jeanne Holm files illuminated the important role of DACOWITS, especially during the 1970s. The America since Hoover Collection explored the role of African Americans in military service, especially during and after World War II. The Martin R. Hoffman papers demonstrated the influence of the Armed Forces Policy Council during the 1970s and recounted the heated debates regarding the AVF during the late 1970s. It also highlighted unique aspects of debates, such as apprehension about the possible unionization of the armed forces.

The Richard M. Nixon Library houses the records of the Nixon administration. It provided valuable understandings of the switch from the draft to the AVF. Especially worthwhile were the White House Central Files, Subject Files, which detail the Nixon administration's policies on a wide range of issues, including the Department of Defense, Department of the Army, Department of the Navy, Department of the Air Force, National Defense, Selective Service System, Defense Manpower Commission, and Commission on an All-Volunteer Armed Force.

William A. Taylor is assistant professor of security studies at Angelo State University in San Angelo, Texas. After graduating from the U.S. Naval Academy with honors and distinction, he participated in the navy's highly selective Voluntary Graduate Education Program, through which he earned an MA degree in history from the University of Maryland. He also completed an MA degree in security studies at Georgetown University, graduating with honors. He then earned MPhil and PhD degrees in history from George Washington University.

Taylor won grants from the Society for Military History/ABC-CLIO (2010), Harry S. Truman Library Institute (2013), and Angelo State University Faculty Research Enhancement Program (2013), and a George C. Marshall/Baruch Fellowship (2012) to research *Every Citizen a Soldier: The Campaign for Universal Military Training after World War II* (Texas A&M University Press, 2014), which won a 2015 Crader Family Book Prize Honorable Mention. Taylor won grants from the Dwight D. Eisenhower Foundation (2014), Gerald R. Ford Presidential Foundation (2014), Harry S. Truman Library Institute (2015), U.S. Army Military History Institute (2015), Lyndon B. Johnson Foundation (2016), and Angelo State University Faculty Research Enhancement Program (2014), and a University of North Texas Libraries Special Collections Fellowship (2015) to research the present book.

Taylor maintains research interests in military service, civil-military relations, military history, security studies, grand strategy, and defense policy. He has contributed to eleven other books and has published more than fifty-five reference articles and book reviews. His work has appeared in *Journal of American History, Choice, Joint Force Quarterly, Journal of Military History, Naval War College Review, Army History, U.S. Naval Institute Proceedings, Strategic Studies Quarterly, On Point: The Journal of Army History, Maryland Historical Magazine, Human Rights Review, Michigan War Studies Review, Journal of America's Military Past, North Dakota History: Journal of the Northern Plains, U.S. Military History Review, H-Net Reviews,* and *African Studies Quarterly,* among others.

In addition to his academic credentials, Taylor served as an officer in the U.S. Marine Corps for more than six years, holding posts in III Marine Expeditionary Force, Expeditionary Force Development Center, and Marine Corps Combat Development Command.

NOTES

FRONT MATTER

1. Paul H. Johnstone, "New Dominion Series no. 87," March 1947, cited in Ambrose Caliver, "Documents in Connection with the Appearance of Federal Security Agency Representatives before the President's Advisory Commission on Universal Training, tab VI, Statement of Dr. Ambrose Caliver, Office of Education, Implications of Universal Military Training in Relation to Negroes," 19 April 1947, p. 14, box 4, folder Commission Kit-13th Meeting 4-18/19-47, Record Group 220 Records of Temporary Committees, Commissions, and Boards, President's Advisory Commission on Universal Training, Harry S. Truman Library. The dedication of this book reflects the words "defense of democracy" in the quotation presented above. A similar practice is used in the chapter titles of this book.

2. Harold Stein, "The Military Services and Their Role in the Making of National Policy," 27 November 1951, p. 2, box 7, folder Civil-Military Relations, Harold Stein papers, Harry S. Truman Library.

3. Robert F. Froehlke, "Notes from Interview with Robert F. Froehlke, Secretary of the Army, 1 July 1971–14 May 1973, Interview Conducted by Robert K. Griffith Jr., General History Branch, Department of the Army," 23 June 1983, p. 3, box 1, folder Official Correspondence—Interviews with Robert Frederick Froehlke, All Volunteer Army Collection, U.S. Army Military History Institute. A handwritten note replaced the phrase "That avoids implying the AVF is the only way" with "When the debate begins by asking whether AVF is working, you force those who are responsible for making it work to go on the defense."

4. John Donne, *Devotions upon Emergent Occasions*, ed. Anthony Raspa (Montreal: McGill-Queen's University Press, 1975), 87.

CHAPTER I. CAMP RED CLOUD

1. Reshema Sherlock, "Last Continuously Serving Draftee Retires after 42 Years of Service," 28 October 2014, available at http://www.army.mil/article/137112/Last_continuously_serving_draftee_retires_after_42_years_of_service/ (accessed 3 June 2015).

CHAPTER 2. THE SELECTIVE SERVICE IDEA

1. Lewis B. Hershey, *Selective Service in Peacetime: First Report of the Director of Selective Service, 1940–1941* (Washington, DC: U.S. Government Printing Office, 1942), 3.

2. War Department, Bureau of Public Relations, Press Branch, "Report of Board of Officers on Utilization of Negro Manpower in the Post-War Army," 4 March 1946, pp. 1–2, box 3, folder Commission Kit-5th Meeting 1-15-47, Record Group 220 Records of Temporary Committees, Commissions, and Boards, President's Advisory Commission on Universal Training, Harry S. Truman Library.

3. Lewis B. Hershey, *Selective Service and Victory: Fourth Report of the Director of Selective Service, 1944–1945, with a Supplement for 1946–1947* (Washington, DC: U.S. Government Printing Office, 1948), 348, entry 43 Annual Reports 1940–1947, box 1, folder 4, Record Group 147 Records of the Selective Service System 1940–, National Archives and Records Administration.

4. Lewis B. Hershey, *Selective Service in Wartime: Second Report of the Director of Selective Service, 1941–1942* (Washington, DC: U.S. Government Printing Office, 1943), 62–64, entry 43 Annual Reports 1940–1947, box 1, folder 2, Record Group 147 Records of the Selective Service System 1940–, National Archives and Records Administration. By 8 December 1941 the U.S. military experienced a huge expansion. The army numbered 683,360, the navy totaled 342,295, the marine corps equaled 69,588, the National Guard counted 264,289, and the coast guard came to 21,928, totaling 1,381,460 Americans in military service. In addition, there were 914,626 selectees, which made the U.S. military equal 2,296,086 personnel.

5. For more on the peacetime draft, see J. Garry Clifford and Samuel R. Spencer Jr., *The First Peacetime Draft* (Lawrence: University Press of Kansas, 1986).

6. For more on public debates and representative opposing views, see L. H. Robbins, "Call to Arms, American Style," *New York Times*, 22 September 1940; Dudley J. Stroup, "Coercion of Conscience Seen: Selective Service Registration Viewed as Unjust to Objectors," *New York Times*, 5 December 1940.

7. Lewis B. Hershey to Franklin D. Roosevelt, 29 August 1942, in Hershey, *Selective Service in Peacetime: First Report*, pp. iii, 2–3, 9. The Militia Act of 1792 defined military service as a common obligation even during peacetime, but the act did not actually induct people into military service. First colonies and later states used conscription during the colonial era, the Revolutionary War, and the War of 1812. In 1863 the Union instituted wartime conscription during the American Civil War. What was new in 1863 was direct federal conscription. The United States continued this trend in World War I, establishing the Selective Service System.

8. Julius Cohen, "Memorandum to Bernard C. Gavit, General Counsel, Subject: Extent of Power of Volunteer for Induction to Control his Assignment to a Branch of the Armed Forces," 15 January 1943, p. 2, entry 161, box 2, folder Voluntary Enlistment in Armed Forces, Record Group 211 Records of the War Manpower Commission, National Archives and Records Administration.

9. The Selective Service System existed during World War I. The Sixty-Fifth United States Congress passed the Selective Service Act on 18 May 1917. For more on the Selective Service System during World War I, see Christopher Capozzola, *Uncle Sam Wants You: World War I and the Making of the Modern American Citizen* (Oxford: Oxford University Press, 2008); Gerald E. Shenk, *"Work, or Fight!" Race, Gender, and the Draft in World War One* (New York: Palgrave Macmillan, 2005); John W. Chambers, *To Raise an Army: The Draft Comes to Modern America* (New York: Free Press, 1987); David M. Kennedy, *Over Here: The First World War and American Society* (Oxford: Oxford University Press, 1980); Daniel R. Beaver, *Newton D. Baker and the American War Effort, 1917–1919* (Lincoln: University of Nebraska Press, 1966).

10. For global dimensions of World War II, see Gerhard L. Weinberg, *A World at Arms: A Global History of World War II* (Cambridge: Cambridge University Press, 1994).

11. Hershey, *Selective Service in Peacetime: First Report*, pp. 3, 9, 11.

12. For more on Osborn, see James J. Cooke, *American Girls, Beer, and Glen Miller: GI Morale in World War II* (Columbia: University of Missouri Press, 2012), 2–3, 23, 26, 29–30, 35–36, 39, 43, 45–48, 57–58, 60–62, 65–66, 92–94, 96–100, 102–104, 108, 120, 124, 134–37, 144, 155, 172–173, 176–177, 180.

13. "Peacetime Draft Put into Effect as President Gives Detailed Rules," *Los Angeles Times*, 24 September 1940.

14. In comparison, it is interesting to note that a 2012 Government Accountability Office (GAO) report to congressional committees found that the current standby Selective Service System "is not resourced to provide first inductees within 193 days of mobilization and 100,000 inductees within 210 days." U.S. Government Accountability Office, "National Security: DOD Should Reevaluate Requirements for the Selective Service System," June 2012, p. 15, available at http://www.gao.gov/assets/600/591441.pdf (accessed 22 January 2016).

15. Hershey, *Selective Service in Peacetime: First Report*, pp. 11–14.

16. A little background on Hershey is instructive. As a major, Hershey participated in a Joint Army and Navy Committee that in 1926 began a study of selective service. He eventually served as the executive officer of the committee. Hershey, *Selective Service in Peacetime: First Report*, pp. 9–11. For more on Hershey, see Nicholas A. Krehbiel, *General Lewis B. Hershey and Conscientious Objection during World War II* (Columbia: University of Missouri Press, 2011); George Q. Flynn, *Lewis B. Hershey, Mr. Selective Service* (Chapel Hill: University of North Carolina Press, 1985).

17. Hershey, *Selective Service in Peacetime: First Report*, pp. 13–14. There were also other smaller registrations to account for U.S. territories outside the continental United States, including Hawaii (26 October 1940), Puerto Rico (20 November 1940), and Alaska (22 January 1941). These registrations accounted for approximately 350,000 registrants in the overall total.

18. Hershey, *Selective Service in Peacetime: First Report*, pp. 14–16. The exact number available for military service was 2,070,000, broken down as follows: 600,000 available for general military service (Class I-A or I-A-o), 610,000 available for limited military service (Class I-B or I-B-o), and 860,000 awaiting local physical examinations but already placed in Class I.

19. Ibid., 17. Of the total 12,138,710 Americans in a deferred class, the Selective Service System deemed 320,000 necessary to civilian activities (Class II-A) and classified 207,000 necessary to national defense (Class II-B). In addition, 10,160,000 had dependents (Class III-A); 268,000 were officials, aliens, or ministers (Class IV-B, IV-C, and IV-D respectively); 5,710 were conscientious objectors (Class IV-E); and 1,178,000 were unfit for military service (Class IV-F).

20. U.S. President's Commission on an All-Volunteer Armed Force, *The Report of the President's Commission on an All-Volunteer Armed Force* (Washington, DC: U.S. Government Printing Office, 1970), 161. The actual U.S. wartime

figure was approximately 15.4 million personnel, including roughly 400,000 women. In contrast, the Soviet Union fielded about 35 million personnel during the war, with around 245,000 killed in action and 400,000 wounded in action per month.

21. Hershey, *Selective Service in Peacetime: First Report*, pp. 17–18. For more on the creation of an independent air force, see Bill Yenne, *Hap Arnold: Inventing the Air Force* (Washington, DC: Regnery History, 2013); Michael S. Sherry, *The Rise of American Air Power: The Creation of Armageddon* (New Haven, CT: Yale University Press, 1987). The close relationship between the army and the draft continued and resurfaced prominently in the transition to the all-volunteer force in the late 1960s and early 1970s.

22. Hershey, *Selective Service in Peacetime: First Report*, p. 19. When surveyed with the question "Do you think the draft has been handled fairly?," 93 percent of respondents answered in the affirmative while only 7 percent answered in the negative.

23. Hershey, *Selective Service and Victory: Fourth Report*, p. 78. On 29 August 1945, President Truman issued Executive Order 9605, which allowed the resumption of recruiting volunteers by both the war and navy departments.

24. Voluntary means also proved insufficient to raise enough men during the American Civil War, as the Union instituted conscription in 1863. In World War I, based on the British experience from August 1914 until early 1916, the United States shunned volunteer military service and instead instituted the Selective Service System. Possible exceptions to this trend after World War II include the Persian Gulf War, Operation Iraqi Freedom, and Operation Enduring Freedom in Afghanistan. In the latter two cases, however, private security contractors (PSCs) fulfilled the same personnel augmentation that the draft served in previous conflicts. For more on PSCs, see Chapter 8.

25. The draft lapsed from 31 March 1947–24 June 1948 during the climax of the campaign for universal military training after World War II.

26. This situation was not new to World War II. For more on African American experiences with military service in World War I, see Chad L. Williams, *Torchbearers of Democracy: African American Soldiers in the World War I Era* (Chapel Hill: University of North Carolina Press, 2010).

27. Hershey, *Selective Service in Wartime: Second Report*, p. 277.

28. Ibid., 277–279, 287. See especially the detailed graph "Inductions by Race excluding White for United States and Territories, November 1940–October 1942" on p. 287, which illustrates the predominance of African Americans as a racial minority during World War II.

29. For African American military service prior to World War II, see Bernard C. Nalty, *Strength for the Fight: A History of Black Americans in the Military* (New York: Free Press, 1986).

30. "The Negro and Defense," *Kansas American*, 14 November 1941.

31. Selective Service System, *Selective Service and Victory: Fourth Report of the Director of Selective Service, 1944–1945, with a Supplement for 1946–1947* (Washington, DC: U.S. Government Printing Office, 1948), 187, entry 43, box 1, folder 4, Record

Group 147 Records of the Selective Service System, 1940–, National Archives and Records Administration.

32. War Department, Adjutant General's Office, "Memorandum to John J. McCloy, Subject: Advisory Committee on Negro Troop Policies," 27 August 1942, box 14, folder McCloy Committee, Record Group 220 Records of Temporary Committees, Commissions, and Boards, President's Committee on Equality of Treatment and Opportunity in the Armed Services, Harry S. Truman Library.

33. J. S. Leonard, Colonel, Infantry, Secretary, Advisory Committee on Negro Troop Policies, "Digest of War Department Policy Pertaining to Negro Military Personnel," 1 January 1944, box 14, folder McCloy Committee, Record Group 220 Records of Temporary Committees, Commissions, and Boards, President's Committee on Equality of Treatment and Opportunity in the Armed Services, Harry S. Truman Library.

34. J. S. Leonard, Colonel, Infantry, Secretary, "Memorandum for Members of the Advisory Committee on Negro Troop Policies, Subject: Duties of the Advisory Committee on Negro Troop Policies," 6 January 1944, box 14, folder McCloy Committee, ibid.

35. Davidson Sommers, "Memorandum for Mr. McCloy," 28 August 1945, box 14, folder McCloy Committee, ibid. Almost four years later, E. W. Kenworthy, executive secretary of the Fahy Committee, connected the earlier work of the McCloy Committee to the subsequent Fahy Committee by way of the Gillem Board. As he stated to Charles Fahy, "I have spent the weekend combing through those files of the Assistant Secretary of War which deal with this committee. It is a history of unrelieved headaches. After reading in this file, I cannot understand how the Army can defend its racial policy by appealing to experience. I was never more certain that we are on the right track." E. W. Kenworthy to Charles Fahy, 8 August 1949, box 14, folder McCloy Committee, ibid.

36. Paul V. McNutt to Henry L. Stimson (identical letter sent to Frank Knox), 17 February 1943, entry 7, box 4, folder Roosevelt, Franklin D., Record Group 211 Records of the War Manpower Commission, National Archives and Records Administration.

37. Paul V. McNutt to Henry L. Stimson (identical letter sent to Frank Knox), 17 February 1943, entry 7, box 4, folder Roosevelt, Franklin D., ibid.

38. Henry L. Stimson to Paul V. McNutt, 14 April 1943, entry 7, box 4, folder Roosevelt, Franklin D., ibid. In his letter to McNutt, Stimson included a memorandum from Brigadier General E. C. McNeil, Acting Judge Advocate General (JAG) of the U.S. Army. See E. C. McNeil, "Memorandum for the Assistant Chief of Staff, G-1, Subject: Interpretation of Selective Training and Service Act," 22 February 1943, pp. 1–3. Stimson focused on the part of the JAG opinion where McNeil argued, "For the reasons above indicated, it is my opinion that the Army's current practice of placing requisitions with the Selective Service System for separate quotas of white and colored troops for training and service under the provisions of the Selective Training and Service Act of 1940 in such numbers as to preserve the same ratio between colored and white men in the Army as exists between colored and white registrants, is in full harmony with the provisions of that act."

39. Paul V. McNutt to Henry L. Stimson, 23 April 1943, entry 7, box 4, folder Roosevelt, Franklin D., ibid.

40. See Paul V. McNutt to Henry L. Stimson, 17 February 1943; McNutt to Knox, 17 February 1943; Stimson to McNutt, 20 February 1943; Knox to McNutt, 26 February 1943; McNutt to Knox, 2 March 1943; Knox to McNutt, 13 March 1943; McNutt to Stimson, 23 March 1943; McNutt to Knox, 23 March 1943; Knox to McNutt, 13 April 1943; McNutt to Knox, 23 April 1943, entry 7, box 4, folder Roosevelt, Franklin D., ibid. It is important to note that throughout the extensive letter exchange, McNutt coordinated his responses with Hershey. Most of McNutt's letters have a handwritten annotation stating "Cleared with Gen Hershey" or something similar.

41. Selective Service System, *Selective Service in Wartime: Second Report of the Director of Selective Service, 1941–1942* (Washington, DC: U.S. Government Printing Office, 1943), 71, entry 43, box 1, folder 2, Record Group 147 Records of the Selective Service System, 1940–, National Archives and Records Administration.

42. Kristy N. Kamarck, "Women in Combat: Issues for Congress," *Congressional Research Service Report*, 18 August 2015, p. 3. Congress only authorized the Women's Army Corps for the duration of World War II and up to six months after its conclusion.

43. For example, during the same time period agricultural workers decreased from 8.3 million to 8.1 million; self-employed workers dropped from 5.8 million to 5.3 million; and unemployed workers declined from 3.8 million to 1.5 million. Total non–war-related industry dwindled more than 27 percent, from 29.2 million to 21.1 million. For more on the breakdown of American labor by category during the first year of World War II see the graph "Estimates of Manpower Requirements to December 1942," in Selective Service System, *Selective Service in Wartime: Second Report*, p. 72.

44. Ibid., 78.

45. Selective Service System, *Selective Service and Victory: Fourth Report*, p. 166. The worst ratio was 75 percent favorable to 25 percent unfavorable.

46. Lewis B. Hershey, "Establishing Selective Service: A Howard Crawley Memorial Lecture Delivered before the Faculty and Students, Wharton School of Finance and Commerce, University of Pennsylvania," 5 November 1941, p. 14, folder P.I. 27 Appendix II B Listed, box 65, entry 42 Copies of Speeches and Congressional Testimony by General Lewis B. Hershey, Director of Selective Service System, Record Group 147 Records of the Selective Service System, 1940–, National Archives and Records Administration.

47. Selective Service System, *Selective Service and Victory: Fourth Report*, p. 175.

48. Selective Service System, *Selective Service as the Tide of War Turns: Third Report of the Director of Selective Service, 1943–1944* (Washington, DC: U.S. Government Printing Office, 1945), 212–214, 220, entry 43, box 1, folder 3, Record Group 147 Records of the Selective Service System 1940–, National Archives and Records Administration.

49. Anonymous to FBI, 12 April 1943, box 13, folder Fan Mail April 1–12, 1943, Record Group 147 Records of the Selective Service System 1940–, National Archives and Records Administration.

50. For representative samples, see W. F. Seguine to FBI, 16 April 1943; Anonymous to FBI, 15 April 1943; An American Mother to FBI, 14 April 1943; H. C. Harris to Department of Justice, 14 April 1943; Juanita Moore to FBI, 13 April 1943, box 13, folder Fan Mail April 13–16, 1943, ibid.

51. H. B. Batleman to Franklin D. Roosevelt, 13 April 1943, box 13, folder Fan Mail April 13–16 1943, ibid.

52. Selective Service System, *Selective Service and Victory: Fourth Report*, pp. 3–6.

53. Ibid.

54. Ibid., 17–18, 21.

55. Ibid., 54–55.

56. Ibid., 154. For more on acquisitions, separations, and overall strength of U.S. armed forces from March 1940 to December 1945, see figure 5.

57. Ibid., 51.

58. D. M. Giangreco, *Hell to Pay: Operation* DOWNFALL *and the Invasion of Japan, 1945–1947* (Annapolis, MD: Naval Institute Press, 2009), 16–17.

59. Selective Service System, *Selective Service and Victory: Fourth Report*, pp. 23, 25, 51–52. On 6 October 1945, the 79th Congress approved Public Law 190.

60. War Department, Bureau of Public Relations, Press Branch, "Report of Board of Officers on Utilization of Negro Manpower in the Post-War Army," 4 March 1946, pp. 1, 10, box 3, folder Commission Kit-5th Meeting 1-15-47, Record Group 220 Records of Temporary Committees, Commissions, and Boards, President's Advisory Commission on Universal Training, Harry S. Truman Library.

61. "Rotary in Atlanta: Monday, December 28, 1953, Meeting, 12:30 at the Ansley," 28 December 1953; "Gen. Gillem Dies; Rites Tomorrow," *Atlanta Constitution*, 14 February 1973, box 8, folder Clippings, Alvan C. Gillem papers, U.S. Military History Institute. Gillem's impressive military legacy continued after his death; his son, Lieutenant General Alvan C. Gillem II, commanded Air University at Maxwell Air Force Base in Montgomery, Alabama.

62. War Department, Bureau of Public Relations, Press Branch, "Report of Board of Officers on Utilization of Negro Manpower in the Post-War Army," 4 March 1946, pp. 1, 4, 6.

63. Ibid., pp. 4, 6–10.

64. Anthony Leviero, "Army Maps Plan for Negro Troops: Wider Use Is Proposed by Generals But Combat Units to Be Cut," *New York Times*, 4 March 1946.

65. "GI's Disgusted with Fort Benning," *Plain Dealer*, 27 September 1946.

66. Alvan C. Gillem, "Utilization of Negro Manpower," 9 March 1949, pp. 30–31, box 14, folder Speeches 1948–1949, Alvan C. Gillem papers, U.S. Army Military History Institute.

67. War Department Circular Number 124, "Utilization of Negro Manpower in the Postwar Army Policy," 27 April 1946, box 7, folder Gillem Board Report, Record Group 220 Records of Temporary Committees, Commissions, and Boards, President's Committee on Equality of Treatment and Opportunity in the Armed Services, Harry S. Truman Library.

68. The four volumes of *Studies in Social Psychology in World War II* were

vol. 1: *The American Soldier: Adjustment during Army Life*; vol. 2: *The American Soldier: Combat and Its Aftermath*; vol. 3: *Experiments on Mass Communication*; and vol. 4: *Measurement and Prediction*.

69. Joseph W. Ryan, *Samuel Stouffer and the GI Survey: Sociologists and Soldiers during the Second World War* (Knoxville: University of Tennessee Press, 2013), 16.

70. Samuel A. Stouffer, Edward A. Suchman, Leland C. DeVinney, Shirley A. Star, and Robin M. Williams Jr., *The American Soldier: Adjustment during Army Life*, vol. 1 of *Studies in Social Psychology in World War II: The American Soldier* (Princeton, NJ: Princeton University Press, 1949), vii, 12, 54, 68, 486–487, 504, 510, 513, 568, 575.

71. Ibid.

CHAPTER 3. A SOUND AND DEMOCRATIC PRINCIPLE

1. James W. Wadsworth and Clifton A. Woodrum, "Statement on Universal Military Training," 1945, Xerox 3258, Marshall Foundation National Archives Project, George C. Marshall Library.

2. War Department, Bureau of Public Relations, "Opinion Survey No. 21," 5 May 1945, p. 1, cited in "Documents in Connection with the Appearance of Federal Security Agency Representatives before the President's Advisory Commission on Universal Training," tab VI, "Statement of Dr. Ambrose Caliver, Office of Education, Implications of Universal Military Training in Relation to Negroes," 19 April 1947, p. 14, box 4, folder Commission Kit-13th Meeting 4-18/19-47, Record Group 220 Records of Temporary Committees, Commissions, and Boards, President's Advisory Commission on Universal Training, Harry S. Truman Library.

3. "One More Job for General Marshall," *Washington Post*, 25 October 1945.

4. Henry L. Stimson to Archibald G. Thacher, 15 August 1944, box 7, folder 1944–1948 Universal Military Training, Courtney H. Hodges papers, Dwight D. Eisenhower Library.

5. For more on changed strategic perceptions that UMT advocates argued made the plan essential, see William A. Taylor, "Target No. 1: USA," in *Every Citizen a Soldier: The Campaign for Universal Military Training after World War II* (College Station: Texas A&M University Press, 2014), 33–41.

6. George C. Marshall, "Circular No. 347," 25 August 1944, box 7, folder 1944–1948 Universal Military Training, Courtney H. Hodges papers, Dwight D. Eisenhower Library.

7. James V. Forrestal to Archibald G. Thacher, 8 December 1944, box 7, folder 1944–1948 Universal Military Training, ibid.

8. For more on Palmer, see I. B. Holley Jr., *General John M. Palmer, Citizen Soldiers, and the Army of a Democracy* (Westport, CT: Greenwood Press, 1982).

9. For letters demonstrating the close friendship and mutual respect between Palmer and Marshall, see John M. Palmer to George C. Marshall, 1 September 1938; George C. Marshall to John M. Palmer, 7 September 1938; John M. Palmer to George C. Marshall, 21 November 1938; George C. Marshall to John M. Palmer, 22 November 1938; George C. Marshall to John M. Palmer, 6 March 1939; and John M. Palmer to George C. Marshall, 15 December 1939, box 78, folder 16,

George C. Marshall papers, George C. Marshall Library. For their relationship in the Infantry Association, see John M. Palmer to George C. Marshall, 13 November 1944, box 87, folder 23; and on their wives' friendship, see John M. Palmer to George C. Marshall, 19 April 1941, box 87, folder 18, George C. Marshall papers, George C. Marshall Library.

10. John M. Palmer to George C. Marshall, 13 November 1944, box 78, folder 23, ibid.

11. John M. Palmer to George C. Marshall, 8 October 1945, box 78, folder 30, ibid.

12. John M. Palmer to Henry L. Stimson, May 1940, box 78, folder 17, ibid.

13. John M. Palmer to George C. Marshall, 24 June 1943, box 78, folder 20, ibid.

14. John M. Palmer, "Memorandum for the Committee on Civilian Components, Subject: Inter-relations between Professional and Non-professional Personnel in the Armed Forces of a Democratic State," 9 January 1948, p. 12, box 78, folder 33, ibid. For more on the concrete-and-steel analogy, see John M. Palmer, "Memorandum for the Chief of Staff, Subject: Estimates of Post-War Troop and Air Strength and Probable Costs," 16 November 1944, box 78, folder 24, ibid. In this document Palmer hinted to Marshall of a widespread predisposition among military officers toward professional forces: "When I showed the metaphor to an Engineer friend of mine, he said, 'You will find it difficult to apply that principle in Uncle Sam's military establishment because all of his planners have a personal interest in selling him just as much steel as possible.'"

15. George C. Marshall, "For the Common Defense: Biennial Report to the Secretary of War, 1 July 1943 to 30 June 1945," 9 October 1945, p. 18, excerpts published in a UMT brochure by the Citizens Committee for UMT of Young Men located at 72 Wall Street, New York, NY, box 7, folder 1944–1948 Universal Military Training, Courtney H. Hodges papers, Dwight D. Eisenhower Library. The representative who sponsored the bill was Jeremiah Wadsworth, cousin to James Wadsworth, who in turn was the great-grandfather of James W. Wadsworth Jr. (R-NY). This was significant because James W. Wadsworth Jr. became the main political proponent of UMT after both World War I and World War II. Wadsworth worked closely with John M. Palmer and George C. Marshall on the campaign for UMT, knew of Jeremiah's role in connection with Washington, and sought to accomplish enactment of the plan that his forebear previously recommended. For more on Jeremiah Wadsworth, see Wayne Mahood, *General Wadsworth: The Life and Times of Brevet Major General James S. Wadsworth* (Cambridge, MA: Da Capo Press, 2003), 6–8.

16. For more on the connection between UMT and Washington's plan, see John M. Palmer, "Summary of Paper upon Washington's 'Plan for a Peace Establishment,'" published in a Citizens Committee for Universal Military Training of Young Men brochure, 18 January 1945, box 7, folder 1944–1948 Universal Military Training, Courtney H. Hodges papers, Dwight D. Eisenhower Library.

17. George C. Marshall, "U.M.T. Washington's Plan," *Biennial Report*, 1 July 1943–30 June 1945, p. 118, Xerox 3208, Marshall Foundation National Archives Project, George C. Marshall Library.

18. George C. Marshall, "The Obligation to Serve," *Army Information Digest* 6, 4 (April 1951): 4.

19. Marshall, "U.M.T. Washington's Plan."

20. George C. Marshall, "Statement on Universal Military Training before the Select Committee on Post-War Military Policy of the House of Representatives," 16 June 1945, pp. 2–4, Xerox 3091, Marshall Foundation National Archives Project, George C. Marshall Library.

21. Ibid.

22. Ibid.

23. Selective Service System, *Selective Service and Victory: Fourth Report of the Director of Selective Service, 1944–1945, with a Supplement for 1946–1947* (Washington, DC: U.S. Government Printing Office, 1948), 56–57, entry 43, box 1, folder 4, Record Group 147 Records of the Selective Service System, 1940–, National Archives and Records Administration.

24. Marshall was *Time* man of the year in both 1943 and 1947.

25. This was not the first time that such a situation emerged. In a previous era, Russell F. Weigley showed, "By proposing a military policy that the country could not accept, Emory Upton helped ensure that the country would continue to limp along with virtually no military policy at all." Russell F. Weigley, *History of the United States Army* (New York: Macmillan, 1967), 281. The period from 1948 to 1973 evidenced many similarities.

26. Jacob L. Devers, "Memorandum to Unit Commanders, Army Ground Forces, Subject: Universal Military Training," 9 November 1945, Xerox 996, Marshall Foundation National Archives Project, George C. Marshall Library.

27. George C. Marshall to Dwight D. Eisenhower, 20 September 1945, pp. 1–2, box 80, folder George C. Marshall (5) [July 1945–December 1947], Dwight D. Eisenhower Pre-Presidential papers 1916–1952, Principal File, Dwight D. Eisenhower Library. Marshall based his assessment on an army proposal of "almost a million men," a navy proposal of 500,000 sailors and 100,000 marines, and an envisioned UMT program of "some 600,000 to 700,000 young men."

28. Ibid. For more on the connection between the experience of demobilization in World War I and planning for the postwar military after World War II, see William A. Taylor, "The Spirit of 1920," in *Every Citizen a Soldier*, pp. 13–26.

29. George C. Marshall to Dwight D. Eisenhower, 20 September 1945, pp. 1–2, box 80, folder George C. Marshall (5) [July 1945–December 1947], Dwight D. Eisenhower Pre-Presidential papers 1916–1952, Principal File, Dwight D. Eisenhower Library.

30. "Music Program," p. 1, box 8, folder Staff Studies—Ft. Knox, Kentucky, Record Group 220 Records of Temporary Committees, Commissions, and Boards, President's Advisory Commission on Universal Training, Harry S. Truman Library.

31. Army Ground Forces UMT Demonstration Unit, "Annex No. 8, Public Relations Plan," entry 91, box 5, folder Regimental Plans, Record Group 337 Records of Headquarters Army Ground Forces, National Archives and Records Administration.

32. John M. Devine, "Interim Report, U.M.T. Experimental Unit, Fort Knox,

Kentucky," 1 August 1947, pp. 6–7, entry 91, box 1, folder UMT General Orders, Record Group 337 Records of Headquarters Army Ground Forces, National Archives and Records Administration.

33. For more on Truman and military service, see D. M. Giangreco, *The Soldier from Independence: A Military Biography of Harry Truman* (Minneapolis: Zenith Press, 2009).

34. President's Advisory Commission on Universal Training, *A Program for National Security: Report of the President's Advisory Commission on Universal Training* (Washington, DC: U.S. Government Printing Office, 1947). See especially the appendices, pp. 99–448.

35. Joseph E. Davies, Harold W. Dodds, Truman K. Gibson Jr., Daniel A. Poling, Anna M. Rosenberg, Samuel I. Rosenman, Edmund A. Walsh, Charles E. Wilson, Karl T. Compton to Harry S. Truman, letter of transmittal, 29 May 1947, in President's Advisory Commission on Universal Training, *A Program for National Security*, p. vii.

36. Ambrose Caliver, "Implications of Universal Military Training in Relation to Negroes," tab VI in "Documents in Connection with the Appearance of Federal Security Agency Representatives before the President's Advisory Commission on Universal Training," 19 April 1947, pp. 1, 4–5, box 4, folder Commission Kit-13th Meeting 4-18/19-47, Record Group 220 Records of Temporary Committees, Commissions, and Boards, President's Advisory Commission on Universal Training, Harry S. Truman Library.

37. Finding aid, Record Group 147 Records of the Selective Service System, 1940–, National Archives and Records Administration.

38. Dwight D. Eisenhower to George C. Marshall, 18 October 1950, pp. 1–2, box 80, folder Marshall, George C. (4) [January 1948–November 1950], Dwight D. Eisenhower papers, Pre-Presidential, 1916–1952, Principal File, Dwight D. Eisenhower Library.

39. George C. Marshall to Dwight D. Eisenhower, 23 October 1950, box 80, folder Marshall, George C. (4) [January 1948–November 1950], ibid. For more on this dynamic, specifically as it relates to UMT, see Taylor, "The Paradox of Preparedness," in *Every Citizen a Soldier*, pp. 161–171.

40. George C. Marshall to Dwight D. Eisenhower, 21 March 1951, box 80, folder Marshall, George C. (3) [December 1950–9 May 1951], Dwight D. Eisenhower papers, Pre-Presidential, 1916–1952, Principal File, Dwight D. Eisenhower Library.

41. James W. Wadsworth Jr. to Archibald G. Thacher, 9 November 1950, box 31, folder 39 UMT 8 November 1950–22 February 1951, James Wadsworth Family papers, Library of Congress.

42. George C. Marshall, "The Obligation to Serve," *Army Information Digest* 6, 4 (April 1951): 7–8.

43. Form letter, George C. Marshall to senator, 6 March 1951, Xerox 2607, Marshall Foundation National Archives Project, George C. Marshall Library. Attached to the letter was a covering note that stated, "Addressed to each Senator, these letters were delivered by hand by Senator Lyndon B. Johnson today for his distribution to the Senators."

44. George C. Marshall to Sam Rayburn, 6 April 1951, p. 2, Xerox 2607, Marshall Foundation National Archives Project, George C. Marshall Library.

45. Quentin R. Mott, "UMT Outlook—Youth Can Rest Easy: It's a Long Road Ahead," *Washington Star*, 12 August 1951.

46. For more on earlier resistance to UMT, see Taylor, "A Pig in a Poke," in *Every Citizen a Soldier*, pp. 67–87.

47. Mott, "UMT Outlook—Youth Can Rest Easy."

48. Ibid.

49. Arthur L. Williston to James W. Wadsworth Jr., 11 July 1951, box 27, folder National Security Training Committee 31 May–21 July 1951, James Wadsworth Family papers, Library of Congress.

50. James W. Wadsworth Jr. to Barber B. Conable Jr., 1 December 1950, pp. 1–2, box 29, folder Postwar Military Policy Woodrum Committee 17 August–22 December 1950, ibid.

51. Anna M. Rosenberg to Dwight D. Eisenhower, 25 June 1952, Xerox 3227, Marshall Foundation National Archives Project, George C. Marshall Library. Rosenberg penned two letters to Eisenhower, one she wrote earlier but held and the other drafted upon hearing his quoted statement on the "threat of creating a militaristic state." On 25 June 1952 she sent both: "For the past few weeks I have been somewhat disturbed over the statements made by General Eisenhower with reference to Universal Military Training and Service so I drafted a letter to him showing the contradictions between his former stand on UMT and the stand he is now taking. Knowing the pressure he is under, I held up the letter for some time until a subsequent statement by him on the 'threat of creating a militaristic state' came to my attention. I then sent him the original letter with covering letter." Anna M. Rosenberg to George C. Marshall, 8 July 1952, Xerox 3227, ibid.

52. Anna M. Rosenberg to Dwight D. Eisenhower, 25 June 1952, Xerox 3227, ibid.

53. Dwight D. Eisenhower to Anna M. Rosenberg, 1 July 1952, Xerox 3227, ibid.

54. Anna M. Rosenberg to George C. Marshall, 8 July 1952, Xerox 3227, ibid.

CHAPTER 4. FREEDOM TO SERVE

1. "Truman K. Gibson Predicts Mixed Army," *Amsterdam Star-News*, 8 December 1945, box 54, folder Minorities—Negro—General—Individuals—News Clippings 1945–1946 [1 of 2], Philleo Nash papers, Harry S. Truman Library.

2. President's Committee on Equality of Treatment and Opportunity in the Armed Services, *Freedom to Serve: Equality of Treatment and Opportunity in the Armed Services, A Report by the President's Committee* (Washington, DC: U.S. Government Printing Office, 1950), 49, box Student Research File (B File) Desegregation of the Armed Forces #20A [1 of 2], folder The Truman Administration's Civil Rights Program: The Desegregation of the Armed Forces [6 of 17], Harry S. Truman Library.

3. Robert K. Carr, "Memorandum to Members of the President's Committee on Civil Rights, Subject: 'Negroes in the Armed Forces' Prepared by Milton D. Stewart and Joseph Murtha," 10 June 1947, p. 1, box 18, folder "Negroes in the Armed

Forces," Record Group 220 Records of Temporary Committees, Commissions, and Boards, President's Committee on Civil Rights, Harry S. Truman Library.

4. Clark M. Clifford, "Confidential Memorandum for the President, Subject: The 1948 Campaign," 17 August 1948, p. 3, box 22, folder Confidential Memo to the President [Clifford-Rowe memorandum of November 19, 1947] [2 of 2], Clark M. Clifford papers, Harry S. Truman Library.

5. James V. Forrestal to Grant Reynolds and A. Philip Randolph, 17 July 1948, p. 2, box Student Research File (B File) Desegregation of the Armed Forces #20A [1 of 2], folder The Truman Administration's Civil Rights Program: The Desegregation of the Armed Forces [1 of 17], Harry S. Truman Library. For details of the conference and a list of all attendees, see the enclosure to the letter.

6. Press release, "Negro Leaders Submit Report and Recommendations on Segregation," 8 September 1948, pp. 1, 7–9, box 55, folder Minorities—Negro—General—Negro Leaders' Report on Segregation, Philleo Nash papers, Harry S. Truman Library. The text of the report is located as an appendix to the press release.

7. "Leaders Offer Seven-Point Plan to End Bias in Army," *Plain Dealer*, 17 September 1948.

8. Grant Reynolds and A. Philip Randolph to Harry S. Truman, 29 June 1948, box Student Research File (B File) Desegregation of the Armed Forces #20A [1 of 2], folder The Truman Administration's Civil Rights Program: The Desegregation of the Armed Forces [1 of 17], Harry S. Truman Library. In 1941, Randolph had also threatened a march on Washington protesting segregation, particularly in the defense industry but also in military service.

9. Mr. and Mrs. Irvin Dagen to Harry S. Truman, 15 June 1948, box Student Research File (B File) Desegregation of the Armed Forces #20A [1 of 2], folder The Truman Administration's Civil Rights Program: The Desegregation of the Armed Forces [1 of 17], Harry S. Truman Library. For similar letters, see Howard H. Davis (President of Richmond Committee for Civil Rights) to Harry S. Truman, 10 May 1948; Richard A. Givens (National Board of Students for Democratic Action) to John R. Steelman, 22 July 1948; Leon Henderson (National Chairman of Americans for Democratic Action) to Harry S. Truman, 22 July 1948, box Student Research File (B File) Desegregation of the Armed Forces #20A [1 of 2], folder The Truman Administration's Civil Rights Program: The Desegregation of the Armed Forces [1 of 17], ibid.

10. Harry S. Truman, "Executive Order 9981," 26 July 1948, box 31, folder Executive Order 9981 (Working Papers and Final [draft] Order), Harry S. Truman papers, Staff Member and Office Files, Philleo Nash files, Harry S. Truman Library.

11. Clark M. Clifford, "Confidential Memorandum for the President, Subject: The 1948 Campaign," 17 August 1948, p. 3, box 22, folder Confidential Memo to the President [Clifford-Rowe Memorandum of 19 November 1947] [2 of 2], Clark M. Clifford papers, Harry S. Truman Library.

12. Alan Gropman, "U.S. Air Force Oral History Interview #879, Mr. James C. Evans," ca. 1973, pp. 2, 4, 18–19, box 168.7061-12 168.7061-25 1940–1970 1970

Gropman, A. L. Col 22, folder 168.7061-12, U.S. Air Force Historical Research Agency.

13. Joseph Beauharnais to Louis A. Johnson (copy to Harry S. Truman), 24 June 1949, box Student Research File (B File) Desegregation of the Armed Forces #20A [1 of 2], folder The Truman Administration's Civil Rights Program: The Desegregation of the Armed Forces [1 of 17], Harry S. Truman Library.

14. Eben A. Ayers, "Press Release, President's Committee on Equality of Treatment and Opportunity in the Armed Forces," 18 September 1948, box Student Research File (B File) Desegregation of the Armed Forces #20A [1 of 2], folder The Truman Administration's Civil Rights Program: The Desegregation of the Armed Forces [2 of 17], Harry S. Truman Library.

15. Kenneth C. Royall to Harry S. Truman, 17 September 1948, box Student Research File (B File) Desegregation of the Armed Forces #20A [1 of 2], folder The Truman Administration's Civil Rights Program: The Desegregation of the Armed Forces [3 of 17], Harry S. Truman Library.

16. Transcript, "Meeting of the President and the Four Service Secretaries with the President's Committee on Equality of Treatment and Opportunity in the Armed Services," 12 January 1949, p. 2, box Student Research File (B File) Desegregation of the Armed Forces #20A [1 of 2], folder The Truman Administration's Civil Rights Program: The Desegregation of the Armed Forces [2 of 17], Harry S. Truman Library.

17. President's Committee on Equality of Treatment and Opportunity in the Armed Services, "Further Interim Report to the President," 6 October 1949, p. 4, box Student Research File (B File) Desegregation of the Armed Forces #20A [1 of 2], folder The Truman Administration's Civil Rights Program: The Desegregation of the Armed Forces [6 of 17], Harry S. Truman Library.

18. President's Committee on Equality of Treatment and Opportunity in the Armed Services, "Memorandum for the President," 14 December 1949, p. 2, box Student Research File (B File) Desegregation of the Armed Forces #20A [1 of 2], folder The Truman Administration's Civil Rights Program: The Desegregation of the Armed Forces [6 of 17], Harry S. Truman Library.

19. William E. Stevenson, "The Road to Democracy," 23 January 1950, box Student Research File (B File) Desegregation of the Armed Forces #20A [1 of 2], folder The Truman Administration's Civil Rights Program: The Desegregation of the Armed Forces [5 of 17], Harry S. Truman Library.

20. E. W. Kenworthy, "Memorandum for Mr. Fahy, Subject: Committee Meeting with the President," 3 June 1949, box 2, folder 7 June 1949—Meeting with President, Record Group 220 Records of Temporary Committees, Commissions, and Boards, President's Committee on Equality of Treatment and Opportunity in the Armed Services, Harry S. Truman Library.

21. Press release, "President's Committee on Equality of Treatment and Opportunity in the Armed Services," 22 May 1950, box 2, folder 22 May 1950 [Final Meeting with President], ibid.

22. Edward H. Brooks, "ACS G-1 to C/S," January 1951, box 22, folder Racial Integration of Armed Forces 1949–1953, J. Lawton Collins papers, Dwight D. Ei-

senhower Library; "Table 11, Black Marines, 1949–1955," available at http://www
.montfordpointmarines.com/History.html (accessed 8 January 2016).

23. Edward H. Brooks, "ACS G-1 to C/S," January 1951, box 22, folder Racial
Integration of Armed Forces 1949–1953, J. Lawton Collins papers, Dwight D. Eisenhower Library.

24. For more on military integration during the Korean War, see Christine
Knauer, *Let Us Fight as Free Men: Black Soldiers and Civil Rights* (Philadelphia:
University of Pennsylvania Press, 2014); Bernard C. Nalty, *Long Passage to Korea:
Black Soldiers and the Integration of the U.S. Navy* (Washington, DC: Naval Histori-
cal Center, 2003); Morris J. MacGregor, *Integration of the Armed Forces, 1940–1965*
(Washington, DC: U.S. Army Center of Military History, 1981).

25. "Yanks End Racial Line Sidelights of Korean War," *Negro Star*, 15 September
1950.

26. Frank Pace Jr. to David K. Niles, 21 February 1951, p. 2, box Student Re-
search File (B File) Desegregation of the Armed Forces #20A [1 of 2], folder The
Truman Administration's Civil Rights Program: The Desegregation of the Armed
Forces [1 of 17], Harry S. Truman Library.

27. Leo Bogart, ed., *Project Clear: Social Research and the Desegregation of the
United States Army* (New Brunswick, NJ: Transaction Publishers, 1992), xviii–xix,
xxxi.

28. Anthony C. McAuliffe, "Summary Sheet," 29 December 1951, p. 1, box
22, folder Racial Integration of Armed Forces 1949–1953, J. Lawton Collins papers, Dwight D. Eisenhower Library. McAuliffe qualified this conclusion by recommending "80–90% white and 10–20% Negro personnel in any unit for which
qualified."

29. Bogart, *Project Clear*, pp. ix, xl.

30. Ibid., 3, 147. Project Clear focused on enlisted soldiers, as evidenced by the
proportion of interviews (150 with officers and 450 with enlisted soldiers); only
"a few company-grade officers" received questionnaires. As with the Korean War
study, most of the continental United States study involved questionnaires, although social scientists conducted approximately 550 personal interviews. For the
actual questionnaires, instructions, tabulations, check lists, and interview guide,
see the appendices on pp. 281–351.

31. Ibid., xxxvii.

32. Ibid., xliii. For "Part I: The Utilization of Negro Troops in Korea," see
pp. 1–144. For "Part II: The Utilization of Negro Troops in the Continental United
States," see pp. 145–279.

33. Ibid., 8, 140–142. Class II referred to segregated units designated solely for
African American personnel. For Project Clear's recommendation for the elimination of this classification, see p. 143.

34. Ibid., xxxix, xli.

35. Ibid., x, xlv–xlviii. Even though the army declassified Project Clear on 7 November 1966, the Research Analysis Corporation (RAC) had subsumed ORO and
on 21 August 1967 copyrighted the report, including all of Project Clear's surveys,
"for the specific purpose of keeping it out of the public domain," according to

RAC's lawyer. The classification and subsequent copyright kept Project Clear out of the public domain until Bogart's publication of his work in 1969.

36. Ibid., ix.

37. Alan Gropman, "U.S. Air Force Oral History Interview #879, Mr. James C. Evans," ca. 1973, pp. 26–28, 46, box 168.7061-12 168.7061-25 1940–1970 1970 Gropman, A. L. Col 22, folder 168.7061-12, U.S. Air Force Historical Research Agency.

38. Maxwell D. Taylor, "Notes from Far East Trip," 10 May 1951, p. 3, box 45, folder General Correspondence: [1951] T–Z (1), Henry S. Aurand papers, Dwight D. Eisenhower Library.

39. George C. Marshall to Herbert H. Lehman and Hubert H. Humphrey, 20 July 1951, box 22, folder Racial Integration of Armed Forces 1949–1953, J. Lawton Collins papers, Dwight D. Eisenhower Library. Marshall noted two exceptions, the 40th and 45th Infantry Divisions, and explained, "Integration within the 40th and 45th Infantry Divisions will follow at a later date and will be accomplished through the normal flow of replacements." This is significant because those two divisions were Army National Guard units, indicating the significant resistance to integration within the Army National Guard even at a time when the army was integrating widely.

40. Anthony C. McAuliffe, "Summary Sheet," 29 December 1951, p. 1, box 22, folder Racial Integration of Armed Forces 1949–1953, J. Lawton Collins papers, Dwight D. Eisenhower Library.

41. Joseph M. Swing to Anthony C. McAuliffe, 10 September 1951, p. 1, box 22, folder Racial Integration of Armed Forces 1949–1953, ibid.

42. Anthony C. McAuliffe to Joseph M. Swing, 17 September 1951, box 22, folder Racial Integration of Armed Forces 1949–1953, ibid.

43. Fred Korth, "Memorandum for the Assistant Secretary of Defense (M&P), Subject: Progress Report on Elimination of Segregation in the Army," 3 September 1952, box 22, folder Racial Integration of Armed Forces 1949–1953, ibid. For context, see the extensive background notes accompanying the document that highlight the relationship between integration and the military personnel policy SR 600-629-1 entitled "Utilization of Negro Manpower in the Army" issued by Army Chief of Staff J. Lawton Collins on 16 January 1950. SR 600-629-1 was a complete revision of War Department Circular Number 124. On p. 3, Korth contended, "It was on the basis of the policy published in this document that all future integration took place."

44. Korth, "Memorandum for the Assistant Secretary of Defense (M&P), Subject: Progress Report on Elimination of Segregation in the Army," 3 September 1952, pp. 4–5, box 22, folder Racial Integration of Armed Forces 1949–1953, J. Lawton Collins papers, Dwight D. Eisenhower Library.

45. Ibid., 5.

46. Ibid., 5–6. All this information is presented under the heading, "What specific orders integrated the army."

47. Harry S. Truman, "The State of the Union Address of the President of the

United States," 9 January 1952, p. 3, box 6, folder 1952 Tax Program Volume I, L. Laszlo Ecker-Racz papers, Harry S. Truman Library.

48. Collins George, "Army Racial Integration 90 Per Cent Complete," *Detroit Michigan Free Press*, 15 May 1953, box 22, folder Racial Integration of Armed Forces 1949–1953, J. Lawton Collins papers, Dwight D. Eisenhower Library.

49. "Army Nears End of Segregation; Only 'Specialist' Negro Units Remain— Normal Turnover to Complete 'Integration,'" *New York Times*, 6 July 1954.

50. Bogart, *Project Clear*, p. xxi.

51. "Mark Clark Attacks Integration in Army," *Washington Post and Time Herald*, 29 April 1956.

52. Wilber M. Brucker, "Memorandum for the President, Subject: Army-Tulane Football Game," 2 May 1957, box 617, folder OF 143-E Football, Dwight D. Eisenhower papers, White House Central Files, Official File, Dwight D. Eisenhower Library.

53. "Army Game Protested, N.A.A.C.P. Urges Ban on '57 Football Clash at Tulane," *New York Times*, 3 November 1956.

54. U.S. President's Commission on an All-Volunteer Armed Force, *The Report of the President's Commission on an All-Volunteer Armed Force* (Washington, DC: U.S. Government Printing Office, 1970), 162.

55. Ibid.

56. Congressional Budget Office, *The All-Volunteer Military: Issues and Performance* (Washington, DC: Congressional Budget Office, 2007), 3.

57. Melvin R. Laird, "Report to the President and the Chairmen of Armed Services Committees of the Senate and of the House of Representatives (P.L. 92-129), Progress in Ending the Draft and Achieving the All-Volunteer Force," August 1972, pp. 11–12, box 8, folder Official Papers—Report—Progress in Ending the Draft and Achieving the All-Volunteer Force, All Volunteer Army Collection, U.S. Army Military History Institute.

CHAPTER 5. WHO SERVES WHEN NOT ALL SERVE?

1. John F. Kennedy to Gesell Committee, quoted by Robert S. McNamara, "Memorandum for the President," 24 July 1963, The President's Committee on Equal Opportunity in the Armed Forces, initial report, "Equality of Treatment and Opportunity for Negro Military Personnel Stationed within the United States," 13 June 1963, p. 45, box 67, folder Wa (2), Dwight D. Eisenhower papers, Post-Presidential papers, Principal File U to War 1963, Dwight D. Eisenhower Library.

2. Arthur Krock, "In the Nation: A Search for Equity in the Draft," *New York Times*, 23 June 1966.

3. National Advisory Commission on Selective Service, *In Pursuit of Equity: Who Serves When Not All Serve?* (Washington, DC: U.S. Government Printing Office, 1967), 3.

4. The President's Committee on Equal Opportunity in the Armed Forces, initial report, "Equality of Treatment and Opportunity for Negro Military Personnel Stationed within the United States," 13 June 1963, pp. 57–58, 92–93, box 67,

folder Wa (2), Dwight D. Eisenhower papers, Post-Presidential papers, Principal File U to War 1963, Dwight D. Eisenhower Library.

5. Ibid., 1.

6. Ibid., 1–2, 4.

7. Gesell Committee members to President John F. Kennedy, transmittal letter, 13 June 1963, box 67, folder Wa (2), ibid.

8. Ibid., 3.

9. Ibid., 5.

10. Ibid., 4.

11. Ibid., 4–5.

12. Ibid., 5–6. For a detailed accounting of African American personnel as a percentage of the American military from 1949 to 1962, see the chart on p. 6. Regarding African American officers, the army had 1.8 percent in 1949, 3.0 percent in 1954, and 3.2 percent in 1962. The navy had 0 percent in 1949, 0.1 percent in 1954, and 0.2 percent in 1962. The air force had 0.6 percent in 1949, 1.1 percent in 1954, and 1.2 percent in 1962. The marine corps had 0 percent in 1949, 0.1 percent in 1954, and 0.2 percent in 1962.

13. Ibid., 10.

14. Ibid., 10–11.

15. Ibid., 20–21, 23.

16. Ibid., 34–35.

17. Ibid., 42, 45.

18. U.S. President's Commission on an All-Volunteer Armed Force, *The Report of the President's Commission on an All-Volunteer Armed Force* (Washington, DC: U.S. Government Printing Office, 1970), 163; "Sobering Statistics for the Vietnam War," available at http://www.nationalvietnamveteransfoundation.org/statistics .htm (accessed 8 January 2016).

19. Deputy Chief of Staff (Personnel), "Impact of 'No-Draft' on Army Personnel Procurement," 1 September 1964, pp. 1–2, box 8, folder Official Papers—Report—Impact of 'No-Draft' on Army Personnel Procurement, Deputy Chief of Staff Personnel Study, All Volunteer Army Collection, U.S. Army Military History Institute.

20. Thomas Morris, "Report on DOD Study of the Draft, Statement of Thomas Morris, Assistant Secretary of Defense (Manpower) before the House Committee on Armed Services," 30 June 1966, pp. 2–4, box 8, folder Official Papers—Report—Department of Defense Study of the Draft, ibid.

21. Ibid., 4–7.

22. U.S. President's Commission on an All-Volunteer Armed Force, *The Report of the President's Commission on an All-Volunteer Armed Force*, pp. 204, 208–209. The cost estimates ranged from $3.67 billion to $16.66 billion.

23. Morris, "Report on DOD Study of the Draft, Statement of Thomas Morris, Assistant Secretary of Defense (Manpower) before the House Committee on Armed Services," 30 June 1966, pp. 4, 13, 22, box 8, folder Official Papers—Report—Department of Defense Study of the Draft, All Volunteer Army Collection, U.S. Army Military History Institute.

24. Roger T. Kelley, "Memorandum for Distribution List, Subject: Project Volunteer," 22 January 1970, p. 17, box 5, folder Official Papers—Memorandum—Report of the Program Evaluation Group on the All Volunteer Force, All Volunteer Army Collection, U.S. Army Military History Institute. Attached to Kelley's memorandum is a copy of the report of the Program Evaluation Group on the All-Volunteer Force.

25. William C. Westmoreland, "Notes for Joint Chiefs of Staff Discussion with President Nixon," 18 August 1970, pp. 2–3, box 1, folder Official Correspondence—General William C. Westmoreland, All Volunteer Army Collection, U.S. Army Military History Institute.

26. Ibid.

27. Don Irwin, "Draft Study Panel Named by Johnson: Advisory Unit Could Call for Wide Revisions," *Los Angeles Times*, 3 July 1966.

28. Lyndon B. Johnson, "Executive Order 11289," 2 July 1966, p. 1. For a copy of Executive Order 11289, see National Advisory Commission on Selective Service, *In Pursuit of Equity*, pp. 66–67.

29. National Advisory Commission on Selective Service, *In Pursuit of Equity*, pp. v–vi.

30. James Reston, "Washington: A Marshall Plan for Youth?" *New York Times*, 16 October 1966.

31. National Advisory Commission on Selective Service, *In Pursuit of Equity*, p. 4.

32. Ibid., iii, vii, 3–4. For more on "The Need for the Draft," see pp. 11–16; for more on "The Structure of the Proposed System," see pp. 31–36; for more on "The Individual in the System," see pp. 37–52; for more on "The Rejected," see pp. 57–60. Marshall failed to acknowledge the elasticity of qualitative personnel standards; since World War II, military service has demonstrated that quantitative and qualitative requirements are inversely proportional. The military services learned to adapt to most fluctuations.

33. For a listing and explanation of all thirteen recommendations, see ibid., 4–8.

34. Ibid., 4–10. For more on "An All-Volunteer Force," see pp. 11–14; for more on "Universal Training," see p. 15; for more on "National Service," see pp. 61–63. For more on social class divisions and the Vietnam War, see Christian G. Appy, *Working-Class War: American Combat Soldiers and Vietnam* (Chapel Hill: University of North Carolina Press, 1993).

35. National Advisory Commission on Selective Service, *In Pursuit of Equity*, pp. 4–10.

36. Press Division, Directorate of Advertising and Publicity, Headquarters, U.S. Air Force Recruiting Service, "History of the United States Air Force Recruiting Service," 1 July 1967–31 December 1967, pp. 3–4, box K289.92-23B, folder K289.92-23B, U.S. Air Force Historical Research Agency.

37. For more on Project 100,000, see Thomas Sticht, "Project 100,000 in the Vietnam War and Afterward," in *Scraping the Barrel: The Military Use of Sub-Standard Manpower* (Bronx, NY: Fordham University Press, 2012), edited by Sand-

ers Marble, 254–269; David A. Dawson, *The Impact of Project 100,000 on the Marine Corps* (Washington, DC: History and Museums Division, Headquarters U.S. Marine Corps, 1995).

38. William Leavitt, "Project 100,000: An Experiment in Salvaging People," *Space Digest* (January 1968): 59, attachment 7, Press Division, Directorate of Advertising and Publicity, Headquarters, U.S. Air Force Recruiting Service, "History of the United States Air Force Recruiting Service," 1 July 1967–31 December 1967, box K289.92-23B, folder K289.92-23B, U.S. Air Force Historical Research Agency.

39. Ibid.

40. Press Division, Directorate of Advertising and Publicity, Headquarters, U.S. Air Force Recruiting Service, "History of the United States Air Force Recruiting Service," 1 July 1967–31 December 1967, p. 4, box K289.92-23B, folder K289.92-23B, U.S. Air Force Historical Research Agency.

41. Leavitt, "Project 100,000: An Experiment in Salvaging People," p. 59. For more on the Universal Military Training Experimental Unit and its attempts to make "every soldier a citizen," see William A. Taylor, "The Fort Knox Experiment," in *Every Citizen a Soldier: The Campaign for Universal Military Training after World War II* (College Station: Texas A&M University Press, 2014), 103–117.

42. Leavitt, "Project 100,000: An Experiment in Salvaging People," pp. 59–61. For more on Project Transition, see the sidebar on p. 60.

43. Ibid., 61.

44. See also William Leavitt, "Project 100,000: A Human Story," *Air Force Magazine* (January 1968).

45. Melvin R. Laird, "Report to the President and the Chairmen of Armed Services Committees of the Senate and of the House of Representatives (P.L. 92-129), Progress in Ending the Draft and Achieving the All-Volunteer Force," August 1972, pp. 1–2, box 8, folder Official Papers—Report—Progress in Ending the Draft and Achieving the All-Volunteer Force, All Volunteer Army Collection, U.S. Army Military History Institute.

46. "Nixon Asks Abolition of Draft after Vietnam War Is Ended," *Washington Post*, 7 March 1968.

CHAPTER **6**. CONSCRIPTION IS A TAX

1. Stewart Alsop, "Mr. Nixon's Second Promise," *Newsweek*, 9 December 1968.

2. U.S. President's Commission on an All-Volunteer Armed Force, *The Report of the President's Commission on an All-Volunteer Armed Force* (Washington, DC: U.S. Government Printing Office, 1970), 9–10.

3. Ted Sell, "GI's Now Gentlemen: The Army, Mr. Jones? Everything but Phones," *Los Angeles Times*, 19 July 1971.

4. George F. Will, "All-Volunteer Armed Force: The Rarest Kind of Achievement," *Los Angeles Times*, 7 August 1974.

5. Richard M. Nixon quoted by Melvin R. Laird, "Report to the President and the Chairmen of Armed Services Committees of the Senate and of the House of Representatives (P.L. 92-129), Progress in Ending the Draft and Achieving the

All-Volunteer Force," August 1972, p. 1, box 8, folder Official Papers—Report—Progress in Ending the Draft and Achieving the All-Volunteer Force, All Volunteer Army Collection, U.S. Army Military History Institute.

6. Richard M. Nixon, "Memorandum for Melvin R. Laird," 29 January 1969, box 5, folder Official Papers—Memorandums Regarding Transition to All Volunteer Force—Creation of Project Volunteer, Provide, and Gates Commission—November 1968–December 1969, All Volunteer Army Collection, U.S. Army Military History Institute.

7. Richard M. Nixon to Melvin Laird, 6 February 1969, box 5, folder Official Papers—Memorandums Regarding Transition to All Volunteer Force—Creation of Project Volunteer, Provide, and Gates Commission—November 1968–December 1969, ibid.

8. Melvin Laird, "Memorandum for Richard M. Nixon," 7 February 1969, box 5, folder Official Papers—Memorandums Regarding Transition to All Volunteer Force—Creation of Project Volunteer, Provide, and Gates Commission—November 1968–December 1969, ibid.

9. Melvin R. Laird, "Report to the President and the Chairmen of Armed Services Committees of the Senate and of the House of Representatives (P.L. 92-129), Progress in Ending the Draft and Achieving the All-Volunteer Force," August 1972, p. 4, box 8, folder Official Papers—Report—Progress in Ending the Draft and Achieving the All-Volunteer Force, All Volunteer Army Collection, U.S. Army Military History Institute.

10. Richard M. Nixon, "Statement by the President Announcing the Creation of the Commission," 27 March 1969, U.S. President's Commission on an All-Volunteer Armed Force, *The Report of the President's Commission on an All-Volunteer Armed Force* (Washington, DC: Government Printing Office, 1970), v. In addition to official members, the commission had an extensive professional staff led by executive director William H. Meckling. David J. Callard was deputy executive director, and Stuart Altman, Harry J. Gilman, David Kassing, and Walter Y. Oi were directors of research.

11. Thomas S. Gates to Richard M. Nixon, 20 February 1970, ibid., i–ii.

12. U.S. President's Commission on an All-Volunteer Armed Force, *The Report of the President's Commission on an All-Volunteer Armed Force*, pp. 1, 5, 6–8. These projections assumed a stable force level of approximately 2.5 million. Even though there were roughly 500,000 enlistments per year at that time, estimates were that only half of them were true volunteers. The other half represented draft-induced volunteers. The commission predicted that increasing first-term basic pay (for both enlisted personnel and junior officers) would inflate the defense budget by approximately $2.7 billion annually. It also advised increasing first-term basic pay "on the ground of equity alone . . . regardless of the fate of the draft." The commission based its assessment on the mid-range force size of 2.5 million personnel. Cost estimates ranged from $1.5 billion annually for a force of 2 million service members to $4.6 billion annually for a force of 3 million service members.

13. Melvin R. Laird, "Report to the President and the Chairmen of Armed Services Committees of the Senate and of the House of Representatives (P.L.

92-129), Progress in Ending the Draft and Achieving the All-Volunteer Force," August 1972, p. 5, box 8, folder Official Papers—Report—Progress in Ending the Draft and Achieving the All-Volunteer Force, All Volunteer Army Collection, U.S. Army Military History Institute.

14. William K. Brehm, "Memorandum for the Assistant Secretary of Defense (Manpower and Reserve Affairs), Subject: Ongoing, Planned and Other Actions to Reduce Reliance on the Draft," 12 July 1969, p. 2, box 5, folder Official Papers—Memorandums Regarding Transition to All Volunteer Force—Creation of Project Volunteer, Provide, and Gates Commission—November 1968–December 1969, All Volunteer Army Collection, U.S. Army Military History Institute.

15. "New and Different Army," *Chicago Daily News*, 22 September 1973.

16. John G. Kester, "Memorandum for the Assistant Secretary of the Army (M&RA), Subject: Haircuts," 5 September 1969, pp. 1, 3–4, box 5, folder Official Papers—Memorandums Regarding Transition to All Volunteer Force—Creation of Project Volunteer, Provide, and Gates Commission—November 1968–December 1969, All Volunteer Army Collection, U.S. Army Military History Institute.

17. Alfred B. Fitt, "Memorandum for the Assistant Secretaries of the Military Departments (Manpower and Reserve Affairs), Subject: Study Plan for 'Project Volunteer,'" 15 November 1968, p. 7, box 5, folder Official Papers—Memorandums Regarding Transition to All Volunteer Force—Creation of Project Volunteer, Provide, and Gates Commission—November 1968–December 1969, ibid.

18. William K. Brehm, "Memorandum for the Assistant Secretary of Defense (Manpower and Reserve Affairs), Subject: Ongoing, Planned and Other Actions to Reduce Reliance on the Draft," 12 July 1969, p. 2, box 5, folder Official Papers—Memorandums Regarding Transition to All Volunteer Force—Creation of Project Volunteer, Provide, and Gates Commission—November 1968–December 1969, ibid.

19. Thomas S. Gates to Richard M. Nixon, 20 February 1970, in U.S. President's Commission on an All-Volunteer Armed Force, *The Report of the President's Commission on an All-Volunteer Armed Force*, pp. i–ii. Even though the report was unanimous, Roy Wilkins was unable to participate in all of the meetings due to poor health. As a result, he did not sign the report. Wilkins generally supported the conclusions and acknowledged, "Although I have been unable to share in its specific recommendations, I would like to endorse the basic idea of moving towards an all-volunteer armed force, and to express my hope that you will be able to take steps in the near future to reduce reliance on conscription." See Roy Wilkins to Richard M. Nixon, 6 February 1970, located on p. iii.

20. U.S. President's Commission on an All-Volunteer Armed Force, *The Report of the President's Commission on an All-Volunteer Armed Force*, p. 10. The pay raise for first-term officers was from $428 to $578 per month.

21. Ibid., 11–19.

22. E. Constantin Jr. to Robert F. Froehlke, 14 November 1972, box 6, folder Official Papers—Memorandums—Regarding Last Year of the Draft—June–December 1972, All Volunteer Army Collection, U.S. Army Military History Institute. The issue of military unionization received serious attention as well. In 1978

Congress specifically addressed the issue in that year's defense authorization act.

23. U.S. President's Commission on an All-Volunteer Armed Force, *The Report of the President's Commission on an All-Volunteer Armed Force*, pp. 169–171.

24. Melvin R. Laird, "Report to the President and the Chairmen of Armed Services Committees of the Senate and of the House of Representatives (P.L. 92-129), Progress in Ending the Draft and Achieving the All-Volunteer Force," August 1972, p. 6, box 8, folder Official Papers—Report—Progress in Ending the Draft and Achieving the All-Volunteer Force, All Volunteer Army Collection, U.S. Army Military History Institute.

25. Richard M. Nixon, "The President's Message to the Congress Outlining Actions and Proposals in a Move Toward Ending the Draft," 23 April 1970, in Weekly Compilation of Presidential Documents, pp. 571–573, 575, box 5, folder Official Papers—Memorandums regarding Transition to All Volunteer Army—Recommendations of Gates Commission—January–September 1970, All Volunteer Army Collection, U.S. Army Military History Institute. Three years earlier, key Nixon aide Martin Anderson relayed to Nixon, "It has been estimated that enlisted men could earn at least $3,600 a year in civilian jobs. Thus, they pay a *hidden tax* of $1,200 a year—twice that paid by the average taxpayer." Because a drafted enlistee earned an annual income of $2,400 during his first tour of duty, Anderson argued that draftees paid "a hidden tax" of $1,200 every year they served. Such sentiments formed the basis for Nixon's "conscription is a tax" argument and equated military service with civilian employment, military organizations with civilian institutions, and military values with civilian principles. They also generated significant contempt among career military personnel. See Martin Anderson, "Memorandum to Richard Nixon, Re: An Outline of the Factors Involved in Establishing an All-Volunteer Armed Force," 1967, p. 3, box 11, folder WHCF: SMOF Martin Anderson All Volunteer Armed Force [2 of 4], White House Central Files, Staff Member and Office Files, Martin Anderson Files, Richard M. Nixon Library.

26. Richard M. Nixon quoted in Melvin R. Laird, "Report to the President and the Chairmen of Armed Services Committees of the Senate and of the House of Representatives (P.L. 92-129), Progress in Ending the Draft and Achieving the All-Volunteer Force," August 1972, pp. 6–7, box 8, folder Official Papers—Report—Progress in Ending the Draft and Achieving the All-Volunteer Force, All Volunteer Army Collection, U.S. Army Military History Institute.

27. Laird, "Report to the President and the Chairmen of Armed Services Committees of the Senate and of the House of Representatives (P.L. 92-129), Progress in Ending the Draft and Achieving the All-Volunteer Force," August 1972, p. 7, box 8, folder Official Papers—Report—Progress in Ending the Draft and Achieving the All-Volunteer Force, ibid.

28. Ibid., 8–9.

29. Modern Volunteer Army Experiment, "Final Evaluation Report, Fort Benning, Georgia," July 1972, pp. tab A-1, 2, box 8, folder Official Papers—Report—Final Evaluation, Modern Volunteer Army Experiment, Fort Benning, Georgia—July 1972 (Part 1 of 2), All Volunteer Army Collection, U.S. Army Military History Institute.

30. Sell, "GI's Now Gentlemen."

31. Special Assistant of the Modern Volunteer Army, "Talking Paper, Subject: Modern Volunteer Army Accomplishments," 23 June 1971, box 6, folder Official Papers—Memorandums Regarding the Special Assistant of the Modern Volunteer Army—18 November 1970, All Volunteer Army Collection, U.S. Army Military History Institute.

32. Modern Volunteer Army Experiment, "Final Evaluation Report, Fort Benning, Georgia," July 1972, p. iii, box 8, folder Official Papers—Report—Final Evaluation, Modern Volunteer Army Experiment, Fort Benning, Georgia—July 1972 (Part 1 of 2), All Volunteer Army Collection, U.S. Army Military History Institute.

33. Laird, "Report to the President and the Chairmen of Armed Services Committees of the Senate and of the House of Representatives (P.L. 92-129), Progress in Ending the Draft and Achieving the All-Volunteer Force," August 1972, pp. 3–4, box 8, folder Official Papers—Report—Progress in Ending the Draft and Achieving the All-Volunteer Force, All Volunteer Army Collection, U.S. Army Military History Institute. The bill was the Draft Extension and Military Pay Bill.

34. William C. Westmoreland, "Address by General W. C. Westmoreland, Chief of Staff, United States Army, Annual Luncheon, Association of the United States Army, Washington, D.C.," 13 October 1970, pp. 1–3, box 1, folder Official Correspondence—General William C. Westmoreland, Office of the Chief of Staff, All Volunteer Army Collection, U.S. Army Military History Institute.

35. William C. Westmoreland to Richard M. Nixon, 30 June 1972, box 1, folder Official Correspondence—General William C. Westmoreland, Office of the Chief of Staff, ibid.

36. Laird, "Report to the President and the Chairmen of Armed Services Committees of the Senate and of the House of Representatives (P.L. 92-129), Progress in Ending the Draft and Achieving the All-Volunteer Force," August 1972, pp. iii, 1, box 8, folder Official Papers—Report—Progress in Ending the Draft and Achieving the All-Volunteer Force, All Volunteer Army Collection, U.S. Army Military History Institute.

37. Howard H. Callaway to Gerald R. Ford, 14 February 1974, box 8, folder Official Papers—Report—The Volunteer Army, One Year Later, All Volunteer Army Collection, U.S. Army Military History Institute.

38. Edward K. Delong, "Concerned: Secretary of Army Callaway Reports Volunteer Troops Face New Problems," *Stars and Stripes*, 24 September 1973, box 2, folder Official Correspondence—Letter to Secretary of the Army Howard H. Callaway from Private William B. Flanagin Jr. Regarding Conditions in Germany—11 October 1973, All Volunteer Army Collection, U.S. Army Military History Institute. For more on racial and drug problems in the post-Vietnam army, see Michael L. Lanning, *The Battles of Peace* (New York: Ivy Books, 1992).

39. Howard H. Callaway to Gerald R. Ford, 14 February 1974, box 8, folder Official Papers—Report—The Volunteer Army One Year Later, All Volunteer Army Collection, U.S. Army Military History Institute.

40. "Secretary Kelley, Brigadier General Montague, Meeting with Deputy Secretary of Defense," 7 May 1973, pp. 1, 3, box 1, folder Official Correspondence—To

Assistant Secretary of Defense Kelley Regarding Transition to AVF—January–May 1973, All Volunteer Army Collection, U.S. Army Military History Institute.

41. Brigadier General Montague, "Memorandum to Secretary Kelley thru Lieutenant General Taber, Subject: First Meeting of DOD Task Force on the All-Volunteer Force," 14 May 1973, p. 3, box 1, folder Official Correspondence—To Assistant Secretary of Defense Kelley Regarding Transition to AVF—January–May 1973, ibid.

42. Lieutenant General Taber, Brigadier General Montague, and Stephen E. Herbits, "Prior Clearance for Mental Standards Changes," 5 June 1973, pp. 1–2, box 1, folder Official Correspondence—To Lieutenant General (LTG) Taber and Brigadier General Montague, Congressman Stephen Herbits Regarding AVF—June–July 1973, All Volunteer Army Collection, U.S. Army Military History Institute.

43. Nick Thimmesch, "Volunteer Army's Soft-Sell Missing Target," *Chicago Tribune*, 2 September 1973, box 2, folder Official Correspondence Regarding Publicity for Modern Volunteer Army Concept, August–October 1973, All Volunteer Army Collection, U.S. Army Military History Institute.

44. For recent incarnations of the national service debate, see John S. McCain III and Stanley A. McChrystal, "Expand Opportunities for Young Americans to Serve Their Country," *CNN*, 10 August 2015, available at http://www.cnn.com/2015/08/10/opinions/mccain-mcchrystal-national-service-legislation/ (accessed 9 January 2016); William A. Galston, "Our National Responsibilities," *U.S. News & World Report*, November 2010, 8. For discussion inside the government, see U.S. Congress, Senate, Committee on Health, Education, Labor, and Pensions, *The Next Generation of National Service: Hearings of the Committee on Health, Education, Labor, and Pensions*, 111th Cong., 1st sess., 10 March 2009.

45. C. L. Sulzberger, "Where Are Volunteers?" *New York Times*, 26 September 1973, box 2, folder Official Correspondence Regarding Publicity for Modern Volunteer Army Concept, August–October 1973, All Volunteer Army Collection, U.S. Army Military History Institute.

46. "The Volunteer Army," *Atlanta Journal*, 29 October 1973, in box 2, folder Official Correspondence Regarding Publicity for Modern Volunteer Army Concept, August–October 1973, ibid. For more on the U.S. Army's publicity efforts, see this folder.

47. Howard H. Callaway to Gerald R. Ford, 14 February 1974, box 8, folder Official Papers—Report—The Volunteer Army, One Year Later, All Volunteer Army Collection, U.S. Army Military History Institute. For the report, see Howard H. Callaway, "The Volunteer Army—One Year Later," 11 February 1974, ibid.

48. William K. Brehm to John C. Stennis, 17 December 1974, box 2, folder Official Correspondence—Letter to John C. Stennis, Chairman, Armed Forces Committee—Population Representation in All-Volunteer Force—17 December 1974, All Volunteer Army Collection, U.S. Army Military History Institute. Brehm entitled the report "Population Representation in the All-Volunteer Force" and included it as an attachment to his letter.

49. Howard H. Callaway to Major General John A. Wickham Jr., Military As-

sistant to the Secretary of Defense, 1 July 1974, box 2, folder Official Correspondence—Secretary of the Army Howard H. Callaway at Authorized Manpower—1 July 1974, All Volunteer Army Collection, U.S. Army Military History Institute.

50. Howard H. Callaway, "FY 74 Volunteer Army Highlights," 1 July 1974, pp. 1, 3, attached to Howard H. Callaway to Major General John A. Wickham Jr., Military Assistant to the Secretary of Defense, 1 July 1974, box 2, folder Official Correspondence—Secretary of the Army Howard H. Callaway at Authorized Manpower—1 July 1974, ibid.

51. Robert F. Froehlke, "Statement before the Defense Manpower Commission Hearing on Future Needs and Methods of Providing Manpower for the Defense of the United States of America," 17 July 1975, pp. 1–3, 13, box 1, folder Official Correspondence—Interviews with Robert Frederick Froehlke, All Volunteer Army Collection, U.S. Army Military History Institute. Froehlke served as secretary of the army from 1 July 1971 to 14 May 1973.

CHAPTER 7. MORE THAN EVER BEFORE

1. Project Volunteer Committee, "Plans and Actions to Move toward an All Volunteer Force: A Report to the Secretary of Defense," 14 August 1970, p. 14, box C1, folder All-Volunteer Force Document 41, Melvin R. Laird papers, Gerald R. Ford Library.

2. Martin Binkin, "Women's Rights and National Security," Washington Post, 7 July 1976.

3. Roper Organization, "Attitudes Regarding the Assignment of Women in the Armed Forces: The Public Perspective," August 1992, p. 3, box 7, folder Poll–The Roper Organization Public Survey, RG 220 Presidential Commission on the Assignment of Women in the Armed Forces, Records Relating to Polls and Surveys of Public and Military Attitudes, Roper Organization Survey and 1992 Survey on Gender in the Military, National Archives and Records Administration.

4. Burrelli, "Women in Combat: Issues for Congress," p. 1.

5. Michelle Sandhoff and Mady Wechsler Segal, "Women in the U.S. Military: The Evolution of Gender Norms and Military Requirements," in The Modern American Military (Oxford: Oxford University Press, 2013), edited by David M. Kennedy, 277.

6. David F. Burrelli, "Women in the Armed Forces," Congressional Research Service Report, 29 September 1998, p. 1.

7. Kristy N. Kamarck, "Women in Combat: Issues for Congress," Congressional Research Service Report, 18 August 2015, p. 3.

8. "First Enlisted Women Are Sworn in by Navy: Sullivan Hails Event as Service Milestone," New York Times, 8 July 1948.

9. "Midnight-Plus-One Service: WACs Here Believed Regular Army Firsts," Atlanta Constitution, 8 July 1948, box 12, folder 1949 [2 of 2], Alvan C. Gillem papers, U.S. Army Military History Institute.

10. Department of Defense, "DACOWITS: Supporting Military Womanpower," Commanders Digest 18, 2 (July 1975): 30, 32, box K141.33, folder History of the Women in the Air Force, 1 July 1975–31 December 1975, U.S. Air Force Histor-

ical Research Agency. Congress removed grade restrictions in 1967. The Supreme Court resolved the issue of a quarters allowance in 1973.

11. Press Division, Directorate of Advertising and Publicity, Headquarters, U.S. Air Force Recruiting Service, "History of the United States Air Force Recruiting Service," 1 July 1967–31 December 1967, pp. 8, 21–23, box K289.92-23B, folder K289.92-23B, U.S. Air Force Historical Research Agency.

12. Burrelli, "Women in Combat: Issues for Congress," p. 1.

13. Burrelli, "Women in the Armed Forces," p. 14.

14. Burrelli, "Women in Combat: Issues for Congress," p. 2.

15. Burrelli, "Women in the Armed Forces," p. 2.

16. Project Volunteer Committee, "Plans and Actions to Move toward an All Volunteer Force: A Report to the Secretary of Defense," 14 August 1970, p. 1, box C1, folder All-Volunteer Force Document 41, Melvin R. Laird papers, Gerald R. Ford Library. The committee membership included all assistant secretaries (manpower and reserve affairs) and all deputy chiefs of staff (personnel). For a full listing of the committee membership, see pp. 1–2.

17. Melvin R. Laird, "Remarks by the Honorable Melvin R. Laird Secretary of Defense before the Defense Advisory Committee on Women in the Services," 13 April 1970, p. 3, box A93, folder Speeches (Laird)—4/13/70—Defense Advisory Committee on Women in the Services, Melvin R. Laird papers, Gerald R. Ford Library.

18. Project Volunteer Committee, "Plans and Actions to Move toward an All Volunteer Force: A Report to the Secretary of Defense," 14 August 1970, pp. 1–27, box C1, folder All-Volunteer Force Document 41, Melvin R. Laird papers, Gerald R. Ford Library.

19. Ibid.

20. Roger T. Kelley, Assistant Secretary of Defense (Manpower and Reserve Affairs), "Memorandum for Distribution List, Subject: Project Volunteer," 22 January 1970, pp. 1, 10, box 5, folder Official Papers—Memorandum—Report of the Program Evaluation Group on the All Volunteer Force—22 January 1970, All Volunteer Army Collection, U.S. Army Military History Institute. Attached to Kelley's memorandum is a copy of the report of the Program Evaluation Group on the All-Volunteer Force.

21. William C. Westmoreland, "Straight Talk from the Chief on the Modern Volunteer Army," May 1971, p. 17, box 1, folder Official Correspondence—General William C. Westmoreland, Office of the Chief of Staff, All Volunteer Army Collection, U.S. Army Military History Institute.

22. Howard H. Callaway, "The Volunteer Army—One Year Later," 11 February 1974, p. V-3, box 8, folder Official Papers—Report—The Volunteer Army, One Year Later, All Volunteer Army Collection, U.S. Army Military History Institute.

23. Melvin R. Laird, "Report to the President and the Chairmen of Armed Services Committees of the Senate and of the House of Representatives (P.L. 92-129), Progress in Ending the Draft and Achieving the All-Volunteer Force," August 1972, p. 26, box 8, folder Official Papers—Report—Progress in Ending the Draft and Achieving the All-Volunteer Force, All Volunteer Army Collection,

U.S. Army Military History Institute. Laird sent similar letters to President Gerald R. Ford, p. iii; Chairman of the Senate Armed Services Committee John C. Stennis (D-MS), p. v; and Chairman of the House Armed Services Committee F. Edward Hébert (D-LA), p. vii.

24. Laird, "Report to the President and the Chairmen of Armed Services Committees of the Senate and of the House of Representatives (P.L. 92-129): Progress in Ending the Draft and Achieving the All-Volunteer Force," August 1972, pp. 1, 31, box A51, folder All-Volunteer Force 1971–1972, Melvin R. Laird papers, Gerald R. Ford Library. Laird titled Chapter IV "The Remaining Problems and How to Solve Them" and dedicated it to a detailed exploration of these topics.

25. Ibid., 32.

26. Ibid., 33.

27. Ibid.

28. Roger T. Kelley, "Memorandum for Distribution List, Subject: Report on AVF to Senate Armed Services Committee," 25 September 1972, pp. 7–8, box 6, folder Official Papers—Memorandum—Report on AVF to Senate Armed Services Committee—25 September 1972, All Volunteer Army Collection, U.S. Army Military History Institute. See especially the chart entitled "Recruiting Military Women."

29. John C. Stennis, "Press Release, The All-Volunteer Force," 23 September 1973, p. 4, box 7, folder Printed Material—Press Release—Senator John C. Stennis, Chairman, Senate Committee on Armed Forces—24 September 1973, All Volunteer Army Collection, U.S. Army Military History Institute.

30. Robert M. Montague Jr. to Stephen E. Herbits, 28 November 1973, box 7, folder Official Papers—Memorandum Regarding Women's Army Corps Emphasis by Command Group—28 November 1973, All Volunteer Army Collection, U.S. Army Military History Institute.

31. Forest G. Crittenden, "Memorandum for Command General, Subject: WAC Emphasis by Command Group," attached to Robert M. Montague Jr. to Stephen E. Herbits, 28 November 1973, box 7, folder Official Papers—Memorandum Regarding Women's Army Corps Emphasis by Command Group—28 November 1973, ibid.

32. Charles W. Dyke, "Memorandum for the Chief of Legislative Liaison, Director of the Army Budget, OCA, Subject: Ideas to Enhance Recruiting for the Volunteer Army," 11 February 1974, box 7, folder Official Papers—Memorandums—Ideas to Enhance Recruiting for the All Volunteer Army—11 February 1974, ibid.

33. Department of Defense, "General Holm Named Journal's 'Woman of the Year,'" *Commanders Digest* 18, 2 (July 1975): 12–13, box K141.33, folder History of the Women in the Air Force 1 July 1975–31 December 1975, U.S. Air Force Historical Research Agency. For more on Holm, see Jeanne Holm, *Women in the Military: An Unfinished Revolution* (New York: Ballantine Books, 1982).

34. Staff of the Directorate, Women in the Air Force, "History of the Women in the Air Force," 1 July 1975–31 December 1975, p. 1, box K141.33, folder History of the Women in the Air Force 1 July 1975–31 December 1975, U.S. Air Force Historical Research Agency.

35. Carole Frings, Office of the General Counsel, Office of the Assistant Secretary of Defense, "Legislative Briefing Made at the DACOWITS 1975 Fall Meeting," pp. C-10–C-11, attachment 15, Staff of the Directorate, Women in the Air Force, "History of the Women in the Air Force," 1 July 1975–31 December 1975, box K141.33, folder History of the Women in the Air Force 1 July 1975–31 December 1975, U.S. Air Force Historical Research Agency.

36. Staff of the Directorate, Women in the Air Force, "History of the Women in the Air Force," 1 July 1975–31 December 1975, p. 6, box K141.33, folder History of the Women in the Air Force 1 July 1975–31 December 1975, U.S. Air Force Historical Research Agency.

37. Frings, Office of the General Counsel, Office of the Assistant Secretary of Defense, "Legislative Briefing Made at the DACOWITS 1975 Fall Meeting," pp. C-6, C-8, ibid.

38. Staff of the Directorate, Women in the Air Force, "History of the Women in the Air Force," ibid.

39. Frings, Office of the General Counsel, Office of the Assistant Secretary of Defense, "Legislative Briefing Made at the DACOWITS 1975 Fall Meeting," pp. C-2–C-3, ibid.

40. Ibid.

41. Kamarck, "Women in Combat: Issues for Congress," p. 4.

42. Department of Defense, *Report of the Task Force on Women in the Military* (Washington, DC: U.S. Government Printing Office, 1988), 8–20.

43. Kamarck, "Women in Combat: Issues for Congress," p. 5.

44. "Public Law 102-190," 5 December 1991, pp. 1–3, box 1, folder Statute-Public Law 102-190-5 December 1991, Record Group 220 Presidential Commission on the Assignment of Women in the Armed Forces, Records Relating to the Commission's Establishment and Organization, National Archives and Records Administration.

45. "Biographies of Commissioners," box 1, folder Biographies of Commissioners, Record Group 220 Presidential Commission on the Assignment of Women in the Armed Forces, Records Relating to the Commission's Establishment and Organization, National Archives and Records Administration.

46. Burrelli, "Women in Combat: Issues for Congress," p. 4.

47. Kamarck, "Women in Combat: Issues for Congress," p. 1.

48. Burrelli, "Women in Combat: Issues for Congress," p. i; Kamarck, "Women in Combat: Issues for Congress," p. i.

49. Burrelli, "Women in the Armed Forces," p. 2.

CHAPTER 8. TO SERVE IN SILENCE

1. Anonymous service member, "Confidential Communication Mechanism," 2010, cited in Department of Defense, *Report of the Comprehensive Review of the Issues Associated with a Repeal of 'Don't Ask, Don't Tell'* (Washington, DC: U.S. Government Printing Office, 2010), 6.

2. Ibid.

3. Barack H. Obama, "Remarks on Signing the Don't Ask, Don't Tell Repeal

Act of 2010," 22 December 2010, number 201001091, Daily Compilation of Presidential Documents.

4. Cited in Aaron Belkin, Morten G. Ender, Nathaniel Frank, Stacie R. Furia, George Lucas, Gary Packard, Steven M. Samuels, Tammy Schultz, and David R. Segal, "Readiness and DADT Repeal: Has the New Policy of Open Service Undermined the Military?" *Armed Forces and Society* 39, 4 (October 2013): 589, 597n8.

5. Les Aspin, *All Volunteer: A Fair System; A Quality Force* (Washington, DC: U.S. Government Printing Office, 1991).

6. Les Aspin and William Dickinson, *Defense for a New Era: Lessons of the Persian Gulf War* (Washington, DC: U.S. Government Printing Office, 1992), 47, box NA-414-Defense for a New Era: Lessons of the Persian Gulf War, folder NA-414-Defense for a New Era: Lessons of the Persian Gulf War, U.S. Air Force Historical Research Agency.

7. Ibid., 45. Especially relevant for this book was the material under the heading entitled "Providing the Forces: U.S. Personnel in the Persian Gulf Crisis," pp. 45–60.

8. Ibid., 47–48.

9. Ibid., 48–49.

10. Ibid., 49.

11. Saundra J. Reinke and Timothy G. Smith, "Out and Serving Proudly: Repealing 'Don't Ask, Don't Tell,'" *Politics and Policy* 39, 6 (December 2011): 926.

12. Beth Bailey, "The Politics of Dancing: 'Don't Ask, Don't Tell,' and the Role of Moral Claims," *Journal of Policy History* 25, 1 (2013): 91–92.

13. John Lancaster, "Powell Relents on Defense Cuts, but Not on Gays," *Washington Post*, 19 November 1992.

14. U.S. Congress, "Homosexuals in the Military: Evolution of the Don't Ask, Don't Tell Policy," *Congressional Digest*, April 2010, p. 103.

15. Jody Feder, "'Don't Ask, Don't Tell': A Legal Analysis," *Congressional Research Service Report*, 6 August 2013, p. 1.

16. U.S. Congress, "Homosexuals in the Military," p. 103.

17. Bailey, "The Politics of Dancing," p. 89.

18. Jeffrey H. Birnbaum, "Clinton Adopts Policy to Ease Military Gay Ban: Asking Sexual Orientation of Recruits Is Barred; Nunn Plans Alternative," *Wall Street Journal*, 20 July 1993.

19. U.S. Congress, "Homosexuals in the Military," p. 103.

20. John Lancaster, "Senators Find Clinton Policy on Gays in the Military Confusing," *Washington Post*, 21 July 1993; John Lancaster, "Policy Tosses Issue to Courts, Ambiguity Seen Leading to Protracted Litigation," *Washington Post*, 20 July 1993. Aspin first declared that homosexual statements were not grounds for discharge, only to concede later in his testimony to Sam Nunn that they in fact were.

21. Section 571 of the law codified the DADT policy.

22. U.S. Congress, "Homosexuals in the Military," p. 104.

23. Office of the Under Secretary of Defense (Personnel and Readiness), "Report to the Secretary of Defense: Review of the Effectiveness of the Application

and Enforcement of the Department's Policy on Homosexual Conduct in the Military," April 1998, p. 1, available at http://www.dod.gov/pubs/rpt040798.html (accessed 1 September 2015).

24. Department of Defense, "Directive 1332.30: Separation of Regular and Reserve Commissioned Officers," 11 December 2008, p. 9, available at www.dtic .mil/whs/directives/corrres/pdf/133230p.pdf (accessed 29 August 2015).

25. Office of the Under Secretary of Defense (Personnel and Readiness), "Report to the Secretary of Defense: Review of the Effectiveness of the Application and Enforcement of the Department's Policy on Homosexual Conduct in the Military," p. 4.

26. David F. Burrelli and Jody Feder, "Homosexuals and the U.S. Military: Current Issues," *Congressional Research Service Report*, 22 July 2009, pp. 4–5.

27. Office of the Under Secretary of Defense (Personnel and Readiness), "Report to the Secretary of Defense: Review of the Effectiveness of the Application and Enforcement of the Department's Policy on Homosexual Conduct in the Military," pp. 2–4, 10. Discharges decreased from 1980 to 1994 but then "increased each year since that time." See especially table 1, "Discharge for Homosexual Conduct, Fiscal Year 1980–1997," on pp. 11–12.

28. "Flag and General Officers for the Military," available at www.cmrlink.org /HMilitary.asp?docID=350 (accessed 29 August 2015).

29. White House Office of the Press Secretary, "Remarks by the President in State of the Union Address," 27 January 2010, p. 19, available at www.whitehouse .gov/the-press-office/remarks-president-state-union-address (accessed 31 August 2015).

30. Department of Defense, *Report of the Comprehensive Review of the Issues Associated with a Repeal of 'Don't Ask, Don't Tell,'* pp. 1–3. DADT was officially known as Section 654 of Title 10 of the United States Code. Of the additional approximately 100,000 service member responses, nearly three-quarters resulted from the online inbox. The G.I. survey led by Samuel Stouffer during World War II was a larger effort in terms of scope, respondents, and results. For more on the G.I. survey, see Joseph W. Ryan, *Samuel Stouffer and the GI Survey* (Knoxville: University of Tennessee Press, 2013). For analysis and results of the G.I. survey, see Samuel A. Stouffer, Edward A. Suchman, Leland C. DeVinney, Shirley A. Star, and Robin M. Williams Jr., *Adjustment during Army Life*, vol. 1 of *Studies in Social Psychology in World War II: The American Soldier* (Princeton, NJ: Princeton University Press, 1949); Samuel A. Stouffer, Arthur A. Lumsdaine, Marion Harper Lumsdaine, Robin M. Williams Jr., M. Brewster Smith, Irving L. Janis, Shirley A. Star, and Leonard S. Cottrell Jr., *Combat and Its Aftermath*, vol. 2 of *Studies in Social Psychology in World War II: The American Soldier* (Princeton, NJ: Princeton University Press, 1949).

31. Department of Defense, "Support Plan for Implementation," 30 November 2010.

32. Department of Defense, *Report of the Comprehensive Review of the Issues Associated with a Repeal of 'Don't Ask, Don't Tell,'* pp. 3–4.

33. Ibid., 8, 10.

34. Ibid., 10–17. Other areas included "Leadership, Training, and Education"; "Privacy and Cohabitation"; "Equal Opportunity"; "Benefits"; "Re-accession"; "UCMJ"; and "Follow-on Review."

35. Saundra J. Reinke and Timothy G. Smith, "Out and Serving Proudly: Repealing 'Don't Ask, Don't Tell,'" *Politics and Policy* 39, 6 (December 2011): 937. As noted by the authors, two seats in the U.S. House of Representatives were vacant at the time of the vote. For detailed analysis of congressional votes on repeal of DADT, see pp. 925–948.

36. Bailey, "The Politics of Dancing," pp. 106–107.

37. Barack H. Obama, "Remarks on Signing the Don't Ask, Don't Tell Repeal Act of 2010," 22 December 2010, p. 1–3, number 201001091, Daily Compilation of Presidential Documents.

38. Feder, "'Don't Ask, Don't Tell,'" pp. i, 3.

39. Ibid., 3.

40. Aaron Belkin, Morten G. Ender, Nathaniel Frank, Stacie R. Furia, George Lucas, Gary Packard, Steven M. Samuels, Tammy Schultz, and David R. Segal, "Readiness and DADT Repeal: Has the New Policy of Open Service Undermined the Military?" *Armed Forces and Society* 39, 4 (October 2013): 587–588. The authors held appointments at the following institutions: San Francisco State University, United States Military Academy, Columbia University, University of California Los Angeles, United States Naval Academy, United States Air Force Academy, United States Marine Corps War College, and University of Maryland.

CHAPTER 9. AN UNEASY RELATIONSHIP

1. Steve Fainaru, "Where Military Rules Don't Apply; Blackwater's Security Force in Iraq Given Wide Latitude by State Department," *Washington Post*, 20 September 2007.

2. Moshe Schwartz, "The Department of Defense's Use of Private Security Contractors in Afghanistan and Iraq: Background, Analysis, and Options for Congress," *Congressional Research Service Report*, 13 May 2011, p. 7.

3. For more on private security contractors, see Allison Stanger, *One Nation under Contract: The Outsourcing of American Power and the Future of Foreign Policy* (New Haven, CT: Yale University Press, 2009); Deborah Avant, *The Market for Force: The Consequences of Privatizing Security* (New York: Cambridge University Press, 2005); Peter Singer, *Corporate Warriors: The Rise of the Privatized Military Industry* (Ithaca, NY: Cornell University Press, 2003).

4. Thomas X. Hammes, "Private Contractors in Conflict Zones: The Good, the Bad, and the Strategic Impact," *Strategic Forum* 260 (November 2010): 1.

5. Matthew Quirk, "Private Military Contractor's: A Buyer's Guide," *Atlantic*, September 2004, available at http://www.theatlantic.com/magazine/archive/2004/09/private-military-contractors/303424/ (accessed 13 October 2015).

6. Schwartz, "The Department of Defense's Use of Private Security Contractors in Afghanistan and Iraq," p. 1.

7. For more on Fallujah, see Bing West, *No True Glory: A Frontline Account of the Battle for Fallujah* (New York: Bantam Books, 2005). It is important to note that

the Second Battle of Fallujah, also known as Operation Al-Fajr, occurred from 7 November to 23 December 2004. It had little to do with the four private security contractors' deaths seven months earlier, but rather sought to eliminate the city as a base for insurgent operations and as a possible negative precedent for other cities throughout Iraq.

8. Jeffrey Gettleman, "4 from U.S. Killed in Ambush in Iraq: Mob Drags Bodies," *New York Times*, 1 April 2004. It is important to note that many private military contractors honorably served with distinction in the U.S. military prior to their employment as contractors. For example, the four Blackwater private military contractors discussed were all prior Special Operations Forces personnel, three having served with the U.S. Navy SEALs and one with the U.S. Army Rangers.

9. Monica Davey, "Americans Are Jolted by Gruesome Reminders of the Day in Mogadishu," *New York Times*, 1 April 2004; Gettleman, "4 from U.S. Killed in Ambush in Iraq." For more on the events in Mogadishu, Somalia, see Mark Bowden, *Black Hawk Down: A Story of Modern War* (New York: Grove Press, 1999). Even with journalistic comparisons, however, the results were starkly different. Few analysts used the Fallujah incident to argue for a withdrawal from Iraq, whereas the earlier events in Mogadishu triggered a departure of U.S. forces from Somalia.

10. John M. Broder and James Risen, "Blackwater Tops All Firms in Iraq in Shooting Rate, Aggressive Reputation: Pentagon Sends a Team to Review the Role of Security Guards," *New York Times*, 27 September 2007.

11. U.S. Congress, House Committee on Oversight and Government Reform, *Private Security Contracting in Iraq and Afghanistan*, 110th Cong., 1st sess., 2 October 2007; U.S. Congress, House Committee on the Judiciary, Subcommittee on Crime, Terrorism, and Homeland Security, *Enforcement of Federal Criminal Law to Protect Americans Working for U.S. Contractors in Iraq*, 110th Cong., 1st sess., 19 December 2007; U.S. Congress, Senate Committee on Homeland Security and Governmental Affairs, *An Uneasy Relationship: U.S. Reliance on Private Security Firms in Overseas Operations*, 110th Cong., 2nd sess., 27 February 2008; U.S. Congress, House Committee on Armed Services, *Contingency Contracting: Implementing a Call for Urgent Reform*, 110th Cong., 2nd sess., 9 April 2008; U.S. Congress, House Committee on Oversight and Government Reform, Subcommittee on National Security and Foreign Affairs, *Commission on Wartime Contracting: Interim Findings and Path Forward*, 111th Cong., 1st sess., 9 June 2009.

12. Of course, militaries have used private security contractors, often referred to as mercenaries, throughout human history. For more on the historical context of private security contractors, see Sean McFate, *The Modern Mercenary: Private Armies and What They Mean for World Order* (Oxford: Oxford University Press, 2014).

13. Some observers estimated that private security contractors in Iraq and Afghanistan represented approximately 10 percent of total military contractors. See Scott L. Efflandt, "Military Professionalism and Private Military Contractors," *Parameters* 44, 2 (Summer 2014): 53.

14. Deborah Avant and Renée de Nevers, "Military Contractors and the Amer-

ican Way of War," in *The Modern American Military* (Oxford: Oxford University Press, 2013), edited by David M. Kennedy, 135–137.

15. Hammes, "Private Contractors in Conflict Zones," pp. 1, 3.

16. Ibid., 3.

17. Heidi M. Peters, Moshe Schwartz, and Lawrence Kapp, "Department of Defense Contractor and Troop Levels in Iraq and Afghanistan: 2007–2014," *Congressional Research Service Report*, 22 July 2015, p. 6. For monthly details of contract obligations in Iraq and Afghanistan, see table 5, "DOD Contract Obligations in Iraq and Afghanistan Theaters of Operation (FY 2007–FY 2014; in FY 2015 dollars)."

18. Ibid., 5. For monthly details of the number of private security contractors in Iraq, see table 4, "DOD PSC Personnel and Troop Levels in Iraq (September 2007–September 2013)."

19. Schwartz, "The Department of Defense's Use of Private Security Contractors in Afghanistan and Iraq," pp. 11, 13.

20. Ibid., 7–8. As of 31 March 2011 there were 18,971 total private security contractors in Afghanistan: 17,989 (95 percent) of them were Afghans, 732 (4 percent) were third-country nationals, and only 250 (1 percent) were Americans. See especially table 1, "Number of Security Contractors in Afghanistan by Nationality."

21. Peters, Schwartz, and Kapp, "Department of Defense Contractor and Troop Levels in Iraq and Afghanistan: 2007–2014," p. 3. For monthly details of the number of private security contractors in Afghanistan see table 2, "DOD PSC Personnel and Troop Levels in Afghanistan (September 2007–December 2014)."

22. Moshe Schwartz and Jennifer Church, "Department of Defense's Use of Contractors to Support Military Operations: Background, Analysis, and Issues for Congress," *Congressional Research Service Report*, 17 May 2013, p. 2.

23. Schwartz, "The Department of Defense's Use of Private Security Contractors in Afghanistan and Iraq," p. 9.

24. Hammes, "Private Contractors in Conflict Zones," p. 1.

25. Ryan Kelty, "Citizen Soldiers and Civilian Contractors: Soldiers' Unit Cohesion and Retention Attitudes in the 'Total Force,'" *Journal of Political and Military Sociology* 37, 2 (Winter 2009): 147–148.

26. James Glanz and Alissa J. Rubin, "From Errand to Fatal Shot to Hail of Fire to 17 Deaths," *New York Times*, 3 October 2007. For a negative portrayal of Blackwater, see Jeremy Scahill, *Blackwater: The Rise of the World's Most Powerful Mercenary Army* (New York: Nation Books, 2007). For a positive depiction of Blackwater, see Erik Prince, *Civilian Warriors: The Inside Story of Blackwater and the Unsung Heroes of the War on Terror* (New York: Portfolio/Penguin, 2013). Due to adverse publicity, Blackwater repeatedly changed its name, first to Xe and then to Academi.

27. It is important to note that private security contractors were not the only ones involved in atrocities. For example, American service members committed abuse at Abu Ghraib in Iraq and locations in Afghanistan. For more on Abu Ghraib, see Seymour M. Hersh, *Chain of Command: The Road from 9/11 to Abu Ghraib* (New York: HarperCollins, 2004).

28. Schwartz, "The Department of Defense's Use of Private Security Contractors in Afghanistan and Iraq," p. 5.

29. U.S. Congress, *To Receive Testimony on the Challenges Facing the Department of Defense: Hearings before the United States Senate Committee on Armed Services,* 110th Cong., 2nd sess., 27 January 2009.

30. Ashton Carter, *Department of Defense Instruction 3020.50: Private Security Contractors (PSCs) Operating in Contingency Operations,* 22 July 2009.

31. Public Law 110-181 established the Commission on Wartime Contracting.

32. Commission on Wartime Contracting in Iraq and Afghanistan, *Transforming Wartime Contracting: Controlling Costs, Reducing Risks* (Washington, DC: U.S. Government Printing Office, 2011), 4.

33. Schwartz and Church, "Department of Defense's Use of Contractors to Support Military Operations," pp. i, 1. For details of this trend see figure 1, "Contractor Personnel as Percentage of DOD Workforce in Recent Operations," on p. 2.

34. Kelty, "Citizen Soldiers and Civilian Contractors," p. 134.

35. Hammes, "Private Contractors in Conflict Zones," p. 7.

36. Scott L. Efflandt, "Military Professionalism and Private Military Contractors," *Parameters* 44, 2 (Summer 2014): 58.

37. David Isenberg, "Private Military Contractors and U.S. Grand Strategy," *International Peace Research Institute Report,* 2009, p. 5. Also see David Isenberg, *Shadow Force: Private Security Contractors in Iraq* (Westport, CT: Greenwood, 2009).

38. Casper Alexander Daugaard, "Blackwater and Private Military Contractors," *Yale Review of International Studies,* August 2012, available at http://yris.yira.org/essays/707 (accessed 13 October 2015).

39. "Private Military Contractors: Beyond Blackwater," *Economist,* 23 November 2013, available at http://www.economist.com/news/business/21590370-industry-reinvents-itself-after-demise-its-most-controversial-firm-beyond-blackwater (accessed 13 October 2015). Academi eventually merged with Triple Canopy to form the Constellis Group.

40. Spencer S. Hsu, Victoria St. Martin, and Keith L. Alexander, "Four Blackwater Guards Guilty in Iraqi Deaths," *Washington Post,* 23 October 2014.

41. "Conviction of Blackwater Guards Closes Painful Chapter for Iraqis," *New York Times,* 15 April 2015.

42. "Blackwater's Legacy Goes beyond Public View," *New York Times,* 15 April 2015.

43. Amnesty International, "The Costs of Outsourcing War," available at http://www.amnestyusa.org/our-work/issues/military-police-and-arms/private-military-and-security-companies (accessed 13 October 2015).

44. Sean McFate, "Reining in Soldiers of Fortune," *New York Times,* 18 April 2015. Also see McFate, *The Modern Mercenary.*

45. Efflandt, "Military Professionalism and Private Military Contractors," pp. 49, 51, 53.

1. Military Leadership Diversity Commission, *From Representation to Inclusion: Diversity Leadership for the 21st-Century Military, Final Report* (Arlington, VA: Military Leadership Diversity Commission, 2011), xvi.

2. Ibid., xix.

3. David R. Segal and Lawrence J. Korb, "Manning and Financing the All-Volunteer Force," in *The Modern American Military* (Oxford: Oxford University Press, 2013), edited by David M. Kennedy, 122.

4. U.S. military operations in Afghanistan continued after December 2014 under Operation Freedom's Sentinel.

5. David F. Burrelli, "Women in Combat: Issues for Congress," *Congressional Research Service Report*, 9 May 2013, p. i.

6. Kristy N. Kamarck, "Women in Combat: Issues for Congress," *Congressional Research Service Report*, 18 August 2015, p. 1. See especially table 1, "Female Casualties in the Global War on Terror." Of the three operations in the Global War on Terror, Operation Iraqi Freedom resulted in the most casualties for American service women, accounting for 110 of the deaths and 627 of the wounded in action. Of the various military services, the army suffered the worst, accounting for 125 of the deaths and 872 of the wounded in action.

7. For more on the shift toward stability operations generally and counterinsurgency specifically, see Jennifer Morrison Taw, *Mission Revolution: The U.S. Military and Stability Operations* (New York: Columbia University Press, 2012); John A. Nagl, *Learning to Eat Soup with a Knife: Counterinsurgency Lessons from Malaya and Vietnam* (Chicago: University of Chicago Press, 2002).

8. Lester L. Lyles to Barack Obama and 112th United States Congress, 15 March 2011, letter of transmittal, Military Leadership Diversity Commission, *From Representation to Inclusion: Diversity Leadership for the 21st-Century Military, Final Report* (Arlington, VA: Military Leadership Diversity Commission, 2011).

9. Military Leadership Diversity Commission, *From Representation to Inclusion*, p. vii.

10. Burrelli, "Women in Combat: Issues for Congress," p. 7.

11. Lester L. Lyles to Barack Obama and 112th United States Congress, 15 March 2011, letter of transmittal, Military Leadership Diversity Commission, *From Representation to Inclusion*, pp. iii–iv.

12. Military Leadership Diversity Commission, *From Representation to Inclusion*, pp. xiv–xvii.

13. Ibid., xvii.

14. Kamarck, "Women in Combat: Issues for Congress," p. i.

15. Burrelli, "Women in Combat: Issues for Congress," pp. i, 12.

16. David Alexander and Phil Stewart, "U.S. Military Opens All Combat Roles to Women," *MSN*, 3 December 2015, available at http://www.msn.com/en-us/news/us/us-defense-chief-to-announce-plan-to-open-military-combat-jobs-to-women-official/ar-AAfZiGq (accessed 11 January 2016).

17. Martin E. Dempsey, "The National Military Strategy of the United States of America," June 2015, p. 14, available at http://www.jcs.mil/Portals/36/Docu

ments/Publications/2015_National_Military_Strategy.pdf (accessed 11 January 2016).

18. Megan Eckstein, "First 4 Enlisted Females Begin Submarine School Today, Ahead of USS *Michigan* Assignment," *U.S. Naval Institute News*, 24 August 2015, available at http://news.usni.org/2015/08/24/first-4-enlisted-females-begin-submarine-school-today-ahead-of-uss-michigan-assignment (accessed 4 September 2015).

19. Scott Newman, "First Female Soldiers Graduate from Army Ranger School," *NPR*, 21 August 2015, available at http://www.npr.org/sections/thetwo-way/2015/08/21/433482186/first-female-soldiers-graduate-from-army-ranger-school (accessed 23 October 2015).

20. "Two Women Pass Army Ranger School, First Female Graduates," *Associated Press*, 18 August 2015, available at www.msn.com/en-us/news/us/2-women-pass-army-ranger-school-first-female-graduates (accessed 4 September 2015).

21. Olivia Cobiskey, "Major Lisa Jaster, 37, First Female Army Reserve Soldier Graduates Army Ranger School," *U.S. Army*, 16 October 2015, available at http://www.army.mil/article/157260/Maj__Lisa_Jaster__37__first_female_Army_Reserve_Soldier_graduates_Army_Ranger_School/ (accessed 23 October 2015).

22. Megan Eckstein, "SECDEF Carter: All Military Specialties Will Be Open to Women, Marine Objections Overruled," *U.S. Naval Institute News*, 3 December 2015, available at http://news.usni.org/2015/12/03/secdef-carter-all-military-specialties-will-be-open-to-women-marine-objections-overruled (accessed 11 January 2016). For Carter's policy, see Ashton B. Carter, "Memorandum for Secretaries of the Military Departments, Acting Under Secretary of Defense for Personnel and Readiness, Chiefs of the Military Services, Commander, U.S. Special Operations Command, Subject: Implementation Guidance for the Full Integration of Women in the Armed Forces," 3 December 2015, available at http://www.defense.gov/Portals/1/Documents/pubs/OSD014303-15.pdf (accessed 11 January 2016). Objection to Carter's policy among senior U.S. Marine Corps leaders has continued. On 8 January 2016 the commander of U.S. Southern Command, Marine General John F. Kelly, publicly pondered whether the move would increase the combat effectiveness of the service. Kelly determined, "If the answer to that is no, clearly don't do it. If the answer to that is, it shouldn't hurt, I would suggest that we shouldn't do it, because it might hurt." He indicated that the policy would likely result in lowered standards. Lolita C. Baldor, "Marine Corps Debate over Women in Combat Continues to Roil," *Marine Corps Times*, 9 January 2016, available at http://www.marinecorpstimes.com/story/military/2016/01/08/marine-general-predicts-lower-standards-women-combat/78526492/ (accessed 11 January 2016).

23. Andrew J. Bacevich, *Breach of Trust: How Americans Failed Their Soldiers and Their Country* (New York: Henry Holt, 2013), 4, 196. Also see Andrew J. Bacevich, *The Limits of Power: The End of American Exceptionalism* (New York, NY: Henry Holt, 2008).

24. Karl W. Eikenberry, "Reassessing the All-Volunteer Force," in *The Modern American Military* (Oxford: Oxford University Press, 2013), edited by David M. Kennedy, 217.

25. David R. Segal and Lawrence J. Korb, "Manning and Financing the All-Volunteer Force," in Kennedy, *The Modern American Military*, pp. 112, 122, 129.

26. Dennis Laich, *Skin in the Game: Poor Kids and Patriots* (Bloomington, IN: iUniverse, 2013), 78–79. For more on the shift from a strategic to an operational reserve, see pp. 77–82.

27. Michael Runey and Charles Allen, "An All-Volunteer Force for Long-Term Success," *Military Review* 95, 6 (November/December 2015): 97–98. See especially figure 1, "The All-Volunteer Force's Strategic Problem." Of the total potential personnel pool, 56 percent were "unwilling and unqualified;" 25 percent were "qualified but unwilling;" and 15 percent were "willing but unqualified." Only 4 percent were "willing and qualified."

28. Kennedy, *The Modern American Military*, p. 4.

29. Robert L. Goldich, "American Military Culture from Colony to Empire," in Kennedy, *The Modern American Military*, p. 79.

30. James Wright, *Those Who Have Borne the Battle: A History of America's Wars and Those Who Fought Them* (New York: Public Affairs, 2012), 23.

31. David R. Segal and Lawrence J. Korb, "Manning and Financing the All-Volunteer Force," in Kennedy, *The Modern American Military*, p. 126.

32. Kelley Holland, "Largest U.S. Employer Proposes New Retirement Plans," *CNBC*, 31 March 2015, available at http://www.msn.com/en-us/money/retirement/largest-us-employer-proposes-new-retirement-plans/ar-AAagtSF?ocid=iehp (accessed 7 September 2015).

33. Congressional Budget Office, "The All-Volunteer Military: Issues and Performance," July 2007, pp. vii–ix, 1.

34. Ibid.

SELECTED BIBLIOGRAPHY

ARCHIVES, COLLECTIONS, AND MANUSCRIPTS

National Archives and Records Administration, College Park, Maryland
    RG 147 Records of the Selective Service System, 1940–
    RG 165 Records of the War Department General and Special Staffs
    RG 211 Records of the War Manpower Commission, 1936–1947
    RG 220 Records of Temporary Committees, Commissions, and Boards
    Presidential Commission on the Assignment of Women in the Armed Forces
    RG 319 Records of the Army Staff
    RG 330 Records of the Secretary of Defense
    RG 337 Records of Headquarters Army Ground Forces
Library of Congress, Manuscript Division, Washington, D.C.
    A. Philip Randolph Papers
    Hanson W. Baldwin Papers
    James Wadsworth Family Papers
    NAACP Collection
    Truman K. Gibson Papers
George C. Marshall Research Library, Lexington, Virginia
    George C. Marshall Papers
    George M. Elsey Papers
    Hanson W. Baldwin Papers
    Marshall Foundation National Archives Project
Harry S. Truman Presidential Library, Independence, Missouri
    Charles Fahy Papers
    Clark M. Clifford Papers
    Earl D. Johnson Papers
    Frank Pace Jr. Papers
    George M. Elsey Papers
    Harold Stein Papers
    Harry S. Truman Papers
    President's Secretary's Files
        Staff Member and Office Files: David H. Stowe Files
        Staff Member and Office Files: Philleo Nash Files
        White House Central Files: Confidential File
        White House Central Files: Official File
    James E. Webb Papers
    J. Howard McGrath Papers
    John Ohly Papers
    J. Thomas Schneider Papers
    L. Laszlo Ecker-Racz Papers

Niles W. Bond Papers
Philleo Nash Papers
Robert A. Lovett Papers
Samuel I. Rosenman Papers
Stephen J. Spingarn Papers
RG 147 Records of the Selective Service System, 1940–
RG 211 Records of the War Manpower Commission, 1936–1947
RG 220 Records of Temporary Committees, Commissions, and Boards
    President's Advisory Commission on Universal Training
    President's Committee on Civil Rights
    President's Committee on Equality of Treatment and Opportunity in the
    Armed Services
Dwight D. Eisenhower Presidential Library, Abilene, Kansas
    Alvan C. Gillem Jr. Collection
    C. D. Jackson Papers
    Courtney H. Hodges Papers
    Dwight D. Eisenhower Papers
        Papers as President of the United States
        Pre-Presidential Papers
        White House Central Files, Official File
    Henry S. Aurand Papers
    J. Lawton Collins Papers
    Maxwell M. Rabb Papers
U.S. Army Military History Institute, Carlisle, Pennsylvania
    All Volunteer Force Collection
    Alvan C. Gillem Papers
    Clifford C. Early Papers
    Darrie Richards Papers
    Frank J. McSherry Papers
    James B. Lampert Papers
    Lewis B. Hershey Papers
    Robert Reader Collection
U.S. Air Force Historical Research Agency, Montgomery, Alabama
    History of the United States Air Force Recruiting Service
    History of the Women in the Air Force
    U.S. Air Force Oral History Interviews
Lyndon B. Johnson Presidential Library, Austin, Texas
    Administrative Histories
        Department of Defense
    Bradley Patterson Papers
    Clark Clifford Papers
    Drew Pearson Papers
    Lewis B. Hershey Papers
    National Security File
    Office Files of the White House Aides

Ramsey Clark Papers
White House Central Files
Wright Patman Papers
Richard M. Nixon Presidential Library, Yorba Linda, California
White House Central Files, Staff Member and Office Files
Martin Anderson Files
White House Central Files, Subject Files
FG 13 Department of Defense
FG 14 Department of the Army
FG 15 Department of the Navy
FG 16 Department of the Air Force
FG 216 Selective Service System
FG 249 Commission on an All-Volunteer Armed Force
ND National Security—Defense
Gerald R. Ford Presidential Library, Ann Arbor, Michigan
America since Hoover Collection
Arthur F. Burns Papers
Gerald R. Ford Vice Presidential Papers
Martin R. Hoffman Papers
Melvin R. Laird Papers
Patricia Lindh and Jeanne Holm Files
Stanley S. Scott Papers
White House Central Files
William J. Baroody Jr. Papers

GOVERNMENT DOCUMENTS

Anastas, Kevin. *Demobilization and Democratizing Discipline: The Doolittle Board and the Post World War II Response to Criticism of the United States Army.* Alexandria, VA: Army Military Personnel Center, 1983.

Aspin, Les. *All Volunteer: A Fair System; a Quality Force.* Washington, DC: U.S. Government Printing Office, 1991.

Aspin, Les, and William Dickinson. *Defense for a New Era: Lessons of the Persian Gulf War.* Washington, DC: U.S. Government Printing Office, 1992.

Burrelli, David F. "Women in Combat: Issues for Congress." *Congressional Research Service Report.* 9 May 2013.

———. "Women in the Armed Forces." *Congressional Research Service Report.* 29 September 1998.

Burrelli, David F., and Jody Feder. "Homosexuals and the U.S. Military: Current Issues." *Congressional Research Service Report.* 22 July 2009.

Commission on Wartime Contracting in Iraq and Afghanistan. *Transforming Wartime Contracting: Controlling Costs, Reducing Risks.* Washington, DC: U.S. Government Printing Office, 2011.

Congressional Budget Office. *The All-Volunteer Military: Issues and Performance.* Washington, DC: Congressional Budget Office, 2007.

Dawson, David A. *The Impact of Project 100,000 on the Marine Corps.* Washington, DC: History and Museums Division, Headquarters U.S. Marine Corps, 1995.

Dempsey, Martin E. "The National Military Strategy of the United States of America." June 2015. Available at http://www.jcs.mil/Portals/36/Documents/Publi cations/2015_National_Military_Strategy.pdf (accessed 11 January 2016).

Department of Defense. *Report of the Comprehensive Review of the Issues Associated with a Repeal of "Don't Ask, Don't Tell."* Washington, DC: Department of Defense, 2010.

———. *Report of the Task Force on Women in the Military.* Washington, DC: U.S. Government Printing Office, 1988.

Devan, Samuel A., and Bernard Brodie. *Universal Military Training.* Library of Congress Legislative Reference Service. Public Affairs Bulletin no. 54. Washington, DC: U.S. Government Printing Office, 1947.

Feder, Jody. "'Don't Ask, Don't Tell': A Legal Analysis." *Congressional Research Service Report.* 6 August 2013.

Feickert, Andrew. "Army Drawdown and Restructuring: Background and Issues for Congress." *Congressional Research Service Report.* 5 March 2013.

Gough, Terrence. *U.S. Army Mobilization and Logistics in the Korean War: A Research Approach.* Washington, DC: U.S. Government Printing Office, 1987.

Griffith, Robert K. Jr. *The U.S. Army's Transition to the All-Volunteer Force, 1968–1974.* Washington, DC: Center of Military History, 1997.

Kamarck, Kristy N. "Women in Combat: Issues for Congress." *Congressional Research Service Report.* 18 August 2015.

Kreidberg, Marvin A., and Henry G. Merton. *History of Military Mobilization in the U.S. Army.* Washington, DC: Department of the Army, 1955.

Laurence, Janice. *The All-Volunteer Force: A Historical Perspective.* Washington, DC: Office of Under Secretary of Defense (Force Management Policy), 2004.

Lee, Ulysses. *The Employment of Negro Troops.* Washington, DC: Office of the Chief of Military History U.S. Army, 1966.

Military Leadership Diversity Commission. *From Representation to Inclusion: Diversity Leadership for the 21st-Century Military.* Arlington, VA: Military Leadership Diversity Commission, 2011.

Military Manpower Task Force. *A Report to the President on the Status and Prospects of the All-Volunteer Force.* Washington, DC: U.S. Government Printing Office, 1982.

Moskos, Charles. *The American Soldier after the Cold War: Towards a Post-Modern Military.* Washington, DC: U.S. Army Research Institute for the Behavioral and Social Sciences, 1998.

National Advisory Commission on Selective Service. *In Pursuit of Equity: Who Serves When Not All Serve?* Washington, DC: U.S. Government Printing Office, 1967.

Office of the Under Secretary of Defense (Personnel and Readiness). "Report to the Secretary of Defense: Review of the Effectiveness of the Application and Enforcement of the Department's Policy on Homosexual Conduct in the Military." April 1998. Available at http://www.dod.gov/pubs/rpt040798.html (accessed 1 September 2015).

Peters, Heidi M., Moshe Schwartz, and Lawrence Kapp. "Department of Defense Contractor and Troop Levels in Iraq and Afghanistan: 2007–2014." *Congressional Research Service Report.* 22 July 2015.

Quattlebaum, Charles A. *Universal Military Training and Related Proposals: Selected Data Basic to a Consideration of the Issues.* Library of Congress Legislative Reference Service. Public Affairs Bulletin no. 43. Washington, DC: U.S. Government Printing Office, 1946.

Schwartz, Moshe. "The Department of Defense's Use of Private Security Contractors in Afghanistan and Iraq: Background, Analysis, and Options for Congress." *Congressional Research Service Report.* 13 May 2011.

Schwartz, Moshe, and Jennifer Church. "Department of Defense's Use of Contractors to Support Military Operations: Background, Analysis, and Issues for Congress." *Congressional Research Service Report.* 17 May 2013.

Selective Service System. *Selective Service and Victory: Fourth Report of the Director of Selective Service, 1944–1945, with a Supplement for 1946–1947.* Washington, DC: U.S. Government Printing Office, 1948.

————. *Selective Service as the Tide of War Turns: Third Report of the Director of Selective Service, 1943–1944.* Washington, DC: U.S. Government Printing Office, 1945.

————. *Selective Service in Peacetime: First Report of the Director of Selective Service, 1940–1941.* Washington, DC: U.S. Government Printing Office, 1942.

————. *Selective Service in Wartime: Second Report of the Director of Selective Service, 1941–1942.* Washington, DC: U.S. Government Printing Office, 1943.

Sparrow, John C. *History of Personnel Demobilization in the United States Army.* Washington, DC: Department of the Army, 1952.

Upton, Emory. *The Military Policy of the United States.* Washington, DC: U.S. Government Printing Office, 1904.

U.S. Congress. House. *Investigation of War Department Publicity and Propaganda in Relation to Universal Military Training: Hearings before the United States House Committee on Expenditures in the Executive Departments, Subcommittee on Publicity and Propaganda.* 80th Cong., 1st sess., 20 June, 16 July 1947.

————. *Investigation of War Department Publicity and Propaganda in Relation to Universal Military Training: Hearings before the United States House Committee on Expenditures in the Executive Departments, Subcommittee on Publicity and Propaganda.* 80th Cong., 2nd sess., 14 January 1948.

————. *Subcommittee Hearings on Universal Military Training (H.R. 4121): Hearings before the United States House Committee on Armed Services.* 80th Cong., 1st sess., 14, 16, 17 July 1947.

————. *Universal Military Training: Hearings before the United States House Committee on Armed Services.* 80th Cong., 1st sess., 11, 18, 19, 27 June, 7, 9–11 July 1947.

————. *Universal Military Training, Part 1: Hearings before the United States House Committee on Military Affairs.* 79th Cong., 1st sess., 8, 13, 15, 16, 19–21, 26–30 November, 3, 6, 7, 10–14, 17–19 December 1945.

————. *Universal Military Training, Part 1: Hearings before the United States House*

Select Committee on Postwar Military Policy. 79th Cong., 1st sess., 4–9, 11–16, 19 June 1945.

———. Universal Military Training, Part 2: Hearings before the United States House Committee on Military Affairs. 79th Cong., 2nd sess., 18–21 February 1946.

U.S. Congress. Senate. To Receive Testimony on the Challenges Facing the Department of Defense: Hearings before the United States Senate Committee on Armed Services. 110th Cong., 2nd sess., 27 January 2009.

———. Universal Military Training: Hearings before the United States Senate Committee on Armed Services. 80th Cong., 2nd sess., 17, 18, 22–25, 29–31 March, 1–3 April 1948.

———. Universal Military Training, Statements by Officials of the American Legion which Organization Sponsored the Bill: Hearings before the United States Senate Committee on Armed Services. 81st Cong., 1st sess., 3 March 1949.

U.S. Government Accountability Office. "National Security: DOD Should Reevaluate Requirements for the Selective Service System." June 2012. Available at http://www.gao.gov/assets/600/591441.pdf (accessed 22 January 2016).

U.S. Library of Congress. General Reference and Bibliography Division. Universal Military Training: A Selected and Annotated List of References. Compiled by Frances Neel Cheney. Washington, DC: U.S. Government Printing Office, 1945.

U.S. President's Advisory Commission on Universal Training. A Program for National Security: Report of the President's Advisory Commission on Universal Training. Washington, DC: U.S. Government Printing Office, 1947.

U.S. President's Commission on an All-Volunteer Force. The Report of the President's Commission on an All-Volunteer Force. Washington, DC: U.S. Government Printing Office, 1970.

U.S. President's Committee on Equality of Treatment and Opportunity in the Armed Services. Freedom to Serve: Equality of Treatment and Opportunity in the Armed Services, a Report by the President's Committee. Washington, DC: U.S. Government Printing Office, 1950.

White House Office of the Press Secretary. "Remarks by the President in State of the Union Address." 27 January 2010. Available at www.whitehouse.gov/the-press-office/remarks-president-state-union-address (accessed 31 August 2015).

MAGAZINES AND NEWSPAPERS
Atlanta Constitution
Atlanta Journal
Atlantic
Chicago Daily News
Chicago Tribune
Detroit Michigan Free Press
Economist
Kansas American (Kansas City, KS)
Los Angeles Times
Negro Star (Wichita, KS)
Newsweek

New York Times
Plain Dealer (Cleveland, OH)
Stars and Stripes
U.S. Naval Institute News
Wall Street Journal
Washington Post
Washington Post and Times Herald
Washington Star

BOOKS AND DISSERTATIONS

Acacia, John. *Clark Clifford: The Wise Man of Washington.* Lexington: University Press of Kentucky, 2009.

Allison, William T., Jeffrey Grey, and Janet G. Valentine. *American Military History: A Survey from Colonial Times to the Present.* 2nd ed. New York: Pearson, 2012.

Ambrose, Stephen E. *Eisenhower: Soldier and President.* New York: Simon & Schuster, 1990.

———. *Upton and the Army.* Baton Rouge: Louisiana State University Press, 1964.

Appy, Christian G. *Working-Class War: American Combat Soldiers and Vietnam.* Chapel Hill: University of North Carolina Press, 1993.

Avant, Deborah D. *The Market for Force: The Consequences of Privatizing Security.* New York: Cambridge University Press, 2005.

Bacevich, Andrew J. *Breach of Trust: How Americans Failed Their Soldiers and Their Country.* New York: Henry Holt, 2013.

———. *The Limits of Power: The End of American Exceptionalism.* New York: Henry Holt, 2008.

———. *The Pentomic Era: The U.S. Army between Korea and Vietnam.* Washington, DC: National Defense University Press, 1986.

Bach, Morten. "None So Consistently Right: The American Legion's Cold War, 1945–1950." PhD diss., Ohio University, 2007.

Bailey, Beth. *America's Army: Making the All-Volunteer Force.* Cambridge, MA: Belknap Press of Harvard University Press, 2009.

Ballard, Jack. *The Shock of Peace: Military and Economic Demobilization after World War II.* Washington, DC: University Press of America, 1983.

Barlow, Jeffrey G. *Revolt of the Admirals: The Fight for Naval Aviation, 1945–1950.* Washington, DC: Brassey's, 1998.

Baskir, Lawrence M., and William A. Strauss. *Chance and Circumstance: The Draft, the War, and the Vietnam Generation.* New York: Vintage, 1978.

Beaver, Daniel R. *Newton D. Baker and the American War Effort, 1917–1919.* Lincoln: University of Nebraska Press, 1966.

Berkowitz, Edward D. *Mr. Social Security: The Life of Wilbur J. Cohen.* Lawrence: University Press of Kansas, 1995.

Bernstein, Barton J., ed. *Politics and Policies of the Truman Administration.* Chicago: Franklin Watts, 1970.

Bernstein, Barton J., and Allen J. Matusow, eds. *The Truman Administration: A Documentary History.* New York: Harper & Row, 1966.

Biank, Tanya. *Undaunted: The Real Story of America's Servicewomen in Today's Military*. New York: NAL Caliber, 2014.

Binkin, Martin. *Who Will Fight the Next War? The Changing Face of the American Military*. Washington, DC: Brookings Institution, 1993.

Bird, Kai. *The Chairman: John J. McCloy and the Making of the American Establishment*. New York: Simon & Schuster, 1992.

Blair, Clay. *The Forgotten War: America in Korea, 1950–1953*. New York: Times Books, 1987.

Boettcher, Thomas D. *First Call: The Making of the Modern U.S. Military, 1945–1953*. Boston: Little, Brown, 1992.

Bogart, Leo, ed. *Project Clear: Social Research and the Desegregation of the United States Army*. New Brunswick, NJ: Transaction, 1992.

Bogle, Lori Lyn. *The Pentagon's Battle for the American Mind: The Early Cold War*. College Station: Texas A&M University Press, 2004.

Borden, William L. *There Will Be No Time: The Revolution in Strategy*. New York: Macmillan, 1946.

Boyer, Paul. *By the Bomb's Early Light: American Thought and Culture at the Dawn of the Atomic Age*. Chapel Hill: University of North Carolina Press, 1985.

Brewer, Susan A. *Why America Fights: Patriotism and War Propaganda from the Philippines to Iraq*. Oxford: Oxford University Press, 2009.

Brodie, Bernard, ed. *The Absolute Weapon: Atomic Power and World Order*. New York: Harcourt, Brace, 1946.

Busch, Andrew E. *Truman's Triumphs: The 1948 Election and the Making of Postwar America*. Lawrence: University Press of Kansas, 2012.

Bynum, Cornelius L. *A. Philip Randolph and the Struggle for Civil Rights*. Urbana: University of Illinois Press, 2010.

Capozzola, Christopher. *Uncle Sam Wants You: World War I and the Making of the Modern American Citizen*. Oxford: Oxford University Press, 2008.

Caraley, Demetrios. *The Politics of Military Unification: A Study of Conflict and the Policy Process*. New York: Columbia University Press, 1966.

Chambers, John W. *To Raise an Army: The Draft Comes to Modern America*. New York: Free Press, 1987.

Clifford, J. Garry. *The Citizen Soldiers: The Plattsburg Training Camp Movement, 1913–1920*. Lexington: University Press of Kentucky, 1972.

Clifford, J. Garry, and Samuel R. Spencer. *The First Peacetime Draft*. Lawrence: University Press of Kansas, 1986.

Coffman, Edward M. *The Regulars: The American Army, 1898–1941*. Cambridge, MA: Belknap Press of Harvard University Press, 2004.

Cohen, Eliot A. *Citizens and Soldiers: The Dilemmas of Military Service*. Ithaca, NY: Cornell University Press, 1985.

———. *Making Do with Less, or Coping with Upton's Ghost*. Carlisle, PA: U.S. Army War College, 1995.

Cook, Martin L. *The Moral Warrior: Ethics and Service in the U.S. Military*. Albany: State University of New York Press, 2004.

Cray, Ed. *General of the Army: George C. Marshall, Soldier and Statesman*. New York: Cooper Square, 1990.

Culver, John C., and John Hyde. *American Dreamer: A Life of Henry A. Wallace*. New York: Norton, 2000.

Cunningham, Frank D. "The Army and Universal Military Training, 1942–1948." PhD diss., University of Texas at Austin, 1976.

Dallek, Robert. *Franklin D. Roosevelt and American Foreign Policy, 1932–1945*. Oxford: Oxford University Press, 1979.

————. *Harry S. Truman*. New York: Times Books, 2008.

Davies, Robert B. *Baldwin of the Times: Hanson W. Baldwin, A Military Journalist's Life, 1903–1991*. Annapolis, MD: Naval Institute Press, 2011.

Davis, Vincent. *Postwar Defense Policy and the United States Navy, 1943–1946*. Chapel Hill: University of North Carolina Press, 1966.

Derthick, Martha. *The National Guard in Politics*. Cambridge, MA: Harvard University Press, 1965.

Donald, Aida D. *Citizen Soldier: A Life of Harry S. Truman*. New York: Basic, 2012.

Donaldson, Gary A. *The Making of Modern America: The Nation from 1945 to the Present*. Lanham, MD: Rowman & Littlefield, 2009.

————. *Truman Defeats Dewey*. Lexington: University Press of Kentucky, 1999.

Dorwart, Jeffrey M. *Eberstadt and Forrestal: A National Security Partnership, 1909–1949*. College Station: Texas A&M University Press, 1991.

Doubler, Michael D. *Civilian in Peace, Soldier in War: The Army National Guard, 1636–2000*. Lawrence: University Press of Kansas, 2003.

Dudziak, Mary L. *Cold War Civil Rights: Race and the Image of American Democracy*. Princeton, NJ: Princeton University Press, 2000.

Dunn, Joe. *The Church and the Cold War: Protestants and Conscription, 1940–1955*. Columbia: University of Missouri Press, 1973.

Eden, Lynn R. "The Diplomacy of Force: Interest, the State, and the Making of American Military Policy in 1948." PhD diss., University of Michigan, 1985.

Eiler, Keith E. *Mobilizing America: Robert P. Patterson and the War Effort, 1940–1945*. Ithaca, NY: Cornell University Press, 1997.

Elsey, George M. *An Unplanned Life*. Columbia: University of Missouri Press, 2005.

Engbrecht, Shawn. *America's Covert Warriors: Inside the World of Private Military Contractors*. Washington, DC: Potomac, 2011.

Erhart, W. D. *Passing Time: Memoir of a Vietnam Veteran against the War*. Jefferson, NC: McFarland, 1986.

Feaver, Peter D., and Richard H. Kohn, eds. *Soldiers and Civilians: The Civil-Military Gap and American National Security*. Cambridge, MA: Massachusetts Institute of Technology Press, 2001.

Finkel, David. *Thank You for Your Service*. New York: Sarah Crichton, 2013.

Fitzpatrick, Edward A. *Universal Military Training*. New York: McGraw-Hill, 1945.

Flynn, George Q. *Conscription and Democracy: The Draft in France, Great Britain, and the United States*. Westport, CT: Greenwood, 2002.

—————. *The Draft, 1940–1973.* Lawrence: University Press of Kansas, 1993.

Foley, Michael. *Confronting the War Machine: Draft Resistance during the Vietnam War.* Chapel Hill: University of North Carolina Press, 2003.

Foot, M. R. D. *Men in Uniform: Military Manpower in Modern Industrial Societies.* London: Weidenfeld, 1961.

Ford, Nancy G. *The Great War and America: Civil-Military Relations during World War I.* Westport, CT: Praeger Security International, 2008.

Foster, Gregory D., Alan Ned Sabrosky, and William J. Taylor Jr., eds. *The Strategic Dimension of Military Manpower.* Cambridge, MA: Ballinger, 1987.

Frank, Nathaniel. *Unfriendly Fire: How the Gay Ban Undermines the Military and Weakens America.* New York: St. Martin's, 2009.

Friedberg, Aaron L. *In the Shadow of the Garrison State: America's Anti-Statism and Its Cold War Grand Strategy.* Princeton, NJ: Princeton University Press, 2000.

Friedman, Norman. *The Fifty Year War: Conflict and Strategy in the Cold War.* Annapolis, MD: Naval Institute Press, 2000.

Gaddis, John L. *Strategies of Containment: A Critical Appraisal of Postwar American National Security Policy.* New York: Oxford University Press, 1982.

—————. *The United States and the Origins of the Cold War, 1941–1947.* New York: Columbia University Press, 1972.

—————. *We Now Know: Rethinking Cold War History.* New York: Oxford University Press, 1997.

Gambone, Michael D. *The Greatest Generation Comes Home: The Veteran in American Society.* College Station: Texas A&M University Press, 2005.

Gerhardt, James M. *The Draft and Public Policy: Issues in Military Manpower Procurement, 1945–1970.* Columbus: Ohio State University Press, 1971.

Giangreco, D. M. *Hell to Pay: Operation DOWNFALL and the Invasion of Japan, 1945–1947.* Annapolis, MD: Naval Institute Press, 2009.

Giangreco, D. M., and Kathryn Moore. *Dear Harry . . . Truman's Mailroom, 1945–1953.* Mechanicsburg, PA: Stackpole, 1999.

Gibson, Truman K. Jr., with Steve Huntley. *Knocking Down Barriers: My Fight for Black America.* Evanston, IL: Northwestern University Press, 2005.

Gilroy, Curtis L., and Cindy Williams, eds. *Service to Country: Personnel Policy and the Transformation of Western Militaries.* Cambridge, MA: Massachusetts Institute of Technology Press, 2006.

Gilroy, Curtis L., Barbara A. Bicksler, and John T. Warner. *The All-Volunteer Force: Thirty Years of Service.* Dulles, VA: Brassey's, 2004.

Gole, Henry G. *General William E. DePuy: Preparing the Army for Modern War.* Lexington: University of Kentucky Press, 2008.

—————. *The Road to Rainbow: Army Planning for Global War, 1934–1940.* Annapolis, MD: Naval Institute Press, 2003.

—————. *Soldiering: Observations from Korea, Vietnam, and Safe Places.* Dulles, VA: Potomac, 2005.

Goodpaster, Andrew J., et al. *Toward a Consensus on Military Service: Report of the Atlantic Council's Working Group on Military Service.* Washington, DC: Atlantic Council, 1982.

Gregory, Raymond F. *Norman Thomas: The Great Dissenter.* New York: Algora, 2008.

Hamby, Alonzo L. *Man of the People: A Life of Harry S. Truman.* New York: Oxford University Press, 1995.

Hammond, Paul. *Organizing for Defense: The American Military Establishment in the Twentieth Century.* Princeton, NJ: Princeton University Press, 1961.

Hanson, Thomas E. *Combat Ready? The Eighth U.S. Army on the Eve of the Korean War.* College Station: Texas A&M University Press, 2010.

Heller, Francis H., ed. *Economics and the Truman Administration.* Lawrence: University Press of Kansas, 1981.

Hersh, Seymour M. *Chain of Command: The Road from 9/11 to Abu Ghraib.* New York: HarperCollins, 2004.

Herzog, Jonathan P. *The Spiritual-Industrial Complex: America's Religious Battle against Communism in the Early Cold War.* Oxford: Oxford University Press, 2011.

Higgs, Robert. *Crisis and Leviathan: Critical Episodes in the Growth of American Government.* Oxford: Oxford University Press, 1987.

Hogan, Michael J. *A Cross of Iron: Harry S. Truman and the Origins of the National Security State, 1945–1954.* Cambridge: Cambridge University Press, 1998.

Hohn, Maria, and Martin Klimke. *A Breath of Freedom: The Civil Rights Struggle, African American GIs, and Germany.* New York: Palgrave Macmillan, 2010.

Holley, I. B. *General John M. Palmer, Citizen Soldiers, and the Army of a Democracy.* Westport, CT: Greenwood, 1982.

Holm, Jeanne. *Women in the Military: An Unfinished Revolution.* New York: Ballantine, 1982.

Hoopes, Townsend, and Douglas Brinkley. *Driven Patriot: The Life and Times of James Forrestal.* Annapolis, MD: Naval Institute Press, 1992.

Horowitz, David A. *Beyond Left and Right: Insurgency and the Establishment.* Urbana: University of Illinois Press, 1997.

House, Jonathan M. *A Military History of the Cold War, 1944–1962.* Norman: University of Oklahoma Press, 2012.

Isenberg, David. *Shadow Force: Private Security Contractors in Iraq.* Westport, CT: Greenwood, 2009.

Karabell, Zachary. *The Last Campaign: How Harry Truman Won the 1948 Election.* New York: Alfred A. Knopf, 2000.

Karsten, Peter M. *The Military in America: From the Colonial Era to the Present.* New York: Free Press, 1986.

Keene, Jennifer D. *Doughboys, the Great War, and the Remaking of America.* Baltimore: Johns Hopkins University Press, 2001.

Keiser, Gordon W. *The U.S. Marine Corps and Defense Unification, 1944–1947: The Politics of Survival.* Washington, DC: National Defense University Press, 1982.

Kennedy, David M., ed. *The Modern American Military.* Oxford: Oxford University Press, 2013.

———. *Over Here: The First World War and American Society.* Oxford: Oxford University Press, 1980.

Kersten, Andrew E. *A. Philip Randolph: A Life in the Vanguard.* Lanham, MD: Rowman & Littlefield, 2007.

Kindsvatter, Peter S. *American Soldiers: Ground Combat in the World Wars, Korea, and Vietnam.* Lawrence: University Press of Kansas, 2003.

Kirkpatrick, Charles E. *An Unknown Future and a Doubtful Present: Writing the Victory Plan of 1941.* Honolulu: University Press of the Pacific, 2005.

Klarman, Michael J. *From Jim Crow to Civil Rights: The Supreme Court and the Struggle for Racial Equality.* Oxford: Oxford University Press, 2004.

Knauer, Christine. *Let Us Fight as Free Men: Black Soldiers and Civil Rights.* Philadelphia: University of Pennsylvania Press, 2014.

Kofsky, Frank. *Harry S. Truman and the War Scare of 1948: A Successful Campaign to Deceive the Nation.* New York: St. Martin's, 1993.

Koistinen, Paul A. C. *State of War: The Political Economy of American Warfare, 1945–2011.* Lawrence: University Press of Kansas, 2012.

Korb, Lawrence J. *The Joint Chiefs of Staff: The First Twenty-Five Years.* Bloomington: Indiana University Press, 1976.

Krehbiel, Nicholas A. *General Lewis B. Hershey and Conscientious Objection during World War II.* Columbia: University of Missouri Press, 2011.

Laich, Dennis. *Skin in the Game: Poor Kids and Patriots.* Bloomington, IN: iUniverse, 2013.

Lanning, Michael L. *The Battles of Peace.* New York: Ivy, 1992.

Larson, Eric V., David T. Orletsky, and Kristin Leuschner. *Defense Planning in a Decade of Change: Lessons from the Base Force, Bottom-Up Review, and Quadrennial Defense Review.* Santa Monica, CA: RAND Corporation, 2001.

Leffler, Melvyn P. *A Preponderance of Power: National Security, the Truman Administration, and the Cold War.* Stanford, CA: Stanford University Press, 1992.

Lewis, Adrian R. *The American Culture of War: The History of U.S. Military Force from World War II to Operation Iraqi Freedom.* London: Routledge, 2007.

Lingeman, Richard. *The Noir Forties: The American People from Victory to Cold War.* New York: Nation, 2012.

Linn, Brian M. *The Echo of Battle: The Army's Way of War.* Cambridge, MA: Harvard University Press, 2007.

Locher, James R. III. *Victory on the Potomac: The Goldwater-Nichols Act Unifies the Pentagon.* College Station: Texas A&M University Press, 2002.

MacGregor, Morris J. *Integration of the Armed Forces, 1940–1965.* Washington, DC: U.S. Army Center of Military History, 1981.

Mahood, Wayne. *General Wadsworth: The Life and Times of Brevet Major General James S. Wadsworth.* Cambridge, MA: Da Capo, 2003.

Mansoor, Peter R. *The GI Offensive in Europe: The Triumph of American Infantry Divisions, 1941–1945.* Lawrence: University Press of Kansas, 1999.

Marble, Sanders, ed. *Scraping the Barrel: The Military Use of Substandard Manpower, 1860–1960.* Bronx, NY: Fordham University Press, 2012.

McCullough, David. *Truman.* New York: Simon & Schuster, 1992.

McGuire, Phillip, ed. *Taps for a Jim Crow Army: Letters from Black Soldiers in World War II.* Santa Barbara, CA: ABC-CLIO, 1983.

Mershon, Sherie, and Steven Schlossman. *Foxholes and Color Lines: Desegregating the U.S. Armed Forces.* Baltimore: Johns Hopkins University Press, 1998.

Miller, William L. *Two Americans: Truman, Eisenhower, and a Dangerous World.* New York: Alfred A. Knopf, 2012.

Millett, Allan R., and Peter Maslowski. *For the Common Defense: A Military History of the United States of America.* Rev. ed. New York: Free Press, 1994.

Mills, Nicolaus. *Winning the Peace: The Marshall Plan and America's Coming of Age as a Superpower.* Hoboken, NJ: John Wiley & Sons, 2008.

Moskos, Charles C. *A Call to Civic Service: National Service for Country and Community.* New York: Free Press, 1988.

Moskos, Charles C., John Allen Williams, and David R. Segal, eds. *The Postmodern Military: Armed Forces after the Cold War.* Oxford: Oxford University Press, 2000.

Nalty, Bernard C. *Long Passage to Korea: Black Soldiers and the Integration of the U.S. Navy.* Washington, DC: Naval Historical Center, 2003.

———. *Strength for the Fight: A History of Black Americans in the Military.* New York: Free Press, 1986.

Neal, Steve. *Harry and Ike: The Partnership that Remade the Postwar World.* New York: Simon & Schuster, 2001.

Neiberg, Michael S. *Making Citizen-Soldiers: ROTC and the Ideology of American Military Service.* Cambridge, MA: Harvard University Press, 2000.

Odom, William O. *After the Trenches: The Transformation of U.S. Army Doctrine, 1918–1939.* College Station: Texas A&M University Press, 1999.

O'Hanlon, Michael. *Healing the Wounded Giant: Maintaining Military Preeminence while Cutting the Defense Budget.* Washington, DC: Brookings Institution, 2013.

———. *The Wounded Giant: America's Armed Forces in an Age of Austerity.* New York: Penguin Group, 2011.

Olson, James C. *Stuart Symington: A Life.* Columbia: University of Missouri Press, 2003.

Osgood, Robert E. *Limited War: The Challenge to American Strategy.* Chicago: University of Chicago Press, 1957.

Palmer, John McAuley. *America in Arms: The Experience of the United States with Military Organization.* Fighting Forces Series. Washington, DC: *Infantry Journal,* 1941.

———. *An Army of the People: The Constitution of an Effective Force of Trained Citizens.* New York: G. P. Putnam's Sons, 1916.

———. *Statesmanship or War.* Introduction by James W. Wadsworth Jr. New York: Doubleday, Page, 1927.

———. *Washington, Lincoln, Wilson: Three War Statesmen.* Garden City, NY: Doubleday, Doran, 1930.

Patterson, James T. *Grand Expectations: The United States, 1945–1974.* Oxford: Oxford University Press, 1996.

———. *Mr. Republican: A Biography of Robert A. Taft.* Boston: Houghton Mifflin, 1972.

Pattison, James. *The Morality of Private War: The Challenge of Private Military and Security Companies.* Oxford: Oxford University Press, 2014.

Perry, Mark. *Partners in Command: George Marshall and Dwight Eisenhower in War and Peace.* New York: Penguin, 2007.

Pfeffer, Paula F. *A. Philip Randolph, Pioneer of the Civil Rights Movement.* Baton Rouge: Louisiana State University Press, 1990.

Phillips, Kimberley L. *War! What Is It Good For? Black Freedom Struggles and the U.S. Military from World War II to Iraq.* Chapel Hill: University of North Carolina Press, 2012.

Pietrusza, David. *1948: Harry Truman's Improbable Victory and the Year That Transformed America.* New York: Union Square, 2011.

Powell, Colin L. *My American Journey.* New York: Random House, 1995.

Prince, Erik. *Civilian Warriors: The Inside Story of Blackwater and the Unsung Heroes of the War on Terror.* New York: Portfolio/Penguin, 2013.

Reynolds, David. *From World War to Cold War: Churchill, Roosevelt, and the International History of the 1940s.* Oxford: Oxford University Press, 2006.

Ridgway, Matthew B. *Soldier: The Memoirs of Matthew B. Ridgway, as Told to Harold H. Martin.* New York: Harper, 1956.

Rostker, Bernard. *I Want You! The Evolution of the All-Volunteer Force.* Santa Monica, CA: RAND Corporation, 2006.

Roth-Douquet, Kathy, and Frank Schaeffer. *AWOL: The Unexcused Absence of America's Upper Classes from Military Service—and How It Hurts Our Country.* New York: HarperCollins, 2006.

Ryan, Joseph W. *Samuel Stouffer and the GI Survey: Sociologists and Soldiers during the Second World War.* Knoxville: University of Tennessee Press, 2013.

Scahill, Jeremy. *Blackwater: The Rise of the World's Most Powerful Mercenary Army.* New York: Nation, 2007.

Schifferle, Peter J. *America's School for War: Fort Leavenworth, Officer Education, and Victory in World War II.* Lawrence: University Press of Kansas, 2010.

Segal, David R. *Recruiting for Uncle Sam: Citizenship and Military Manpower Policy.* Lawrence: University Press of Kansas, 1989.

Sharp, Bert. *"Bring the Boys Home": Demobilization of the United States Armed Forces after World War II.* East Lansing: Michigan State University Press, 1977.

Shenk, Gerald E. *"Work or Fight!" Race, Gender, and the Draft in World War One.* New York: Palgrave Macmillan, 2005.

Sherry, Michael S. *Preparing for the Next War: American Plans for Postwar Defense, 1941–1945.* New Haven, CT: Yale University Press, 1977.

Sherwin, Martin J. *A World Destroyed: Hiroshima and Its Legacies.* 3rd ed. Stanford, CA: Stanford University Press, 2003.

Singer, Peter. *Corporate Warriors: The Rise of the Privatized Military Industry.* Ithaca, NY: Cornell University Press, 2003.

Spalding, Elizabeth E. *The First Cold Warrior: Harry Truman, Containment, and the Remaking of Liberal Internationalism.* Lexington: University Press of Kentucky, 2006.

Sparrow, James T. *Warfare State: World War II Americans and the Age of Big Government*. Oxford: Oxford University Press, 2011.

Spector, Ronald H. *Advice and Support: The Early Years, 1941–1960*. Washington, DC: U.S. Army Center of Military History, 1985.

Stanger, Allison. *One Nation Under Contract: The Outsourcing of American Power and the Future of Foreign Policy*. New Haven, CT: Yale University Press, 2009.

Stentiford, Barry M. *The American Home Guard: The State Militia in the Twentieth Century*. College Station: Texas A&M University Press, 2002.

Stoler, Mark A. *Allies and Adversaries: The Joint Chiefs of Staff, the Grand Alliance, and U.S. Strategy in World War II*. Chapel Hill: University of North Carolina Press, 2000.

———. *George C. Marshall: Soldier-Statesman of the American Century*. Boston: Twayne, 1989.

———. *The Politics of the Second Front: American Military Planning and Diplomacy in Coalition Warfare, 1941–1943*. Westport, CT: Greenwood, 1977.

Stouffer, Samuel A., Arthur A. Lumsdaine, Marion Harper Lumsdaine, Robin M. Williams Jr., M. Brewster Smith, Irving L. Janis, Shirley A. Star, and Leonard S. Cottrell Jr. *The American Soldier: Combat and Its Aftermath*. Vol. 2 of *Studies in Social Psychology in World War II: The American Soldier*. Princeton, NJ: Princeton University Press, 1949.

Stouffer, Samuel A., Edward A. Suchman, Leland C. DeVinney, Shirley A. Star, and Robin M. Williams Jr. *The American Soldier: Adjustment during Army Life*. Vol. 1 of *Studies in Social Psychology in World War II: The American Soldier*. Princeton, NJ: Princeton University Press, 1949.

Stur, Heather M. *Beyond Combat: Women and Gender in the Vietnam War Era*. New York: Cambridge University Press, 2011.

Sweeney, Jerry K., ed. *A Handbook of American Military History: From the Revolutionary War to the Present*. 2nd ed. Lincoln: University of Nebraska Press, 1996.

Swomley, John M. "A Study of the Universal Military Training Campaign, 1944–1952." PhD diss., University of Colorado at Boulder, 1959.

Taylor, William A. *Every Citizen a Soldier: The Campaign for Universal Military Training after World War II*. College Station: Texas A&M University Press, 2014.

Trauschweizer, Ingo. *The Cold War U.S. Army: Building Deterrence for Limited War*. Lawrence: University Press of Kansas, 2008.

Unger, David C. *Emergency State: America's Pursuit of Absolute National Security at All Costs*. New York: Penguin, 2012.

Vogel, Steve. *The Pentagon: A History*. New York: Random House, 2008.

Ward, Robert D. "The Movement for Universal Military Training in the United States, 1942–1952." PhD diss., University of North Carolina at Chapel Hill, 1957.

Weigley, Russell F. *The American Way of War: A History of United States Military Strategy and Policy*. Bloomington: Indiana University Press, 1973.

———. *History of the United States Army*. New York: Macmillan, 1967.

———. *Towards an American Army: Military Thought from Washington to Marshall*.

New York: Columbia University Press, 1962.

West, Bing. *No True Glory: A Frontline Account of the Battle for Fallujah.* New York: Bantam, 2005.

Wheeler, Winslow T., and Lawrence J. Korb. *Military Reform: A Reference Handbook.* Westport, CT: Praeger Security International, 2007.

Williams, T. Harry. *The History of American Wars.* New York: Alfred A. Knopf, 1981.

Winton, Harold R. *Corps Commanders of the Bulge: Six American Generals and Victory in the Ardennes.* Lawrence: University Press of Kansas, 2007.

Wolk, Herman S. *Planning and Organizing the Postwar Air Force, 1943–1947.* Washington, DC: Office of Air Force History, 1984.

Wright, James. *Those Who Have Borne the Battle: A History of America's Wars and Those Who Fought Them.* New York: Public Affairs, 2012.

ARTICLES

Arant, Morgan Jr. "Government Use of the Draft to Silence Dissent to War." *Peace and Change* 17, 2 (April 1992): 147–171.

Armor, David, and Curtis Gilroy. "Changing Minority Representation in the U.S. Military." *Armed Forces and Society* 36, 2 (January 2010): 223–246.

Avant, Deborah, and Lee Sigelman, "Private Security and Democracy: Lessons from the U.S. in Iraq," *Security Studies* 19, 2 (2010): 230–265.

Bacevich, Andrew. "Emory Upton: A Centennial Assessment." *Military Review* 61, 12 (December 1981): 21–28.

———. "Losing Private Ryan: Why the Citizen-Soldier is MIA." *National Review* 51, 15 (August 1999): 32–34.

———. "One Percent Republic: Without Citizen Soldiers, Plutocracy Rises Unchecked." *American Conservative* 12, 6 (November/December 2013): 20–23.

———. "Who's Bearing the Burden? Iraq and the Demise of the All-Volunteer Army." *Commonweal* 132, 13 (July 2005): 13–15.

———. "Whose Army?" *Daedalus* 140, 3 (Summer 2011): 122–134.

———. "Who Will Serve?" *Wilson Quarterly* 22, 3 (Summer 1998): 80–91.

Bailey, Beth. "The Army in the Marketplace: Recruiting an All-Volunteer Force." *Journal of American History* 94, 1 (June 2007): 47–74.

———. "The Politics of Dancing: 'Don't Ask, Don't Tell,' and the Role of Moral Claims." *Journal of Policy History* 25, 1 (2013): 89–113.

Belkin, Aaron. "'Don't Ask, Don't Tell': Does the Gay Ban Undermine the Military's Reputation?" *Armed Forces and Society* 34, 2 (2008): 276–291.

Belkin, Aaron, Morten G. Ender, Nathaniel Frank, Stacie R. Furia, George Lucas, Gary Packard, Steven M. Samuels, Tammy Schultz, and David. R Segal. "Readiness and DADT Repeal: Has the New Policy of Open Service Undermined the Military?" *Armed Forces and Society* 39, 4 (October 2013): 587–601.

Bell, David A. "When the Levee Breaks: Dissenting from the Draft." *World Affairs* 170, 3 (Winter 2008): 59–68.

Bennett, Scott. "Conscience, Comrades, and the Cold War: The Korean War Draft

Resistance Cases of Socialist Pacifists David McReynolds and Vern Davidson."
Peace and Change 38, 1 (January 2013): 83–120.

Blum, Albert A. "The Farmer, the Army and the Draft." *Agricultural History* 38, 1 (January 1964): 34–42.

Bredbenner, Candice L. "A Duty to Defend? The Evolution of Aliens' Military Obligations to the United States, 1792 to 1946." *Journal of Policy History* 24, 2 (April 2012): 224–262.

Britt, Jason. "Unwilling Warriors: An Examination of the Power to Conscript in Peacetime." *Northwestern Journal of Law and Social Policy* 4 (2009): 400–423.

Burk, James. "Debating the Draft in America." *Armed Forces and Society* 15, 3 (Spring 1989): 431–448.

———. "The Military Obligations of Citizens since Vietnam." *Parameters* 31, 2 (Summer 2001): 48–60.

Butler, Jack. "The All-Volunteer Armed Force: Its Feasibility and Implications." *Parameters* 2, 1 (Summer 1972): 17–29.

Card, David, and Thomas Lemieux. "Going to College to Avoid the Draft: The Unintended Legacy of the Vietnam War." *American Economic Review* 91, 2 (May 2001): 97–102.

Clifford, John G. "Grenville Clark and the Origins of Selective Service." *Review of Politics* 35, 1 (January 1973): 17–40.

Coffman, Edward M. "The Duality of the American Military Tradition: A Commentary." *Journal of Military History* 64, 4 (October 2000): 967–980.

Cooling, B. Franklin. "Civil Defense and the Army: The Quest for Responsibility, 1946–1948." *Military Affairs* 36, 1 (February 1972): 11–14.

Cox, Marcus. "'Keep Our Black Warriors out of the Draft': The Vietnam Antiwar Movement at Southern University, 1968–1973." *Educational Foundations* 20, 1–2 (Winter/Spring 2006): 123–144.

Cram, W. A. "Universal Training for War and Peace." *School Review* 53, 7 (September 1945): 401–408.

Cunningham, Frank D. "Harry S. Truman and Universal Military Training, 1945." *Historian* 46 (Summer 1984): 397–415.

Curzon, Myron W. "The Nation's Military Security." *Scientific Monthly* 62, 1 (January 1946): 66–70.

Davenport, Roy K. "Implications of Military Selection and Classification in Relation to Universal Military Training." *Journal of Negro Education* 15, 4 (Autumn 1946): 585–594.

Dorey, Halstead. "The Plattsburg Contribution to Military Training." *Proceedings of the Academy of Political Science in the City of New York* 6, 4 (July 1916): 229–233.

Dunn, Joe P. "UMT: A Historical Perspective." *Military Review* 61, 1 (January 1981): 11–18.

Earhart, Mary. "The Value of Universal Military Training in Maintaining Peace." *Annals of the American Academy of Political and Social Science* 241 (September 1945): 46–57.

Efflandt, Scott L. "Military Professionalism and Private Military Contractors," *Parameters* 44, 2 (Summer 2014): 49–60.

Eikenberry, Karl W. "Reassessing the All-Volunteer Force." *Washington Quarterly* 36, 1 (Winter 2013): 7–24.

Elliott, Allen R. "The Plus Values of Military Training." *Journal of Criminal Law and Criminology* 35 (January 1946): 324–325.

Fautua, David. "The 'Long Pull' Army: NSC-68, the Korean War, and the Creation of the Cold War U.S. Army." *Journal of Military History* 61, 1 (January 1997): 93–120.

Fitzpatrick, David J. "Emory Upton and the Army of a Democracy." *Journal of Military History* 77, 2 (April 2013): 463–490.

———. "Emory Upton and the Citizen Soldier." *Journal of Military History* 65, 2 (April 2001): 355–389.

Fitzpatrick, Edward. "The Volunteer and the Conscript in American Military History." *Current History* 38, 224 (February 1960): 205–213.

Flynn, George Q. "American Medicine and Selective Service in World War II." *Journal of the History of Medicine and Allied Sciences* 42, 3 (July 1987): 305–326.

———. "Selective Service and American Blacks during World War II." *Journal of Negro History* 69, 1 (January 1984): 14–25.

Forman, Sidney. "Thomas Jefferson on Universal Military Training." *Military Affairs* 11, 3 (Autumn 1947): 177–178.

Galston, William A. "Should the All-Volunteer Force Be Replaced by Universal Mandatory National Service." *Congressional Digest* 85, 7 (September 2006): 208–220.

———. "Thinking about the Draft." *Public Interest* 154 (Winter 2004): 61–73.

Garcia, Daniel. "Class and Brass: Demobilization, Working Class Politics, and American Foreign Policy between World War and Cold War." *Diplomatic History* 34, 4 (September 2010): 681–698.

Gard, Robert Jr. "The Military and the American Society." *Foreign Affairs* 49, 4 (July 1971): 698–710.

Graham, Robert A. "Universal Military Training in Modern History." *Annals of the American Academy of Political and Social Science* 241 (September 1945): 8–14.

Grandstaff, Mark R. "Making the Military American: Advertising, Reform, and the Demise of an Antistanding Military Tradition, 1945–1955." *Journal of Military History* 60, 2 (April 1996): 299–323.

Griffith, Robert K. Jr. "About Face? The U.S. Army and the Draft." *Armed Forces and Society* 12, 1 (Fall 1985): 108–133.

Hammes, Thomas X. "Private Contractors in Conflict Zones: The Good, the Bad, and the Strategic Impact," *Strategic Forum* 260 (November 2010): 1–15.

Hausrath, Alfred. "Utilization of Negro Manpower in the Army." *Journal of the Operations Research Society of America* 2, 1 (February 1954): 17–30.

Hershey, Lewis B. "Procurement of Manpower in American Wars." *Annals of the American Academy of Political and Social Science* 241 (September 1945): 15–25.

Holborn, Hajo. "Professional Army versus Military Training." *Annals of the American Academy of Political and Social Science* 241 (September 1945): 123–130.

Hoskins, Halford L. "Universal Military Training and American Foreign Policy."

Annals of the American Academy of Political and Social Science 241 (September 1945): 58–66.

Janowitz, Morris. "Making the All-Volunteer Military Work?" *Bulletin of the Atomic Scientists* 37, 2 (February 1981): 7–9.

———. "National Service: A Third Alternative?" *Teachers College Record* 73, 1 (September 1971): 13–25.

———. "Volunteer Armed Forces and Military Purpose." *Foreign Affairs* 50, 3 (April 1972): 427–443.

Janowitz, Morris, and Charles C. Moskos Jr. "Five Years of the All-Volunteer Force: 1973–1978." *Armed Forces and Society* 5, 2 (Winter 1979): 171–218.

Kelty, Ryan. "Citizen Soldiers and Civilian Contractors: Soldiers' Unit Cohesion and Retention Attitudes in the 'Total Force.'" *Journal of Political and Military Sociology* 37, 2 (Winter 2009): 133–159.

Korb, Lawrence J. "Fixing the Mix." *Foreign Affairs* 83, 2 (March/April 2004): 2–7.

———. "Should Congress Approve Legislation Reinstating the Military Draft? Pro." *Congressional Digest* 83, 5 (May 2004): 146–148.

Korb, Lawrence J., and David R. Segal. "Manning and Financing the Twenty-First-Century All-Volunteer Force." *Daedalus* 140, 3 (Summer 2011): 75–87.

Krebs, Ronald. "The Citizen-Soldier Tradition in the United States: Has Its Demise Been Greatly Exaggerated?" *Armed Forces and Society* 36, 1 (October 2009): 153–174.

Lee, R. Alton. "The Army of 'Mutiny' of 1946." *Journal of American History* 53, 3 (December 1966): 555–571.

MacKenzie, Megan H. "Let Women Fight: Ending the U.S. Military's Female Combat Ban." *Foreign Affairs* 91, 6 (November/December 2012): 32–42.

Marquit, Erwin. "The Demobilization Movement of January 1946." *Nature, Society, and Thought* 15, 1 (Winter 2002): 5–39.

Maxwell, Donald. "Young Americans and the Draft." *OAH Magazine of History* 20, 5 (October 2006): 37–39.

McCloy, John J. "The Plan of the Armed Services for Universal Military Training." *Annals of the American Academy of Political and Social Science* 241 (September 1945): 26–34.

Miller, Karen. "'Air Power Is Peace Power': The Aircraft Industry's Campaign for Public and Political Support, 1943–1949." *Business History Review* 70, 3 (Autumn 1996): 297–327.

Modell, John, and Timothy Haggerty. "The Social Impact of War." *Annual Review of Sociology* 17 (January 1991): 205–224.

Moos, Felix. "History and Culture: Some Thoughts on the United States All-Volunteer Force." *Naval War College Review* 26, 1 (July 1973): 16–27.

Moskos, Charles C. Jr. "Racial Integration in the Armed Forces." *American Journal of Sociology* 72, 2 (September 1966): 132–148.

Nelson, Anna K. "Anna M. Rosenberg, an 'Honorary Man.'" *Journal of Military History* 68, 1 (January 2004): 133–161.

O'Hanlon, Michael. "The Need to Increase the Size of the Deployable Army." *Parameters* 41, 4 (Autumn 2004): 4–17.

Perri, Timothy J. "The Evolution of Military Conscription in the United States." *Independent Review* 17, 3 (Winter 2013): 429–439.

Persico, Joseph E. "The Day When We Almost Lost the Army." *American Heritage* 62, 1 (Winter/Spring 2012): 38–45.

Platt, Kenneth B. "What Is National Defense?" *Scientific Monthly* 62, 1 (January 1946): 71–78.

Reinke, Saundra J., and Timothy G. Smith. "Out and Serving Proudly: Repealing 'Don't Ask, Don't Tell.'" *Politics and Policy* 39, 6 (December 2011): 925–948.

Runey, Michael, and Charles Allen, "An All-Volunteer Force for Long-Term Success." *Military Review* 95, 6 (November/December 2015): 92–100.

Rutenberg, Amy. "Drafting for Domesticity: American Deferment Policy during the Cold War, 1948–1965." *Cold War History* 13, 1 (February 2013): 1–20.

Sager, John. "Universal Military Training and the Struggle to Define American Identity during the Cold War." *Federal History Journal* 5 (January 2013): 57–74.

Saunders, Paul. "The Speaker and the Draft." *American History* 36, 3 (August 2001): 42–46.

Schickele, Rainer, and Glenn Everett. "The Economic Implications of Universal Military Training." *Annals of the American Academy of Political and Social Science* 241 (September 1945): 102–112.

Segal, David R., Thomas J. Burns, William W. Falk, Michael P. Silver, and Bam Dev Sharda. "The All-Volunteer Force in the 1970s." *Social Science Quarterly* 79, 2 (June 1998): 390–411.

Segal, David R., Mary S. Senter, and Mady W. Segal. "The Civil-Military Interface in a Metropolitan Community." *Armed Forces and Society* 4, 3 (Spring 1978): 423–448.

Segal, Mady W. "Women in the Military: Research and Policy Issues." *Youth and Society* 10, 2 (December 1978): 101–126.

Segal, Mady W., and David R. Segal. "Social Change and the Participation of Women in the American Military." *Research in Social Movements, Conflicts, and Change* 5 (1983): 235–258.

Simon, Curtis J., and John T. Warner. "Managing the All-Volunteer Force in a Time of War." *Economics of Peace and Security Journal* 2, 1 (January 2007): 20–29.

Sinaiko, Wallace. "The Last American Draftees." *Armed Forces and Society* 16, 2 (Winter 1990): 241–249.

Spiller, Roger. "Military History and Its Fictions." *Journal of Military History* 70, 4 (October 2006): 1081–1097.

Sprout, Harold. "Trends in the Traditional Relation between Military and Civilian." *Proceedings of the American Philosophical Society* 92, 4 (October 1948): 264–270.

Stone, Marshall H. "Universal Military Service in Peacetime." *Science* 103, 2680 (May 1946): 579–581.

Teachman, Jay D., Vaughn R. A. Call, and Mady W. Segal. "The Selectivity of Military Enlistment." *Journal of Political and Military Sociology* 21, 2 (Winter 1993): 287–309.

Thacher, Archibald G., and W. Randolph Montgomery. "The Relation of the Militia Clause to the Constitutionality of Peacetime Compulsory Universal Military Training." *Virginia Law Review* 31, 3 (June 1945): 628–666.

Thomas, Norman. "Arming against Russia." *Annals of the American Academy of Political and Social Science* 241 (September 1945): 67–71.

Tompkins, William F. "Future Manpower Needs of the Armed Forces." *Annals of the American Academy of Political and Social Science* 238 (March 1945): 56–62.

Tresidder, Donald B. "My Hands to War." *Journal of Higher Education* 16, 7 (October 1945): 343–350.

Trow, William C. "The Case against Compulsory Military Training." *Journal of Criminal Law and Criminology* 35, 5 (January/February 1945): 325–326.

Villard, Oswald G. "Universal Military Training and Military Preparedness." *Annals of the American Academy of Political and Social Science* 241 (September 1945): 35–45.

Walker, Wallace E. "Emory Upton and the Officer's Creed." *Military Review* 61, 4 (April 1981): 65–68.

Warner, John, and Beth Asch. "The Record and Prospects of the All-Volunteer Military in the United States." *Journal of Economic Perspectives* 15, 2 (Spring 2001): 169–192.

Weigley, Russell F. "The Soldier, the Statesman, and the Military Historian." *Journal of Military History* 63, 4 (October 1999): 807–822.

Wood, Leonard. "Citizenship Obligation: National Training for Defense." *Proceedings of the Academy of Political Science in the City of New York* 6, 4 (July 1916): 157–165.

Woodruff, Todd, Ryan Kelty, and David Segal. "Propensity to Serve and Motivation to Enlist among American Combat Soldiers." *Armed Forces and Society* 32, 3 (April 2006): 353–366.

Ylvisaker, Hedvig. "Public Opinion toward Compulsory Peacetime Military Training." *Annals of the American Academy of Political and Social Science* 241 (September 1945): 86–94.

INDEX

Feder, Jody, 166
Federal Bureau of Investigation (FBI), 23, 24
Federal Security Agency, 49
Filipino Americans in World War II, 15
First Infantry Division, 124 (photo)
Fitt, Alfred B., 116
Flora, Ruth, 135
Ford, Gerald, 147
Forrestal, James V., 36–37, 59, 65 (photo), 66
Fortas, Abe, 90
Fort Benning, 121
Fort Carson, 121
For the Common Defense (Marshall), 40
40th Infantry Division, 220n39
Fort McPherson, 135
Fort Ord, 121
45th Infantry Division, 220n39
Freedom to Serve (Fahy Committee report), 68–69
Friedman, Milton, 113–114
Frings, Carole, 149–150
Froehlke, Robert F., 131–132
From Representation to Inclusion: Diversity Leadership for the 21st-Century Military (report), 181
"FY 74 Volunteer Army Highlights" (report), 131

Gallup, George, 12–13
Gallup polls, 12–13, 22
Gates, Robert M., 175, 182
Gates, Thomas S., Jr., 100, 113
Gates Commission
    agreements and differences with Project Volunteer, 118–119
    establishment and members of, 113–114
    on mandatory national service and universal military training, 118
    transition from the draft to an all-volunteer force and, 111, 112–113, 114–115, 132

General Officer Steering Committee on Women in the Army, 145
George, Collins, 83–84
Gesell, Gerhard A., 90
Gesell Committee, 88, 90–96, 108
Gettleman, Jeffrey, 171
Gibson, Truman K., 59, 63
Gillem, Alvan C., Jr., 28–29, 135
Gillem Board, 18, 28–31, 32, 61
Gilpatric, Roswell, 89–90
Gilpatric memorandum, 88, 89–90, 108
Goldich, Robert L., 185
Granger, Lester B., 59, 61, 64, 65–66
Granger report, 60–61, 87
Gray, Gordon, 67, 71 (photo)
Greenewalt, Crawford, 114
Greenspan, Alan, 114
Grenada, 150
Grew, Joseph Clark, 53
Griest, Kristen M., 183
Gropman, Alan, 76–77
Gruenther, Alfred, 114

haircuts, 116
Haislip, Wade H., 73
Ham, Carter F., 162–165
Hammes, Thomas X., 170, 172, 176
Hancock, Joy B., 135
Harris, Joseph P., 10
Hastie, William H., 63
Haver, Shaye L., 183
Hawaiians in World War II, 15
Hays, Anna, 146 (photo)
Hébert, F. Edward, 123
Hector, Louis J., 90
Herbits, Stephen, 114, 127, 144
Herres, Robert T., 151–152
Hershey, Lewis B., 120 (photo)
    on the congressional debate about peacetime conscription, 9
    director of the Selective Service System, 10 (photo), 11
    on employment of women during World War II, 20

military personnel policy, *continued*
  impact of Project Clear and
    integration on American
    society, 75, 76 (*see also* military
    integration/desegregation)
  issues of citizenship and military
    service with the all-volunteer
    force, 184, 185
  McCloy Committee, 16–18
  as the nation's conscience, 3, 6,
    188–189, 190–191
  progress against racial
    discrimination during and after
    World War II, 16–20, 28–31
  Project 100,000, 104–107, 109
  transformative effect of the selective
    service idea, 32–33, 35
  Truman's use of to leverage change
    in civil society, 66
  War Manpower Commission,
    18–20
  women in military service and, 136
military retirement, 184, 185–186
military service academies, admission
  of women to, 147
Militia Act (1792), 206n7
Miller, Scott, 183
minorities
  access to leadership positions and,
    180–181
  issues of representativeness in the
    all-volunteer force, 156–157
  numbers inducted during World
    War II, 15, 16
  See also African Americans
Modern Volunteer Army Program,
  121–122
Montague, Robert J., 125–126, 127,
  144–145
Moorer, Thomas H., 126
moral waivers, 185
Morgan, Thomas, 121
Morris, Thomas, 96–98, 99
Morse, Winslow C., 28
Moskos, Charles, 152

Mott, Quentin R., 53
Mullen, Michael, 166
Muse, Benjamin, 90

National Association for the
  Advancement of Colored People
  (NAACP), 63, 86
National Defense Act (1920), 38
National Defense Act for Fiscal Year
  2011, 181
National Defense Authorization Act for
  Fiscal Year 1994, 160
National Defense Authorization Act for
  Fiscal Year 2008, 174
National Defense Authorization Act for
  Fiscal Year 2009, 174–175, 180
National Defense Authorization Act for
  Fiscal Year 2011, 165
National Defense Authorization Act for
  Fiscal Year 2016, 185–185
National Defense Authorization Act for
  Fiscal Years 1992 and 1993, 151
National Defense Conference on Negro
  Affairs, 59–61, 87
National Guard
  draft-induced enlistments and,
    107–108
  impact of all-volunteer force on,
    184–185
  impact of private security contractors
    on, 174
  in Operations Iraqi Freedom
    and Enduring Freedom in
    Afghanistan, 158
  in the Persian Gulf War, 157–158
  resistance to integration in the Army
    National Guard, 220n39
National Security Training Committee
  (NSTC), 53–54
national service
  Gates Commission on, 118
  O'Mahoney-Kilgore bill, 26
  supporters of at the end of World
    War II, 25, 26
National Service Act, 25, 26